THE MIRAGE OF CONTINUITY:

RECONFIGURING ACADEMIC INFORMATION RESOURCES FOR THE 21ST CENTURY

The Mirage of Continuity:

*Reconfiguring Academic Information Resources
for the 21st Century*

Edited by

BRIAN L. HAWKINS and PATRICIA BATTIN

Council on Library and Information Resources

and
Association of American Universities

A
A
U

Washington, D.C.

Published by the Council on Library and Information Resources, 1755 Massachusetts Avenue, N.W., Washington, D.C. 20036 and the Association of American Universities, 1200 New York Avenue, N.W., Washington, D.C.

First published 1998

Typeset in Sabon

Library of Congress Cataloging-in-Publication Data

The mirage of continuity : reconfiguring academic information
   resources for the 21st century / edited by Brian L. Hawkins and
   Patricia Battin.
      p. cm.
   Includes bibliographical references and index.
   ISBN 1-887334-59-9 (hc. : alk. paper)
      1. Academic libraries—United States—Data processing.
   2. Libraries—United States—Specific collections—Electronic
   information resources.   3. Digital libraries—United States.
   4. Universities and colleges—United States—Data processing.
   I. Hawkins, Brian L.   II. Battin, Patricia.   III. Council on Library
   and Information Resources.   IV. Association of American
   Universities.
   Z675.U5M546   1998
   027.7 ' 0285—dc21   98-28434
                                                        CIP

Contents

Foreword

From the earliest days of the Council on Library and Information Resources (CLIR), leadership has been the focus of one of its core programs. With the emergence of digital technology, the need for attention to the topic has become even more insistent. This volume of essays is a response to the need. At its heart is a pervasive concern for developing the leadership that must shape the transformation of the American university campus in the digital era.

CLIR and the Association of American Universities (AAU) have joined forces as sponsors of the book, which brings together two highly esteemed leaders, Brian Hawkins and Patricia Battin, for an unusually productive collaboration. Hawkins, a university administrator who has recently accepted the presidency of EDUCAUSE and a contributor to the most provocative articles in the information technology field, and Battin, an outstanding university librarian and former president of the Commission on Preservation and Access, explore the many facets of the transformation that is occurring on campuses because of the technology. The essays they have assembled illuminate for all of us the opportunities and the dangers inherent in that transformation.

Hawkins and Battin want to help administrators and others of influence on campuses understand the fundamental changes that must be made in the institutional infrastructure to manage the powers of the technology. They argue that the traditional conceptions of "library" and "information technology division" must be completely rethought. The collective goal of the contributors to the volume is to reconceive the enterprise that defines how instruction, learning, research, management, and finances are conducted on campuses in the global digital society of the 21st century. All of these functions, which have been shaped by the characteristics of print-on-paper technology, must change in the digital environment. But productive change will occur only when leaders of the previously compartmentalized functions engage in imaginative collaboration and identify and cultivate the leadership skills they and their successor generation will need to control a process of radical adjustment.

CLIR has invested in this volume with full recognition that what it describes goes far beyond "a library problem." We are convinced that all segments of the university community must turn their energies to a dramatic restructuring of the institution, despite the discomfort that may accompany the change. We believe that the call to arms issued by Hawkins,

vii

Battin, and their colleagues will hasten development of the requisite new leadership on campuses and encourage universities to function effectively, indeed to flourish, in the transformed circumstances.

Deanna B. Marcum
President
Council on Library and Information Resources

* * * * * * * * * * * * * * * * * * *

The Association of American Universities is pleased to co-publish these essays on reconfiguring academic information resources for the future. The explosive development of digital technology has engaged every sector of the academic community, but the future impact of the technology will be even more sweeping. Digital information technology will profoundly influence the production, dissemination, and management of information; its impact may affect the structure, operation, and governance of the higher education enterprise as well.

As institutions responsible not only for passing cumulative knowledge to succeeding generations but also for expanding the boundaries of that knowledge, universities have a strong vested interest in harnessing the power of the digital revolution to advance their teaching and research missions. But the impacts of this revolution will not automatically be benign. In sorting through the promises and perils of digital technology, university administrators and faculty will have to think as hard about the core university values and practices that need to be preserved as they do about those programs and policies that should be changed.

The debate about continuity and change that underpins the discussion of digital technology has strong polar advocates: some advocates of change—indeed, some within these pages—criticize the conservatism of universities and their leaders; others dismiss digital technology as another mere instrumentality and question any serious discussion of its applications to fundamental institutional missions.

These thoughtful and provocative essays provide a valuable framing of the issues for university presidents and other senior administrators. They may not present views with which all will agree, but they offer points-of-view that should be considered by all who will play a role in incorporating digital technology into higher education's future.

Cornelius J. Pings
President
Association of American Universities

Acknowledgments

We wish to express our heartfelt gratitude to our colleagues who generously responded to our insistent pressure to contribute the insightful and provocative articles in this volume. We asked our friends and partners in the academic process to write on topics that we identified for them, and without exception, they exceeded our every expectation. We are truly grateful for their willingness to participate in this effort and to share their wisdom with a wider audience.

We also want to express our appreciation to the Council on Library and Information Resources (CLIR) and the American Association of Universities (AAU) for their support in sponsoring and underwriting this volume. Their willingness to breach tradition made it possible to publish this volume as an example of a new concept of scholarly communication. While the book itself is copyrighted, the individual authors retain the copyright of their own work, thus allowing them to disseminate their work as they see fit. Many of them intend to place their chapters in the public domain by making them available on the Web. We thank these two innovative professional associations for supporting this modest initiative to transform scholarly publishing.

We are especially grateful to our colleagues, Deanna Marcum and James Morris, President and Vice President of CLIR respectively, for their substantial contributions to our effort. From the beginning of this project, Deanna provided counsel and advice as the framework of the book took shape, through the stages of writing, and through final publication. Jim not only provided us with impeccably edited copy; he served as sounding board and conscience, insuring intellectual rigor and clarity in every chapter. Any errors are ours, not theirs. We are deeply indebted to these two splendid colleagues.

We also appreciate the continuing support and interest of CAUSE and Educom recently merged into EDUCAUSE, an association focused on information technology in higher education. These two organizations brought the two of us together professionally and afforded us the opportunity, through service on their boards, to collaborate for more than fifteen years. During our membership on the boards of CAUSE and Educom, on committees of the Commission on Preservation and Access (now a CLIR program), and other affiliated venues, we have provoked, irritated, infuriated, challenged, and educated each other, each more clearly understanding the difficulties, challenges, and necessity of collaboration between and among various segments of the broadly defined information resource community.

Most recently, we joined Deanna Marcum of CLIR, Joan Gotwals and Billy Frye of Emory University, and Jane Ryland of CAUSE to conceptualize an institute to develop the transformational leadership for information resources in higher education. It was out of this planning effort that the need for such a book emerged. We hope the book will be useful to all members of the higher education community who have the opportunity and the responsibility to transform the information resource infrastructure for the 21st century.

Contributors

Patricia Battin is former Vice President for Information Services and University Librarian at Columbia University and former President of the Commission on Preservation and Access.

John Seely Brown is Chief Scientist of the Xerox Corporation and Director of the Xerox Palo Alto Research Center.

Stanley Chodorow is a Professor of History at the University of Pennsylvania and former Provost of the University. He serves as current Chairman of the Board of the Council on Library and Information Resources.

Paul Duguid is a Research Specialist at the University of California, Berkeley, and has been a consultant at the Xerox Palo Alto Research Center for ten years.

Douglas Greenberg is President and Director of the Chicago Historical Society.

José-Marie Griffiths is the Chief Information Officer of the University of Michigan.

Brian L. Hawkins is President of EDUCAUSE and former Senior Vice President for Academic Planning and Administrative Affairs at Brown University.

Susan Hockey is a professor in the Faculty of Arts and Director of the Canadian Institute for Research Computing in the Arts at the University of Alberta.

Richard N. Katz is Vice President of EDUCAUSE.

Donald Kennedy is Bing Professor of Environmental Science and President Emeritus of Stanford University.

Michael E. Lesk is Director of Information and Intelligent Systems at the National Science Foundation.

Paula Kaufman is Dean of Libraries at the University of Tennessee, Knoxville.

Peter Lyman is a professor in the School of Information Management and Systems at the University of California, Berkeley, and former University Librarian.

Deanna B. Marcum is President of the Council on Library and Information Resources.

Susan Rosenblatt is Deputy University Librarian at the University of California, Berkeley.

Donald J. Waters is Director of the Digital Library Federation at the Council on Library and Information Resources.

Samuel R. Williamson is President of the University of the South.

Section 1

Defining the Problem

1

Setting the Stage: Evolution, Revolution or Collapse?

PATRICIA BATTIN AND BRIAN L. HAWKINS

> *That faiths by which my comrades stand*
> *Seem fantasies to me,*
> *And mirage-mists their Shining Land,*
> *Is a strange destiny.*
>
> —Thomas Hardy The Impercipient
> (1898) Stanza I

Much has been written about the current crisis in American higher education. Annual increases in tuition are well above inflation rates, and the costs of financial aid, scientific research and instructional facilities, libraries, and technology appear to rise inexorably. Organizational and budgetary changes that seem logical and are demanded by the characteristics of technology use across the campus for teaching, learning, research, administrative operations, and provision of information resources are met by debilitating resistance. The growing dysfunctional paralysis, although widespread throughout the institution, is most clearly apparent in the deadly embrace of past, present, and future in libraries and information technology divisions. The congeries of "information resources" that is replacing our traditional concepts of library, computer center, media services, and instructional technology represents the leading edges of both change and paralysis. Efforts to resolve the conflicts over budgetary concerns and services to users within traditionally conceived boundaries of "libraries" and "information technology divisions" compound the problems and create unnecessary costs. Resolution of the inherent conflicts in these areas can occur only through a broadly conceived enterprise that redefines instruction, learning, research, management, and finances for the global digital society of the 21st century. And,

3

as William Plater said in his essay *The Labyrinth of the Wide World,* "More than any other traditional asset, the library is the means by which American universities will transform themselves into something entirely new."[1]

In *The Age of Social Transformation,* Peter Drucker asserts that "no century in recorded history has experienced so many social transformations and such radical ones as the 20th century. They, I submit, may turn out to be the most significant events of this, our century, and its lasting legacy. In the developed free-market countries—which contain less than a fifth of the earth's population but are a model for the rest—work and work force, society and polity, are all, in the last decade of this century, qualitatively and quantitatively different not only from what they were in the first years of this century but also from what has existed at any other time in history: in their configurations, in their processes, in their problems, and in their structures."[2] Drucker supports his argument by tracing the rise and fall of farmers, service workers, and blue-collar workers as the dominant labor force, culminating in today's knowledge-based work force. According to Drucker, the shift to knowledge-based work poses enormous social challenges: "What it means—what are the values, the commitments, the problems, of the new society—we do not know. But we do know that much will be different."[3]

In the past, the social forces transforming the general society have not significantly penetrated the ivory tower. Continuing incremental changes to an entrenched conservative tradition have perhaps created an illusion of receptivity in academe to new circumstances. But with the rise of a society based on the knowledge worker, we are now experiencing a different kind of change. It is no longer incremental. It is no longer even exponential. It is discontinuous and transformational. Transformational change occurs when something comes about that is so radical it alters the basic performance of daily activities. When simple change becomes transforming change, the desire for continuity becomes a dysfunctional mirage.

If the basic issue is not "whether" but "how," why is the transformation process in higher education so slow, so disorderly, so expensive, and

---

[1] William M. Plater, "The Labyrinth of the Wide World," *Educom Review* 30:2 (1995): 39.

[2] Peter Drucker, "The Age of Social Transformation," *The Atlantic Monthly* 275:5 (1994): 53.

[3] Ibid.

so resisted? A possible explanation is the tendency to reason from contemporary circumstances in a period of discontinuous change. The mirage of continuity encourages well-meaning efforts to modify or reform discrete units rather than to recognize the need for fundamental reorganization of the enterprise. Gertrude Himmelfarb, in her essay, *Revolution in the Library,* explores the implications for scholarship of the use of technology to improve traditional activities. She underscores the need to distinguish between the enhanced technological capacity to amass facts and the exercise of informed critical thought. She makes the crucial distinction that the use of information technology has enabled "a revolution, not only in library services but in the very conception of the library. But—and this is a large *but*—all this will be to the good only if the virtues of the new library are made to complement, rather than supplant, those of the old."[4] Although Himmelfarb's remarks reflect a keen analysis of the future, they also ignore the critical interrelationship between the library and the higher education enterprise. The transforming impacts of information technology cannot be confined to the library but imply a fundamental reorganization of the host institution. The digital library, as the epistemological center of the university, is certainly positioned to serve as the catalyst for transforming the university to meet the needs of the 21st century society dominated by electronic technology.

For the past two decades, libraries and computer centers have radically altered both themselves and the higher education landscape, albeit in an incremental fashion. True transformational change continues to be constrained by the misguided belief that the technological revolution can be contained within the old organizational structures. Succumbing to the mirage of continuity that denies the need for financial and management reorganization and the belief in a technological panacea that will miraculously transform an historic tradition of knowledge creation and transmission by the simple substitution of digital for analog technology will only increase dysfunction and paralysis. To recognize the new conception of the library is to recognize and accept the inevitability of a new conception of the university.

The characteristics of digital technology both sustain and alter the habits, mores, and institutions of democratic society. This particular du-

---

[4] Gertrude Himmelfarb. "Revolution in the Library," *American Scholar* 275:5 (1997). Reprinted in *The Key Reporter* 62:3 (1997): 5.

ality has created a mesmerizing appearance of continuity, most clearly reflected in conservative organizations such as higher education. The apparent ease of initial, incremental uses of technology readily obscures the fact that the fundamental differences between the characteristics of print-on-paper and digital technologies inevitably require a completely different set of social and institutional infrastructures. Information technologies have consistently enabled the continuation of traditional values and missions at the same time as their use actively encourages the unrestrained exploration of new frontiers in the creation of knowledge. Applications of this new knowledge in turn radically influence individual and organizational capabilities, thought, and behavior.

Traditional instructional and research methodologies, governance structures, and financial formulas for the higher education enterprise have been shaped by the characteristics of print-on-paper technology. Consequently, digital technologies, characterized by unrelenting change, irrelevancy of time and place, the need for unprecedented and often unwelcome collaboration, and the potential for unmanageable costs, simply do not fit comfortably into the existing infrastructure.

Ironically, the strongest barriers to creating an affordable and efficient array of digital information resources are the existing organizational and financial structures that have created and supported the development of our internationally admired higher education system. The most difficult challenge to be faced in an era of transformational change is the recognition that what has been our strength will become our liability if we do not act in time. The brittle books on library shelves, the deferred maintenance of campus buildings, and the Year 2000 computing conundrum are powerful cautionary examples of great assets becoming crushing liabilities.

The initial incremental nature of technological change encouraged the widespread belief that the new technologies could be easily integrated into the existing management systems. As a result, the discontinuous revolutionary potential of digital technology and its implications for wrenching changes in enshrined assumptions have been widely ignored, misunderstood, and feared.

Exciting new possibilities of electronic publication and storage are enthusiastically hailed as the uncomplicated and less costly substitution for the constraining limitations of print-on-paper technology. But, instead of what was initially promised—unfettered global access to information sources, a paperless society, and reasonably stable and affordable technology—the higher education landscape is littered with an overwhelming volume of paper and confronts runaway costs, increasingly uneven access to information, alarming security and privacy concerns, serious questions of personal and institutional ethics and liability, and ineffectual, fragmented management systems.

It has become clear in the past decade that traditional notions of libraries and information technology organizations are no longer intellectually and economically sustainable. Digitally produced volumes of paper publications rendered obsolete the concept of self-sufficient site-dependent collections. College and university libraries can no longer meet the information needs of their faculty and students through the traditional avenue of simply adding to their collections.

So too is it becoming all too obvious that traditional notions of supporting access to the continually changing technological infrastructure are no longer adequate. During the past two decades, the applications of digital technologies to the storage and dissemination of information have demonstrated that the promise of a rapid transformation was premature and oversimplified by technical mavens whose interest focused on the technical potential rather than the specialized information requirements of working scholars in a variety of disciplines. Cost formulas emphasized initial investments without recognizing the unrelenting need for continuing hardware and software replacements and upgrades; technical access was widely enhanced at the expense of intellectual access and archival reliability; the capacity to handle the rapidly increasing volume of demand as users adapted to new options and services quickly became inadequate; the costs and technical complexity of digitizing existing print resources were seriously underestimated; and requirements for continuing educational opportunities for both information users and providers were vastly misunderstood.

From microfiche libraries in a shoebox to the concept of the digital library, the history of information technology is replete with the incremental introduction of new technologies designed to eliminate the site-bound, labor-intensive constraints of print-on-paper. Each new technology predicted monolithic simplicity, ease of access, relief from steadily increasing costs and from cumbersome management of books and buildings. Each new technology—radio, television, microfilm, video disk, laser disk, music CD's, CD-ROM's, fiber optic networks, and digital scanning—contributed to a growing heterogeneity of media and format, complexity of access, increased expenditures, and a chaotic spectrum of choices. No formats, media, or communications technologies disappeared or superseded others; they continue to appear in new combinations and evolving functionality.

Computer-produced catalog cards evolved into computerized public access catalogs. Centrally maintained and serviced mainframe computers were replaced by networked personal computers. Both these incremental changes exploded into a demand for new skills and new resources as technology invaded the library, and responsibility for information content permeated information technology divisions. But rather than bringing together and integrating the functions and responsibilities of these two disparate professional groups—librarians and information technologists—the traditionally compartmentalized budgeting and management structure of academic institutions served to solidify the incipient dysfunction.

Traditionally, information requirements and habits have been essentially shaped by the constraints of centralized systems of libraries and computer centers. In many instances, the courses of instruction and the pursuit of research have largely depended upon the availability of information resources and services that were determined by the central allocation of institutional funds and by decisions regarding the use of those funds by librarians and computer specialists. Print-on-paper supports a command and control model; in contrast, digital technology not only permits customized information services, depending upon the task at hand, but it destroys the artificial barriers inherent in print-on-paper technology.

The availability of site-independent information resources, the workstation capacity for accessing and manipulating scholarly information, and the multi-media capacity for creating new representations of knowledge release faculty members and students from sole reliance on the linear characteristics of print-on-paper teaching, learning, and research. The capacity to distribute responsibility for communications capability and information access to the desktop in the office, the dormitory, the home, and, ultimately, the laptop, allows the provision of truly customized information services—and the individual at the workstation, the "electronic student/scholar/administrator," can now demand those services.

The increasing decentralization of technology and access to information available to the student and the scholar at the workstation in a variety of media and formats means that we can now respond in kind to customized inquiries and searches. We can provide the book when that particular format will expand the mind; we can provide machine-readable full-text when that format will contribute to different ways of thinking about a problem; and we can provide the tools with which to convert numbers and texts into graphic images to enhance the learning process.

Consequently, it is the scholar, the student, the administrator who becomes the central focus—not the organizational unit in its traditional form as library or information technology division. In like manner, digital technology enables the potential replacement of the traditional classroom approach by customized teaching and learning, matching the knowledge resources with the individual's cognitive style. But our management systems and financial formulas are still geared to the organizational unit—the department, the division, the library, the information technology division—as the center of the institution, and this cripples the inherent power of the technology to decentralize access and control. In the digital university, this welcome and beneficent capacity must be carefully balanced with a new concept of central coordination mechanisms to achieve maximum connectivity, technical platform interoperability, equitable access to information resources, and reasonable cost control. As a further consequence, new interrelationships and organizational structures will be necessary to manage, finance and coordinate the choices and opportunities made possible by digital information resources.

The organizational structures, financial policies, pedagogy, and research methods of academic institutions reflect the characteristics of print-on-paper technology, which include the following:

- site-based information resources
- class and lecture-based teaching techniques
- discipline-oriented departmental structures
- compartmentalized financial formulas and budgets based on predictable stability of print-on-paper technology

The vastly different properties of digital technology include the following:

- rapid, unpredictable and continuing change of hardware/software
- the capacity to combine print-on-paper with multi-media representations of human creativity
- the capacity to customize information services on demand
- continuing changes in learning, teaching, and research methodologies with the application of technology
- the site-independent nature of information resources, teaching, and learning

- increasing volumes of easily disseminated information
- the need for new financial formulas to fund mix of intra- and interinstitutional networks, knowledge bases, and services
- a new conception of "information professional," who is now required to have knowledge of bibliographic sources, discipline, and technology

Two important insights are key to understanding the transformational imperative of digital technologies. First, other media and formats, such as paper, CD-ROM, and magnetic tape, can be generated from knowledge stored as an electronic signal. This particular property means that knowledge can be created, stored, disseminated, and used in a variety of formats and media, depending upon the need of the information seeker. This capability essentially destroys the traditional assumptions of library and computer center services and effectively inverts the conventional relationships between "keepers" and "users." Second, because of the capability to customize knowledge media and formats, effective management of a hybrid environment of both analog and digital technologies must respond to the characteristics of digital technology, which defy time, space, and disciplinary limitations.

A further implication of digital technology is that, just as there is no end game, so is there no obvious starting point for planning the transformation into the 21st-century institution. Linear planning strategies, so well adapted to the characteristics of print-on-paper, are useless in predicting the course and cost of digital technology. We must adopt an exceedingly agile approach, capable of balancing a variety of beginnings, and we must do so with the certain knowledge that anything we do has implications for the total higher education environment—teaching, learning, research, scholarly communication, information resources, governance, and financial support.

It is difficult to plan for and predict with any certainty the outcome of the transformational process. The pace of change will be governed by many factors—the status and maturity of technologies available at any given time; their relevance to different aspects of the complex world of research libraries and their host institutions; the sources of funding available; institutional priorities measured against alternative methodologies; and the availability of appropriate materials in digitally encoded form. In addition, management strategies for digital technology are complicated by the fact that no managerial structures, best practices, or solutions inherent in the technology are immediately apparent.

The essays in this volume confront the issues surrounding the transformation of academic institutions by digital technology, and the organization of the book reflects the fluidity and decentralizing capacity of digital technology. Although organized into four sections reflecting recurring themes, the individual contributions are designed to be read either as separate essays or as loosely connected chapters in the larger volume.

The introductory section provides a brief historical context for the rapid changes occurring today. The authors describe the urgent need for faculty members, librarians, information technology specialists, and administrators to devise creative and thoughtful initiatives to adapt traditional values and missions to a digital environment.

The essays in the second section describe the challenge of blending digital strengths and resources with our past and present assets. How does technology change and support our concept of liberal education? What is the nature and future of scholarly communication in a digital university? Is there a role for print collections? What are the implications of changing scholarly requirements for the funding and management of new information resources?

Contributors in the third section consider the reasons why the revolution is not occurring as rapidly or as simply as predicted. The overwhelming statistical evidence indicates that the traditional reliance on comprehensive library collections is no longer a tenable course. And, as the essay on *Why The Web Isn't a Library* illustrates, many of the proposed solutions raise unresolved questions. What are the fundamental institutional changes necessary to benefit from the transforming power of technology, and do we have both the will and the means to embrace them? Do the implications of scholarly research and differential markets create a new uncertainty for institutional budgets? Will the economics of electronic publications prove as intractable as the economics of publication on paper? Can the archiving function, previously dispersed among many sites and cost centers, be effectively centralized and funded to insure the maintenance of digitally encoded knowledge? What are the technical—in addition to economic and copyright—limits to the concept of the digital library?

The essays in the final section address the issues of leadership and of management for a productive transitional period. A major ingredient for success will be the nurturing of a new generation of leaders with skills and expertise drawn from previously compartmentalized professions—librarians, technologists, and faculty members. Methods for establishing assessment tools and standards for identifying effective results will be important as we move away from reliance on the size of book collections and the number of hits on a Web site.

The range of perspectives represented by the individual authors illustrates the overwhelming influence of digital technology on every aspect of higher education. Its use influences every component of the institution—learning, instruction and research activities, faculty organization and governance, administrative functions, information technologies, and library resources. The essays reflect a lively debate about the advantages, disadvantages, financial benefits, and new liabilities of these innovative technologies and about the ease, or degree of difficulty, with which the technologies will replace traditional activities and resources, as we persist in our efforts to define and manage the transition to a higher education enterprise for the 21st century.

2

To Change

DONALD KENNEDY

Universities are in a dynamic equilibrium with society. On the one hand, they appear to lag behind it, acting as conservators of its history and archivists of its highest cultural attainments. On the other hand, they are seen as leaders, adventuring into new knowledge domains, developing transforming technologies, and serving as the seedbed for novel and often disturbing ideas.

Both these roles are part of the university's academic duty. Institutions of higher education reflect society to itself, and at the same time challenge that self-image by asking difficult questions: What have we become? Why don't we do things differently? Not surprisingly, the university thus sometimes finds itself seemingly at odds with society, especially during periods of rapid social change. The pace of technological change, the transient character of employment, calls for the political reformulation of everything from welfare to health and safety regulation, and the increasingly critical character of public discourse all create a climate in which traditional institutions, perhaps especially universities, feel besieged. The one thing that the university's critics agree on is that academic institutions have to change along with the rest of society—or fail to fulfill their duty. Change will not be easy. But neither is the requirement for it unique in recent history.

The shape of higher education in America has been repeatedly refigured in episodes of dramatic, even wrenching change. The contemporary form of the modern research university was set at the end of the nineteenth century, as the notion of the German graduate school took hold. This revolution helped set the course for the developing land-grant institutions that had been established through the Morrill Act, and it changed forever the future even of those liberal arts colleges that did not become universities, because it put in place the system that would soon supply the nation's professoriate.

After World War II came another revolution, the "endless frontier," which transformed the leading universities into engines for achieving world preeminence in the sciences. If the first revolution was scholarly, this one was surely utilitarian. Its accomplishment was the enlistment of universities as instruments of national economic purpose.

To many who see the contemporary university at the edge of a dynamic but troubled society, it seems probable that the end of the 20th century will usher in a wave of change as dramatic and far-reaching as the two that preceded it. Others, familiar with the innate conservatism of academic institutions and the enormous size to which the enterprise has grown, doubt that any revolutionary (that is, nonincremental) change is possible. I am among the former, but I recognize that predictions of this kind are full of risk. How can we judge the prospects for change? To begin with, what driving forces are at work?

One force is surely public disaffection with higher education, evident not only in the media attention given to all forms of academic scandal, from research misconduct to athletic recruiting violations, but also in the more thoughtful and private criticism of employers, government leaders, and parents. The public attention given to colleges and universities shows just how much they mean to Americans. But our ambivalence about learning—respect for its invitation to self-improvement, suspicion over its potential for creating elites—helps to explain why the American public is prepared to turn hostile when the news is bad. There has been no shortage of bad news, and the attention lavished on it by the media has put academic leaders on the defensive.

A second force is the impending transformation of education by economic and technological changes taking place all around it. The life-cycle of nearly everything in the United States has shortened—of useful information, of technologies, and of special skills. In the new corporate lexicon, "buy don't make" and "outsource where possible" have become watch-words. Organizations that once invested heavily in human development and rewarded loyalty in order to reduce turnover now engage in extensive job-shopping. Consulting firms are growing in number and influence, and organizations that supply temporary employees are prospering as never before. The most admired executives are those who can engineer corporate "turnarounds" by "downsizing," and if they are especially successful they may gain a coveted place among America's Toughest Bosses in *Business Week*.

The result has been a new occupational obsolescence in which large numbers of employees are being cast aside before they reach what was once called normal retirement age. Their transient replacements in the specialty job shops will follow them out of the workforce, because their special knowledge is so vulnerable to technological displacement. In many parts of this country, prematurely retired forty-five and fifty-year-olds with expert knowledge and good educations are becoming commonplace.

Spot employment has become a way of life. New kinds of placement firms specialize in finding executives for one- or two-year appointments, to repair a company or serve in an interim capacity in a unit put into receivership or scheduled for rebuilding. Displaced workers will be pressed to specialize in whatever new technological niche is going at the moment—thus becoming the architects of their own premature retirement once that specialty has superseded. It is ironic that just as we are eliminating mandatory retirement on the basis of age, we are substituting involuntary retirement on the basis of disability.

In effect, we are stretching the envelope of retirement as we have known it. At the far end, it has been extended by increased longevity and by the uncapping of mandatory retirement. And at the near end, it is expanding to include the new wave of involuntary retirees. There will be important consequences for society, both positive and negative. Spot employment may bring new opportunities for part-time or home work through telecommuting. By contrast, finding creative and challenging occupations will be very difficult for unemployed people of high ability. The resulting problem will be exacerbated by the present demographic structure of the U.S. population. The baby-boom generation, with its peak about twenty years from the traditional retirement age, is the largest in our history. Following it, and being counted on to provide the kind of support retirees have traditionally received from our society, is an unusually thin generation. If the baby-boomers retire prematurely in significant numbers, an already heavy prospective burden will become heavier still.

These changes have significant implications for higher education. They suggest the importance of educating young people for flexibility and adaptability. Particular skills will lose their utility fast; the ability to think, reason, and analyze well will be much more durable. Knowledge about our national culture and its historical antecedents will be an increasingly important asset, as the need to learn about and penetrate new occupational environments grows. We will need to wean ourselves from the idea that education is something that happens at a particular, early phase of the lifecycle and then stops. Instead, higher education will have to create abundant, accessible opportunities for relearning—including taking advantage of unusually accomplished but prematurely retired people as teachers as well as learners. In short, the new demography of employment suggests that the universities will be forced to think more imaginatively about how to provide education throughout life. Academic duty may expand from its present single-generation focus to encompass "students" at a number of different phases of their careers, becoming, in effect, "multicohort" education.

Institutions and individuals will also have to adapt to the revolution being brought about by computer technology, which has radically revised the way in which data and information are stored, retrieved, and communicated. Scientific communication, including publication, has been transformed by the Internet. Educational software is proliferating, and it now plays a significant role in instruction. The traditional tasks of editorial criticism and evaluation of problem sets can now take place electronically, in ways that—at their best—link professor and students more closely for more of the work than ever before. Yet despite these important and promising changes, we will be wise to look with some caution on the potential of computer technology for transforming higher education. A quarter of a century ago, it was freely predicted that television would make then-current university teaching methods obsolete. A tour of the typical "modern" classroom built in the early 1970s will almost always reveal expensive installations for videotaping and for display on television monitors. Yet no one can remember when the TV facilities were last used. At best, TV turned out to be a useful adjunct.

Still, there are reasons to believe that academic computing can engage students with their own learning in new and powerful ways. The best examples of effective academic software involve "manipulables": programs that invite students to plan and undertake their own inquiry. Although the best-known cases are in the sciences, there is a wealth of opportunity in other fields; indeed, stimulating courseware exists in which the student can plot, through a series of decisions, his or her own rise through 18th century French society, or arrange the stage sets and actors for a Shakespeare play. Perhaps the most potent idea in the growing literature of educational reform, whether at K–12 or in the university, is that students learn best by active engagement with a subject, through decisions they make themselves. Computers may not reshape the teaching function in the university, but this idea may well do so.

Meanwhile, the Internet and the World Wide Web are vastly expanding students' access to information. The more entrepreneurial and computer-literate undergraduates now routinely probe a depth of bibliographic material heretofore available only to sophisticated doctoral candidates. Recently I suggested to a junior that she consult the Government Documents Library to get a particular Federal Register notice. She responded, "Oh, I picked it off the Web last night . . . It was quite helpful." Indeed, the level of familiarity and comfort that the best students now have with this extraordinarily rich source of information represents the opportunity for an increased emphasis on analysis as opposed to information acquisition—on working with facts instead of accumulating them.

But that opportunity comes attached to some challenges. For example, there is now an awkward and growing generation gap between computer-literate young people and their professorial elders. Differential access to the technology is widening another gap, between adolescent and post-adolescent "haves" and "have-nots." In many institutions, computing has increased the access that ambitious students have to their professors, thus creating new pressures on workload. Perhaps most troublesome of all is the danger of too much "research information" available on the Internet and the World Wide Web and too little quality control. Students need to develop the intellectual taste that will make them discriminating customers in what is rapidly becoming an information flea market.

The international character of the problems most Americans consider important will be another force for change in higher education. International competitiveness; arms control and disarmament; linkage of world financial markets; "sustainable development"; global environmental change; terrorism and the refugee problem—these are but a few examples of the kinds of issues that are rapidly spawning new centers of interdisciplinary activity in U.S. universities. At the same time, postgraduate (and, increasingly, undergraduate) students from abroad are seeking educational opportunity in this country. Our system of higher education has become a magnet for students from all over the world. Almost no sector of the U.S. economy enjoys such a favorable balance of international trade, and surely none is as important in spreading understanding of (and sympathy for) U.S. aims and institutions around the world. The increasingly international nature of our concerns will challenge us to create innovations in curriculum and the organization of scholarly work.

Finally, there is growing concern that the public and private financial resources that have been placed at the disposal of higher education are becoming more constrained, and that the constraints will tighten further, at least until the end of this century. Since the late 1980s, that concern has claimed a major share of the attention of college and university administrators, who worry that resource scarcity will increasingly limit what they can do. When resource constraints increase, institutions tend to examine their programs and make hard choices. Sometimes, in fact, they make changes that lead to dramatic improvement—changes that they invariably fail to make in good times.[1] Hardship, in short, often lowers institutional resistance to change.

It also tends to diminish self-confidence. Sometimes that, too, can be an agent for restructuring: turnover increases, the roots of established habits and ideas are loosened, and new ones find it easier to become established. But it can also build resistance, causing institutions and their leaders to hunker down and hope they can ride out the storm.

In the hierarchical structure found in typical corporate or governmental settings, changes in direction are achieved by the capacity to enforce accountability to some central authority, and to bring in new people to replace others. But in the university, long-standing traditions of delegation (as well as of academic freedom and peer review) locate the power of appointment with departmental faculties; tenure imposes strong limits on replacement, and accountability to the center is minimal. Strong academic leadership from deans and department chairs could overcome these influences. But, in fact, the trend is toward weaker and not stronger leadership at these levels in the research universities, where the traditions of peripheral (that is, faculty) control are strongest. Departments and schools within the university are accorded the dominant voice in selecting their own leaders. These positions are becoming both less desirable and more transitory as constraints increase. It is rare for a department chair to serve more than a three-year term. Deans—once relatively permanent fixtures—move in and out almost as quickly. The current group

---

[1] This seminal notion about organizational change comes from Herbert Simon; for a brief account of its origin and significance, see J. March, *Science* 202 (1978): 858–861.

of deans at Stanford have been in office for an average of only about four years. The frequency of rotation makes it likely that leadership at these levels reflects consensus below rather than any call for change from above.

The dominant patterns of departmental-level choice of chairs and deans favor cautious incrementalism over broad-scale change. The practical requirement that new faculty appointments be supported by a super-majority leads to a form of log-rolling, in which subdisciplines enter into unspoken agreements that act to retain their current representation. Faculty members are heavily invested in their own special fields; each belongs to an invisible transinstitutional academy that commands its loyalty, and each knows that if the discipline prospers, he or she prospers too.

Presidents and governing boards, however influential they may appear, have sharply limited powers. Although the university is sometimes seen from the outside as a relatively apolitical institution, it is in fact intensely political. Without faculty support, leadership from the administration building simply does not work. Proper respect for the faculty's prerogatives in the academic domain restricts the zone of possible intervention. For example, administrations sometimes seek to intervene at the school or department level by the use of visiting committees, from whom they solicit objective evaluations about the quality and effectiveness of academic programs. But those programs and their parent disciplines have strong advocates and effective mechanisms for injecting their views into the decision-making process. Program alumni are often vociferously loyal to the educational units in which they were trained. The visiting evaluations as a result are often less objective than their appointing agencies hoped. In forty years of serving on, or being advised by, dozens of these bodies, I never heard one propose significant reductions in the department it visited. Instead, the committee members usually become advocates for their area—one of unique potential—or, in the words of one overly enthusiastic colleague, "a virgin field, pregnant with possibilities."

At every hand, universities display their devotion to programs and physical plants that endure. Most buildings are constructed as monuments for the ages, not as flexible, inexpensive, modular faculties that invite changes in function. Appointments are made at senior levels in preference to junior ones whenever the opportunity presents itself. Programs are designed and launched with elaborate care, and longevity is often cited as the primary criterion on which their success is to be judged. Perhaps as cause and perhaps as consequence, universities seek to endow nearly everything. Endowment is an attractive form of fund-raising, because it can attach a program or a building to a donor's name and because it has such a reassuring ring of permanence. But it inevitably builds in longevity, often causing programs to outlive their usefulness and to resist change.

In short, nearly every aspect of the university has a long product life-cycle and is associated with a high "regret function." The immediate consequence is that it is difficult to envision a new or radically altered condition, and the eventual result is a set of policies and practices that favor the present state of affairs over any possible future. It is a portrait of conservatism, perhaps even of senescence.

This description does not apply to all institutions. The comprehensive public institutions, in which most U.S. undergraduates are enrolled, are driven more by student enrollment levels and the perceived needs of the communities they serve; the same is true of community colleges. Administrative decision making, sometimes following negotiation with unionized faculties and always more responsive to external governance, is more the rule in such places. Independent liberal arts colleges are more communitarian and faculty-led, but much more attention is given to institutional as opposed to sectional interests. Church-related colleges have their own rules and customs, often more hierarchical in character. There is less endowment in these sectors, and therefore less in the way of lingering obligation. But in every sector, there is a powerful attachment to the status quo.

This notable resistance of universities can hardly preclude change entirely. The task is to evaluate what new directions seem probable, which ones we prefer, and what patterns of institutional response are most likely to deliver the best outcome.

One trend in higher education that has already demonstrated limited effectiveness is the implementation of policies and devices that have proven successful in the for-profit sector. The professionalization of administrative staffs, the adoption of more carefully considered and managed human resources policies, and the design of better benefits programs are all examples of good corporate practices that have been adopted by universities after what has seemed an unconscionably long delay.

But corporatization must be viewed with some caution. It is a little alarming to hear admissions officers (now sometimes called directors of enrollment management) talk authoritatively about marketing and the business managers speak of total quality management. These notions are not without value, but their adoption increases the estrangement between the administrative and academic cultures—already a serious problem in the university. Academic culture strongly favors individual initiative and a pioneering kind of creativity, whereas those of the administrative culture stress accountability, team loyalty, and discipline. Wherever there is interaction at the boundary, these values are often in conflict.

The newer "business values" run counter to the traditional image of the university and its people as less self-interested and more devoted to non-commercial values than other institutions. When outsiders hear university people talking about productivity enhancement, or learn of deals with industry that involve research agreements, they wonder whether higher education is really free of the values that motivate for-profit companies. While this trend is neither all bad nor all good, it bears careful watching. Many trustees press for the adoption of such corporate values, which they bring with them into the boardroom.

Another trend is the enhancement of American higher education's pluralism. In most industrial nations large, publicly supported institutions dominate the scene; but in the United States a wide range of choice is possible—from small, intensely focused liberal arts colleges, through medium-sized public or private institutions and comprehensive state universities, to a rich and heterogeneous array of research universities. Competition is brisk among similar entities; in the view of some it may be too brisk, acting to forestall the sharing of resources and thus forgoing savings. But others would argue that the competitive character of the enterprise is one that encourages high achievement.

Because heterogeneity is regarded as a virtue, because competition is much admired, and because "freedom of choice" among a broad range of possibilities is an American hallmark, the differentiation of higher education in the United States is very likely to increase. The better liberal arts colleges across the country are flourishing. Formerly "lesser" campuses in big state university systems, such as the University of California at San Diego, and earlier UCLA, have grown to rival the flagships; and in the same state, the comprehensive California State University system is improving and adding campuses. The predicted demise of "women's colleges" has been reversed by new evidence that they offer special opportunities not available to women in other settings. Never has it been clearer that there is an extraordinary incentive to quality in our diverse system. The Harvards, Stanfords, and MITs may deserve praise as centers of innovation, but remarkable things are happening at many institutions that receive less attention: Bowdoin, Portland State, Alverno College, Miami-Dade Community College, and Carnegie-Mellon—to take a sampling across the entire spectrum.

Another positive trend is the increasing awareness of our duty to undergraduate students, especially in the research universities. A lively source of controversy in such places is the question of how much attention ought to be paid to the education of undergraduates. Even though these institutions are responsible for only a small fraction of the baccalaureate degrees awarded annually in the United States, it is in them that the tension between the research and the teaching commitments of faculty members is at its highest. Because they are prestigious and highly visible, they are often seen as models. They are also the places in which future faculty are trained—and thus they are the incubators of the academic culture for the next generation.

The improvement of undergraduate education has become a national movement, visible on many fronts. The NAS, the most prestigious organization of research scientists, instituted in the last century to advise the government on scientific and technical matters, has expanded a center devoted to the improvement of science teaching for undergraduates. Calls for revision of the requirements for promotion to tenure so as to place greater emphasis on teaching are heard in many places, and even heeded in a few. Thoughtful observers like the late Ernest Boyer have called for redefining scholarship to include original efforts in the instructional sphere. In short, educational reform is again at the center of concerned conversation in colleges and universities.

That said, it must be admitted that the results are still meager. At Stanford a highly visible faculty commission completed a review of undergraduate instruction in 1994. Its recommendations were thoughtful—including, for example, a clear call for peer review of teaching effectiveness—and occasionally bold; the commission mandated a first-year interdisciplinary science course to be developed and required of all students. But the course is still being tested, and the new evaluation system is not fully installed. Here as in many places, we have what looks like a lit fuse, but no explosion yet.

Reform in undergraduate education has a deeper and more philosophical side. Particularly in the most selective and rigorous undergraduate programs, the academic "atmosphere" is intensely competitive. Though it has softened somewhat in the past two decades, the practices of grading large courses on a curve, of making seminar discussions a form of debate competition, and of discouraging group projects are still quite common. To describe a course as "rigorous" is to give it high praise, and often the test of its rigor is how many students fail to make the grade.

The larger society invites and encourages this view of education through its insistence that colleges and universities serve a credentialing function—telling employers and others that John is a better bet than Julie. The national anger and frustration over the problem of grade inflation are manifestations of the perceived importance of that function.

Yet the larger society also complains that it doesn't like the results of all this competition. Organizations, whether government agencies, companies, or nonprofits, get things done by grouping people with different skills and telling them to solve problems. The effective employee in such a setting is the one who can apply skills constructively through cooperation with others, and if necessary recruit those others through the exercise of personal leadership. Why, employers are asking, are we being sent young men and women who know how to compete but find it difficult to harmonize their efforts with others?

This concern is finding resonance with several movements in higher education. One is toward public and community service organizations, which are becoming more visible on campus, and the commitment of undergraduate students to them. Such organizations have been accompanied by an emphasis on service learning—academic experiences coupled closely with national or community work toward particular objectives. The experiences themselves most often entail group projects, and the academic venues for follow-up courses are especially promising opportunities for cooperative efforts. Campus Compact, a consortium founded by several university presidents in the early 1980s and now including more than five hundred institutions, has been a leading force for examining and extending service learning, a distinctively new and promising approach to higher learning.[2]

In another movement, many faculty members are finding opportunities in their own teaching to assign cooperative work and deliver group

[2] See, for example, *Service Counts: Lessons from the Field of Service and Higher Education* (Campus Compact, Brown University 1995).

rewards for outstanding performance. In writing courses, reciprocal peer review is being used effectively. In schools of engineering, teams of students compete in design competitions in which the outcome is a device and success is determined by, say, its duration of flight rather than the percentage of correct answers. Frequently, the most important lesson of a group project is only loosely connected to its primary academic purpose: students have to deal with the skilled colleague who has a difficult personality, or solve the "free-rider" problem.

There are real but usually unspoken disagreements among faculty as to whether a university education ought to focus entirely on intellectual development or entail some efforts to direct and encourage personal maturation as well. Advocates of the latter are often associated with a "student-affairs mentality" and seen as intellectually soft by many faculty members. Advocates of the former may come across as "hard-nosed" or inflexible to those in the other camp. This philosophical split is vital to the institution's purpose, but unfortunately the contest is now being waged in the dark. We need to recognize that there are substantive choices to be made, and that they ought to be the subject of careful and public deliberation. The change to a more holistic view of our educational responsibility is well under way, but until it becomes the active subject of policy debate we can only guess at whether change is forthcoming.

A very different force is to be found in the growing demand, on the part of students as well as external critics, for policy studies and other work relevant to real-world problems. This is not a new problem for universities; indeed, they have always wavered between "academic" detachment and worldly engagement. The university's reluctance to be "relevant," a lingering after-effect of the painful 1960s, is being eroded by an increasing realization that the great problems confronting the world are too interesting and important to be ignored—and that they do not come in disciplinary packages. The list of challenges is endlessly fascinating and thoroughly "academic" in the sense of being analytically demanding and intellectually exciting. Arms control and disarmament; ethical issues in genetic testing and counseling; contemporary extinction rates and their implications for conservation policy; utilization incentives in health-care systems; the influence of education and economic status of women on fertility rates—this is only a partial list of issues on the academic agenda of one institute in one university in one month. Students find these problems gripping; they insist on learning about them. And increasingly, faculty members want to work on them. Reluctance to do so comes partly from the considerable difficulty of being an interdisciplinary scholar.

Most "interdisciplinary" work should properly be called multidisciplinary; it harnesses different specialties toward some common objective, but without asking students to master them all. Some programs, however, actually try to train students to gain competence in several disciplines. This approach is open to the criticism that it involves "watereddown" biology or "soft" economics. Critics are right to insist on rigorous disciplinary review; indeed, that is probably necessary to keep interdisciplinary work honest. But to insist that the combination of disciplines inevitably involves weakening each of them is merely stubborn and perhaps fearful adherence to traditional approaches.

Members of Congress, foundation executives, the most experienced journalists, and other thoughtful observers of the American scene are all asking the same question—"Can the universities really make a difference with respect to the Big Problems facing us?" The question stems from real concern about the seriousness of the problems, and equally from a mistrust of the ability of the academic sector to mobilize in a way likely to produce solutions. It is not that there is a lack of respect for the intellectual fire-power of the universities, or even for their capacity to make major contributions of a practical sort. The success of university research in bio-medicine and the physical and engineering sciences has been spectacular, and it is widely appreciated. The skepticism is about the universities' ability to recognize to marshal the diverse talents necessary to approach complex problems of large scale. Whether the academy can overcome the resistance of departmental structure and long tradition to "re-engineer" itself in the face of these challenges is an open question.

In the first two-thirds of the 20th century, university faculty members played a dominant role among the nation's "public intellectuals." Today there is growing doubt that academic scholars enjoy that level of prominence or have that much influence in the shaping of public awareness. This is partly the result of an admirable growth of intellectual resources in other sectors. The emergence of more reflective and critical journalism, the increasing role of foundations and think tanks in public life, and the expanded capacity of government and the for-profit sector have all enriched the quality of national thought. But it is difficult to avoid the conclusion that the role of universities has been diminished in part by their own failure to exercise intellectual leadership in the areas that a thoughtful public believes to be important. Critics point to the faddish and often incomprehensible preoccupations of the humanities, to the absorption of the social sciences with the detailed quantification of not very important problems, and to the resistance of various diseases to the ambitious claims of molecular biologists. They wonder at the time and energy expended on internal discussions of whether this or that is politically correct.

It is perhaps neither necessary nor possible for the universities to exert the dominant influence they once had; the nation is a more complicated and pluralistic place, and it has lots of thinkers in lots of areas. But an important role will be reserved for the university and its faculty if, and only if, they can reconnect to the society that nurtures them. The question is how to do that.

One way is through strong leadership from the top. Yet to many critics of the university, presidential leadership has become an oxymoron, like amateur athletics. Where are the Nicholas Murray Butlers and the William Rainey Harpers? Or, to take a somewhat more recent example, could a James Bryant Conant exist now? The "great presidents" of yesteryear are actually more admired for their visibility and influence in national affairs than for what they did within their own institutions. Conant as ambassador to Germany was better understood than Conant as president of Harvard. The much-admired president of Notre Dame, Father Theodore Hesburgh, is better known for his splendid service on various presidential commissions or the wisdom of his observations about American society than for his service to Notre Dame.

It is doubtful whether university presidents can, in this day and age, gain the kind of celebrity status enjoyed by their most noted predecessors. Mass media, visibility, and shifting cultural ideals tend to give the spotlight to athletes, rockers, politicians, and even computer giants. The most noted academic death of 1996, to judge by the front page of the New York Times, was that of Timothy Leary, a Harvard professor noted chiefly for having persuaded his students (and many others) to break the law and put their central nervous systems at risk with various recreational drugs. At bottom, perhaps managing, which is what presidents do most of the time, simply lacks glamour.

Managing a university is harder and more consuming work than it once was. Institutions of higher education are more complicated places, with more constituencies, more government involvement, and more stress. There are often too few hours in the day to deal with every constituency and every emergency. That reality received national attention when Harvard's president, Neil Rudenstine, took a prolonged leave for what was described as exhaustion. The national press treated this with uncharacteristic but deserved compassion, but for many it raised the question, "Are these jobs too tough?" The answer obviously depends on who is doing them, and how much dedication the president insists on bringing to each aspect of the task. But it is clear that escalating obligations and the expanded scale of the university have imposed more stringent limits on the kind of public visibility and outreach that presidents can achieve.

Within the university itself, administrative responsibility is a key ingredient in the design of the institution's objectives. Although presidents don't make curriculum decisions, vital choices about what should be taught and how are arenas for the assertion of presidential leadership. The proposed revisions of the Western Culture course at Stanford brought one such arena to the surface. Others loom. What should be done to improve the scientific "literacy" of college graduates? What should be done about the prevalence of postmodern teaching in some humanities departments, through which students learn that all of the objective reality claimed by scientists is entirely constructed from their system of values? When academic legitimacy is asserted for propositions of this kind, departments and committees can do little. Strong persuasion and mediation from the top are necessary to fulfill the institution's responsibility to its students. And when interdisciplinary approaches to such vital subjects as environmental policy or arms control cannot break departmental monopolies on the budget or the curriculum, presidential initiative should be brought to bear.

Questions arise not only about what we should teach but about whom and how many. At the undergraduate level, particularly for those colleges and universities that admit selectively, the question almost no one asks is, "Are we concerned with value, or with value added?" Admissions officers in such places compete avidly for the "best" applicants, by which they usually mean those who are most likely to graduate with the highest probability of subsequent success. A strong case, at least in some institutions, could be made for accepting those students for whom the institution is likely to make the greatest difference. Such a choice, which would seem heretical in most places, would clearly have to be made at the top.

There is hardly a subject more prominent in the national conversation about higher education than "affirmative action" and its role in admissions decisions. With hefty political leadership from the governor, the Board of Regents of the University of California resolved to abolish racial preference (while, of course, saying nothing about other, much steeper preferences, such as those regularly exercised on behalf of athletes and the children of influential persons). The president of Stanford, Gerhard Casper, issued a strong and thoughtful explanation of why his university would continue to pursue an admissions policy that employed preferences to assure diversity in its student population. It was a splendid example of presidential leadership at the right moment, emphasizing a strong academic consensus that a diverse student body confers educational advantages on all students.[3]

Financial aid, so closely related to admissions in the policy context, raises questions all its own. It is the primary device for determining access: poor and minority students simply cannot come to the more selective institutions without substantial help. Financially favored selective private colleges and universities have maintained policies of "need-blind" admissions; by doing so, they guarantee that no student will be denied admission on the grounds of inability to pay. Unfortunately, this policy is fading fast as budget constraints tighten. The capacity of private colleges and universities to assemble diverse and highly selected student bodies depends on how they arrange financial aid packages. This capacity is limited, of course, by available funds—the vast majority of which, following a long spell of reduction in federal student aid, come from private sources.

In the best of all possible worlds, a student with a given amount of financial need would be offered a standard amount of financial aid, which would vary from institution to institution, since tuition and other charges also vary. The student would then be able to choose according to the suitability of the academic program, not the price. To most of us in higher education, this seems the best possible outcome. Price competition—offering fat scholarship assistance to especially desired admittees—merely wastes scarce resources that could be applied to other students with need. It pits institutions against one another in a kind of "tragedy of the commons," in which the victims are qualified students who don't get helped.

---

[3] This proposition, much as I believe it, is, unfortunately—in the words of my colleague Robert Rosenzweig—based on "rhetoric supported by anecdote."

In 1991 the Department of Justice served more than fifty institutions with Civil Investigative Demands, requiring them to submit reams of documents on the history of tuition-setting and financial aid policy. The theory was that the similarity of financial aid packages and of tuition charges at the selective private institutions amounted to an antitrust violation. Eventually the government narrowed the case to the eight Ivy League institutions and MIT, which had met annually in a so-called overlap group to compare awards and deal with differences in the institutional estimates of financial need by joint applicants. In staff time, institutions the size of Harvard and MIT had to spend between half a million and a million dollars each to satisfy the federal investigative demand. The government eventually sued, and the eight Ivies settled before the case came to trial—agreeing to abandon the practice of overlap analysis. In a courageous exercise of presidential leadership, Charles Vest of MIT decided to stay in the fight. MIT lost at the district court level; the attorney general, Richard Thornburgh, had decided to try the case in Pennsylvania, where he was then running for the U.S. Senate. MIT persevered and won at appeal. Although its victory may not have made much difference in financial aid policy in the long run, it put an emphatic punctuation mark at the end of an overbroad and unreasonable exercise harassment on the part of the U.S. government. Vest's determination in this matter boldly underscores the value of institutional leadership: sometimes university presidents must protect their institutions against powerful outside forces.

Perhaps the most visible and influential presidential role is that of spokesperson. The president of any well-known institution has a "bully pulpit," and there is no shortage of temptation to use it. Students want support from the top on any issue that is deeply felt at the moment. Outside organizations hope for the same. And the presidents themselves, as human beings, have strong convictions that they sometimes want to express in the most public and forceful way. Others, of course, feel differently. Trustees generally hope that their presidents, like 19th century children, will be often seen and seldom heard. They know that any strong view expressed publicly is remembered far longer by those who differ with it than by those who agree. They regularly hear from their friends— in another boardroom, or at the club—whenever "their man" or "their woman" says something controversial. Furthermore, they understand, quite correctly, that when their president tries to take positions as a private individual, members of the public will not make the distinction between person and institution. Most presidents therefore heed these warnings, temper their impulses with judgment, and avoid taking public positions.

When the matter entails a challenge to their own universities or is highly relevant to some institutional interest, academic leaders should be heard. With respect to issues or controversies outside the university, there is more room for doubt. If a matter relates to a specific interest of the institution or of higher education generally, then it is a proper subject for the president to take on in a public way. But if the issue does not matter to the institution itself or to one of its constituencies, then it does not warrant depleting a valuable resource (the public's attention). For example, the institution might not have a direct interest in a particular federal provision regarding student aid if it doesn't affect the university's finances; but if it adversely affects the welfare of its students, the president would certainly be justified in speaking out on their behalf.

It was not difficult to apply these criteria to two of the issues on which I spent the most time during my years as the president of Stanford. One of them was the students' engagement in public and community service. It seemed clear to me that it was in the interest of our students, and of our sense of institutional self-worth, to encourage them to seek outlets for helping, both on the campus and in the community outside. With other presidents, I tried to make this a national effort through the founding of Campus Compact. The second was to move universities toward a recognition of their responsibilities for the quality of elementary and secondary public education. The interest of higher education in that subject seems to me self-evident, and I think our neglect of the rest of the educational system contributed to the erosion of public esteem for all our institutions.

On some other important issues, the case for engagement was not so clear. In the mid-1980s, apartheid in South Africa was a hot topic on many campuses, including ours. Students in large numbers demanded that we divest our stock in corporations doing business in that country to protest human rights violations there. At Stanford we insisted on a case-by-case review, divesting only companies with poor performances under the principles devised by Reverend Leon Sullivan to evaluate corporate citizenship in South Africa. Even then, we divested only after some jawboning to persuade them to improve. Of course this policy did not satisfy many of the students. At the same time, the Congress was considering trade sanctions, and I was urged to comment publicly on those proposals. I did so in the belief that the issue had become so linked to our own institutional policy that it was impossible to separate them.

Finally, there are issues that, even though they do not directly concern the university and fail to meet the criteria I have just suggested, seem of such transcendent importance that the consciences of many people are deeply stirred. A widespread outburst of racial violence, or an episode of unjust and unlawful government action, might justify a presidential statement. If the matter is highly controversial, as it is likely to be, taking a position will entail considerable cost. But the purpose of a self-denying policy, after all, is not absolute constraint. Rather, it serves to remind one of those costs, and to permit only the most carefully considered exceptions.

The vital activity of Ph.D. training is a domain in which the faculty, not the institution's leadership, plays the key role. In the early years of this century, the Ph.D. degree, newly imported from Europe, was represented as a highly advanced scholarly credential. But it soon evolved into a required credential for teaching at the college or university level, across the board. Now lower-tier institutions regularly advertise the proportion of their faculty members who hold Ph.D.s, as though that fact alone were a reliable indicator of the quality of instruction. In fact, it is anything but that: doctoral study has always trained people to do research first. Thus intent and reality drew further apart. William James recognized the problem early on; he talked of the "Ph.D. octopus," and indeed it was, reaching out from the research university to wrap its tentacles around the system of higher education.

To modify higher education in America it is necessary to change the ways in which doctoral students are trained. That is not easy; doctoral training is hard work, and the workers have always done it in a certain way. But there are promising indicators of movement. A new program entitled Preparing Future Faculty, sponsored by the Pew Trusts and the Association of Graduate Schools, is centered on several research university campuses; each institution is part of a consortium that includes a liberal arts college, a community college, a comprehensive public institution, and (often) one or more others. The doctoral candidates at the research university do supervised teaching in the other places, and have the opportunity not only to develop their skills but to absorb and perhaps appreciate the norms in different kinds of settings.

The attitudes of researchers trained in the usual way may be changing. There is an annual convocation of Presidential Young Investigators, recipients of highly prestigious postdoctoral awards from the National Science Board. The fellows choose their own topic, and at a recent meeting they selected undergraduate science education. This decision, somewhat unexpected given that the group is selected on the basis of research accomplishment, led eventually to a serious set of recommendations about how to improve the teaching function.[4]

Indeed, there is real ferment about undergraduate education in the sciences, and about the way we are preparing future faculty for the teaching profession. A major convocation at the NAS in April of 1995 led off a "year of national dialog," during which regional symposia on the subject were held across the country.[5] The NSF has sponsored additional meetings, with participation from other government agencies that support research.

In the humanities, where graduate life is often more isolating than in the sciences, and may lead to a more unrealistic view of the future, a major ten-year study of doctoral education is under way with the support of the Andrew W. Mellon Foundation. That two of the nation's major private foundations and its leading academies are engaged with the problem of how we train Ph.D. candidates is important news. It tells us that there is a problem, but it also suggests that we may be on our way to a solution.

When I was a graduate student, close to finishing a doctorate, some of us would entertain one another with visions of a place we would all like to work. With only the slightest blush, I confess that we called it Good Guy U. Its central feature was the nearly complete collapse of most of the hierarchical traditions that had rubbed us raw in our lowly status as graduate students. The professoriate at GGU consisted of sympathetic people who spent lots of time with students and shared credit generously, not only with students but with their colleagues. At GGU many of the competitive features that characterize research environments were replaced by widespread sharing of ideas, equipment, and space. Interdisciplinary scorn was notably absent, and respect and resources were doled out even-handedly by a supportive administration. Faculty roles in insti-

---

[4] *America's Academic Future: A Report of the Presidential Young Investigator Colloquium on U.S. Engineering, Mathematics and Science Education for the Year 2010 and Beyond* (Washington, D.C.: National Science Board, 1994).

[5] National Academy of Sciences, *From Analysis to Action: Undergraduate Education in Science, Mathematics, Engineering and Technology* (Washington, D.C.: National Academy Press, 1996).

tutional governance were strong, but departmental decision making had much less influence over academic appointments. Students were given a larger role in institutional affairs, which led to a greater sense of belonging to the institution. Junior members of the various student affairs staffs were recognized as real members of the academic profession. GGU's athletic teams, naturally, won regularly—with bona fide students who displayed relentless good sportsmanship.

In this bit of 1950s fantasy, there are a few hints of what a reinvented university ought to be like; and indeed, much has happened since then to convert some of our youthful imagination into institutional reality. Students and their views are much more thoroughly integrated into evaluation and even policy determination. Faculty participation in university governance is both more extensive and more meaningful. Course planning and thinking about curriculum are done more thoroughly, too; indeed, anyone comparing the quality of higher education in the United States, then and now, has to agree that it is better now.

But in some respects the changes have been meager, and in others they have moved in the wrong direction. Departments are still the focus of academic development in the university, but their leadership has tended to narrow its vision and interests, thereby losing its public voice and regard. A kind of pessimism has set in, both about the future of scholarship and about the capacity of universities to be part of the solution to the problems that beset society.

The central force in institutional change, the faculty, has experienced severe crises of morale and status. Feeling pressed from the bottom by students and parents and from the top by administrators, they often feel like scapegoats for everyone's complaints. Yet they remain the heart and mind of the university. Their commitment is essential for university health. Wherever creative energy and institutional loyalty abound, the faculty is willing to experiment and to engage actively with the needs of students. Wherever they are lacking, things seem to stay where they are. Visiting many other institutions and watching the history of my own has convinced me that faculty engagement can be reliably summoned under the right circumstances.

Innovation and commitment are most evident in colleges and universities below the top rung of the prestige ladder. Elites find it difficult to modify a winning formula in this arena, as in many others. The "transforming institutions" are often those that perceive a special mission—for example, to a particular urban center, as is the case with Portland State or Indiana University/Purdue University at Indianapolis. Or they may be founded on the idea of a particular kind of experiment, like Hampshire College or Evergreen State. In such cases a number of faculty members are either gathered to, or convinced by, an explicit vision of institutional goals. Sometimes a college or university is empowered by circumstances or competitive zeal to raise its rank, and the momentum of improvement builds faculty enthusiasm and carries it along. Stanford in the 1960s was described by David Riesman as "a meteor in our business," and those of us on the faculty, exhilarated by the sense of moving up fast, invested heavily in the institution.

In more stable situations, faculty engagement does not come so naturally. Loyalty is often fragmented, and morale is low. Institutional commitment can be summoned, but it will require new ways of making faculty members feel responsible for the institution and for its students. A big part of the task is to develop a more centralized sense of direction, yet maintain a shared governance structure in which faculty members (and, to a degree, students as well) feel more like stakeholders. It is also important to make the institution more flexible and responsive to newly arising needs and opportunities, by deliberately retaining funds for new initiatives and by cultivating the spirit of innovation.

University leadership is critical here. The faculty's confidence in the institution depends on a sense that its role is accepted, appreciated, and protected. Faculty work and faculty service are often poorly understood and rarely congratulated. The university administration needs to be a more active advocate for its own faculty and for a public understanding of its role. If presidents and Boards of Regents, trustees, deans, and administrators would express pride in, and understanding of, them, the work of teaching and scholarship, faculty morale, and faculty responsibility would benefit greatly.

These are the dimensions along which institutional redesign must proceed. It can happen if boards and presidents and faculties come together on the need for change and set out to accomplish it together. It will *not* happen by *obiter dicta*, from boards or the administration; the traditions of academic governance are too strong for that. Reconstruction of the relationship between the legal owners of the university and its academic proprietors is an essential condition. It will be met in a few especially enterprising and imaginative places, and from there it will spread to the rest.

The commanding feature of this process of redesigning the university will be the reclamation of its central mission. It is, after all, society's agent for cultural transmission and cultural change. It works by the thoughtful, participatory transfer of knowledge and excitement from one generation to the next. Accordingly, its improvement must entail putting students and their needs first. Once that is done, the rest falls into place: the complex challenges posed by intellectual property disputes, the tension between teaching and research, the ethical problems in faculty-student relationships, professional misconduct issues, the need for creative thinking about undergraduate education reform—indeed, all the manifold difficulties so prominent in the growing public mistrust of our academic institutions. Placing students first is a simple design principle, but it has great power.

None of this will happen, of course, without some attitudinal change. That is why, in the vast and pluralistic landscape of American higher education, the research universities must be the agents of change. They are the nurturers of the ambitions and the values of the next academic generation. The difficulty is that they are both successful and prestigious, and they lack the natural appetite for renovation and reform that characterizes the striving, transforming institutions. But unless they change, little else will.

It is perhaps not too hopeful to foresee a new understanding of academic duty emerging from that change. For the university, the essential task will be to maintain its special role with respect to the larger society: independent, provocative, but dutiful in its attention to the successor generation. From the faculty, one can hope for a shift in loyalty: more scrupulous attention to the needs of the institution and its students, and a passionate commitment to new ways of knowing and of teaching. And those who manage and lead the institution will need to summon both a readier willingness to assert vigorously, and if necessary defend, the university's values to the public, and the capacity to envision opportunity and welcome change.

Section 2

Integrating Information Resources
with Institutional Mission

3

Universities in the Digital Age

JOHN SEELY BROWN AND PAUL DUGUID

What will the university of the digital age look like? We really ought to have some idea by now. It's been twenty-five years since Donald Schön urged universities to start considering life "beyond the stable state." At about the same time, the futurist Alvin Toffler confidently predicted that the information age would force academia to accommodate an "accelerating pace of change," prepare for "life-long learning," and even consider "learning contracts" instead of the conventional degree.

A flood of reports and a deluge of technological innovations have followed. Yet beyond the replacement of the library catalog by computer terminals, the use of PCs as sophisticated typewriters, and the explosion of campus e-mail, things don't look very different. Perhaps, as an acquaintance suggested to George Landow, hypertext champion and author of *Hypertext: The Convergence of Contemporary Critical Theory and Technology*, (Baltimore: Johns Hopkins University Press, 1991), it's just a matter of lag: "It took only twenty-five years for the overhead projector to make it from the bowling alley to the classroom. I'm optimistic about academic computing; I've begun to see computers in bowling alleys."

Most campuses, of course, are rife with computers. Landow's own Institute for Research into Information and Technology is based at Brown University. Schön teaches at MIT, the spiritual parent of such early high-tech successes as Wang and DEC. Colleagues there include such irreproachable frontiersmen of the digital age as Nicholas Negroponte, Marvin Minsky, and Bill Mitchell. Each is more likely to give you a home Page URL than a business card. Their universities aren't waiting for the Internet: they form its major intersections.

So computational backwardness cannot explain the apparent inertia in campus life over the past twenty-five years. Indeed, it's more likely that campuses are schizophrenic: combinations of high-powered computational infrastructures *and* highly conventional institutional practices. Moreover, strength in technology can sometimes be a good indicator of institutional conservatism. Those institutions that were able to accumulate the resources (financial, intellectual, social) to develop a computer-intensive infrastructure were most likely to be large, wealthy, and above all—despite Schön's pleas—profoundly stable.

This institutional conservatism doesn't arise in the easy-to-criticize administrative bureaucracies alone. Tenured faculty, for both good and bad reasons, tend to cling to the institutional and disciplinary sources of their own hard-won security. (It took an English academic to say to one of us "We've done things this way for 500 years, why should we change now?" but similar currents of conservatism run through American faculty senates.) Alumni and parents, too, as the March 15, 1995, *New York Times* noted, often militate against change. People who have paid a lot for a chunk of tradition usually will resist attempts to dismember it. (In a whirl of medieval costumes and dead languages, commencement invests both parents and alumni with the value of tradition.)

Nonetheless, for all the institutional inertia, universities are changing. Their student bodies are forcing them to. The archtypal 18-to-22-year-old undergraduate going through school in four consecutive years and financed by parents is becoming increasingly rare and unconventional. People are taking up their degrees later and over longer periods, assembling them out of one course here and a few credit hours there, snatched between jobs and bank loans, as time, money, interest, and opportunity arise. It's probably less helpful, then, to say simply that higher education will change because of changing technologies than to say the emerging computational infrastructure will be crucially important in shaping an already changing system.

In contemplating what the future might look like, some suggest that it won't so much "look" as "be"—that the campus of the future will be "virtual," with no need of the physical plant that has been the visible center of academia for so long. This notion of a virtual campus, we suspect, both underestimates how universities as institutions work and overestimates what communications technologies do. Learning, at all levels, relies ultimately on personal interactions and, in particular, on a range of implicit and peripheral forms of communication, some of which technology is still very far from being able to handle proficiently.

Communications technology nonetheless can undoubtedly support many of the interactions between teachers and learners. Moreover, the lower marginal cost of on-line teaching makes it tempting to ignore what teaching does not support. The practical and financial viability of the "on-line academy" may, however, become as much a cause for concern as celebration, threatening to polarize further an already divided system. The more expensive, conventional campus, with all its rich and respected resources, is less likely to disappear than to become the increasingly restricted preserve of those who can afford it. Net access will be for those who cannot. An on-line degree will almost certainly not command the same respect as its distant campus cousin. In consequence, despite conventional concerns about "have-nots" lacking access to technology, technology may in fact become the only access they have to experiences whose full value actually develops off-line.

An alternative approach, and one more in tune with the way people learn, is not to divide the student body between those who get to go to school and those who are only get to go on-line. It will, we argue here, be wiser to arrange things so each student can divide his or her career between time better spent on campus or in communities and time better spent on-line. All learners need to experience both. So, in contrast to those who suggest that the university of the 21st century will not so much "look" as "be," we suggest that it may "look" in many ways much as it does now but "be" very different, because the most profound changes may occur in the institutional arrangements rather than the physical infrastructure that makes up what people currently think of as a university.

WHAT DO SCHOOLS DO?

Our own view of how the college or university of the next millennium may look and be is based on our sense of what it is they do, what roles they play in society, and why people think they are worth the often huge sums of money invested in higher education.

"Higher education" covers a wide spectrum, of course. In 1993, the U.S. Department of Education's National Center for Educational Statistics (NCES) reported that there were 10,800 postsecondary institutions, of which 5,400 offered diplomas for less than two years' work. Of the

3,600 regarded as accredited colleges of higher education, some 2,700 offered four-year degrees, 800 MAs, and 660 doctorates. About 170 of these institutions are designated research universities. Given this range, much that has been written focuses only on a small part of the higher education enterprise, such as the "research university" or a particular school or discipline. But, as Daniel Alpert has argued, part of the failure to change has arisen from the failure to address "the system as a whole." If only at a very general level then, we attempt here to discuss the core of that system—degree granting colleges and universities—and to raise some systemwide issues involving teaching, learning, and credentialing.

We begin by adopting a strategy from business consultants who have to evaluate huge and diversified corporations that address manifold interests. What, we want to ask, are higher education's "core competencies"? What do its accredited institutions do that other institutions don't? Why are individuals, families, states, and government agencies willing to invest so much in it? What is it they want—and the system offers—that's so valuable? The easiest answer—and one in line with the distinctions made in the NCES report—is that it offers degrees.

People in the system don't, of course, like to think of their work in terms of credentials. Many have higher aims and higher goals, and for some, education is an end in itself. But for a large proportion of its clientele, education is an investment—a down payment on a career, social status, or, more immediately, just a job. Most students take the degrees they do to get the jobs they want, knowing or hoping that these jobs will repay the investment. For the vast majority, college implicitly provides a route into the general job "draft," much as it more explicitly prepares athletes for the NBA or NFL draft. Academic aspirations and career aspirations are very tightly entwined. Undoubtedly, providing credentials is far from all that colleges do. Nevertheless, crass though it may seem, any discussion that does not acknowledge the central importance to colleges and their students of credits and credentials, degrees and diplomas, simply cannot get very far.

Distaste for credentialing causes people to look on credentials themselves in very different ways. Some see a vulgar misrepresentation of what schools really do in detail. Others see them as a succinct and useful representation of the experience gained in a college career. Within the system, many rightly want to consider "how you play the game," but outside the system, what matters most is whether you won or lost. These two views are not entirely separable. Public perception of degrees can exert strong influence on university practice at the highest levels. As Peter Eisenberger, professor of physics at Princeton University, notes in a March, 1995, *Physics Today* article, "Once students hear that investing years and thousands of dollars in a Ph.D. has little or no economic value or intellectual satisfaction, they will start changing their plans." So although it can seem a crude measure, a diploma remains a fairly sensitive indicator of the market status—the economic as well as the intellectual value—of a university, a degree, a discipline, and a graduate.

In the degree market then, degrees usefully encapsulate or represent several years of work. Simultaneously, they also "usefully misrepresent" much of what goes on in those years, providing both schools and society with important slack in a system that should not be too taut. While its market value remains high, the very crude semiotics of a degree gives both universities and students a certain license to do what the degree doesn't necessarily register. It allows students to "play the game" in a variety of creative ways, on the simple condition that in the end they meet the requirements for "winning" a degree. Behind a front of public respectability, students and faculty undertake activities that are socially valuable but not readily valued in the market. In the end, this slack provides the job market and society as a whole more diverse and versatile candidates than they probably know to request. To shift our metaphor to legislative terms, the degree is an "omnibus package" intended to draw broad public support. While that support holds, an array of important but not always justifiable measures can be unobtrusively "tacked on" without question. It would help neither students, faculty, nor society to open the package to a "line item veto." In this way, credentialing serves everyone's purposes.

LEARNING AND LADING

The degree, then, is useful for what it mis/represents. As long as it represents certain things about a degree-holder with reasonable accuracy, it can creatively obscure other aspects to advantage. But that still leaves the question, What does a degree represent?

When people look too hard at degrees, we suspect they see a sort of intellectual bill of lading, a receipt for knowledge-on-board. Teaching, in this view, is a delivery service and school a loading site. No one actually says this, but a delivery view nonetheless underlies much of what people perceive about schools. An implicit delivery view also leads some to think of educational technology as a sort of intellectual fork-lift truck. If it's true that the most effective technology in the classroom is still the overhead projector, this may well be because it and many of the alternatives have been designed with delivery in mind.

The knowledge-delivery view, however, profoundly misunderstands how people learn, where they learn, and when they learn. In the first place, it portrays students as vessels into which the university pours information. This is an extraordinarily passive view of how people learn, one which takes no account of the active participation necessary for learning and knowing. And, second, the knowledge-delivery view overlooks all the things that people learn on campus outside as well as inside the classroom. These can be as important to a student's career as teacher-delivered knowledge. People leave college knowing not just things, but knowing people, and knowing not just academic facts, but knowing social strategies for dealing with the world. Reliable friendships and complex social strategies can't be delivered and aren't picked up through lectures, but they give an education much of its value.

Furthermore, people don't usually treat a degree like a bill of lading. Employers, for whom most degrees are ultimately earned, usually look at a degree with infinitely less care than they would a bill of lading. Few outside academia want to examine a transcript. And those who receive degrees rarely act as though it was information delivery that mattered most to them. Alumni tend to blur on classroom information. Details of what they were taught fade exponentially after finals. Few would easily forgive someone who asked them to retake their exams a couple of years—or possibly even a couple of weeks—later.

Short though they may be in some respects, alumni memories do, however, provide some insight into what a degree represents. Alumni do remember groups they joined, scholars they worked with, tasks they accomplished, and friendships they made. We don't have to look much further than the group of Rhodes Scholars around our current president to see how college activities and networks can be far more important in later life than a degree's formal content.

Such networking is not simply a campus sideshow. The groups people join at university, some social, some academic, are important. There's much truth in the old saying "It's not what you know, but who you know," although that doesn't quite reflect the intricate connection between "what" and "who." It's this connection that ultimately explains why parents pay high fees for "good" schools; why students and faculty compete so hard to get to a few campuses, while the vast majority of institutions often struggle to fill their places; why academics are so concerned about where someone received his or her degree and with whom; why diplomas are taken as significant indicators of job worthiness, though transcripts are not; and how university experience helps people find their way through life after university. For the core competency of universities is not transferring knowledge, but developing it, and that's done within intricate and robust networks and communities.

COLLEGES, COMMUNITIES, AND LEARNING

The delivery view of education assumes that knowledge comprises discrete, pre-formed units, which learners ingest in smaller or greater amounts until graduation or indigestion takes over. To become a physicist, such a view suggests, you need to take in a lot of formulas and absorb a lot of experimental data. But, on the one hand, knowledge is not a static, pre-formed substance: it is constantly changing. Learning involves active engagement in the processes of that change. And, on the other hand, people don't become physicists by learning formulas any more than they become football players by learning plays. In learning how to be a physicist or a football player—how to act as one, talk as one, be recognized as one—it's not the explicit statements, but the implicit practices that count.

Indeed, knowing only the explicit—mouthing the formulas or the plays—is often exactly what gives an outsider away. Insiders know more. By coming to inhabit the relevant community, they get to know not just what the standard answers are, but the real questions and why they matter. You don't pick up those things in textbooks any more than you learn to talk like a native by studying grammar books. Learning involves inhabiting the streets of a community's culture. The community may be include astrophysicists, architects, or acupuncturists, but learning involves experiencing its cultural peculiarities.

By describing universities in terms of community, we may seem to be putting academic disciplines somewhere on a cozy line running from neighborhood watch groups to football-team boosters—the sorts of communities that some communitarians have in mind. The communities we have in mind, however, are quite different. These hold together not through voluntarism but through the enduring interpersonal relations that form around shared practices. People come to share this sort of community by sharing the same tasks, obligations, and goals.

Stephen Toulmin, who has explored the community character of academic disciplines, argues that through a complex of shared practices and institutional arrangements (in which the university has come to play a major part), disciplines form "communities of concept users." What is often thought of as "concept-acquisition," he maintains, is really a rich process of "enculturation" as newcomers become members of the community. More recently, two learning researchers, Jean Lave and Etienne Wenger, broadened the scope of Toulmin's analysis by arguing that all learning, whether specifically "academic" or not, involves enculturation in communities. At base, their work suggests, academic communities are quite similar to other communities of practitioners, or "communities of practice," as Lave and Wenger call them.

Communities of practice are, we think, essential and inevitable building blocks of society. Being an inevitable rather than optional form of social arrangement, they have the same credits and debits as society as a whole. They are as likely to be hierarchical as egalitarian; to be restrictive as open; to resist change as welcome it; to be internally divided as united. It is the practice and the concepts they share that connect members of a community, not a warm glow of communitarian fellow feeling. So we are not claiming, as communitarians do, that it would be useful to form communities and that universities are a good place to form them. Rather, we claim that communities, with all their strengths and shortcomings, grow inevitably and inescapably out of ongoing, shared practice. Learning a community's ways always requires access to that community and that practice.

The real test of a school, then, is the quality of access it provides to academic communities—Toulmin's communities of concepts. A degree reflects not simply the quality of participation of a particular individual, but also the quality of access made available by the institution. That is why choosing a school is so important. Moreover, it's exactly because some schools give credentials without ever giving suitable access to knowing communities that the relationship between learning and credentials is always problematic. People can and do end up with the label but without having had the necessary experience. Consequently, the central thrust of any attempt to retool the education system must involve expanding direct access to communities, not simply to credentials.

But our concern about technological retooling also comes at this issue from the opposite direction. Those who have the label but not the experience present one problem. Those who might have the experience but not the label face another. This is a central problem for proponents of "open learning." Experience without a formal representation has very limited exchange value—as those whose experience comes from the university of life well know. Consequently, we believe that any retooling must be two-pronged: it must seek to provide wider access to communities—and not just to information—and it must expand ways to represent new forms of access and practice.

GRADUATES AND UNDERGRADUATES

Graduate education and research illustrate the attempt to bring newcomers into the disciplinary community. Collaboration between aspiring students and established scholars introduces the former to a discipline's practice. With the help of mentors, graduate students work their way ever deeper into a community and its institutions, moving away from a toe-hold on the periphery toward increasingly full participation, like apprentices being led into a craft by masters of the practice. In such a process, medical students learn to treat patients, law students to compose briefs, historians to undertake historical research, physics students to engage in the practice of physics rather than merely learn about it, and so on. It isn't abstract theory but concrete, community practice that's at the top of the pyramid.

Things are obviously different for undergraduates. They, after all, are prime targets of mechanisms of delivery. Nevertheless, as colleges are currently configured, undergraduates usually do gain some forms of community access. If only for didactic purposes, schools usually put before them practitioners from within particular fields or graduate students working on the periphery. These community members, some intentionally and some unintentionally, give undergraduates a glimpse of the reality of what life in those communities is like. Indeed, behind several of the reform movements one sees on campus today—undergraduate research, problem-based learning, field-based senior capstones, and so on—might lie a new sense of the value of introducing undergraduates to real-life aspects of disciplinary practice.

One of the most important things undergraduates gain from such exposures is an implicit sense of how society comprises innumerable distinct communities of practice. From a distance, academic disciplines appear engaged in the collective and seamless pursuit of knowledge. As students begin to engage with the discipline, as they move from exposure to experience, they develop a sense that the different communities on a campus are quite distinct, that apparently common terms have different meanings, apparently shared tools have different uses, and apparently related objects have different interpretations. Coming to understand this, however unconsciously, is a key outcome of a college career. Furthermore, as well as spotting the differences, undergraduates also tend to understand the common social demands all professional communities make. This is an important part of the socializing effect of schools that makes their graduates congenial to corporations.

BEYOND THE CAMPUS

In the past it was quite easy to regard universities as society's unique and separate centers to which students went for a specified period to learn what they needed for life. The opposition of "town" to "gown" and the notion of the "ivory tower" represented a classic division between the university and its locale. Today that division has little meaning. Schools must respond to a growing demand for further education in the town, and they must draw on the knowledge created there, as well.

Demand is growing as people need to go on learning long after the conventional years of school are past. The insights acquired during a four-year degree never really sufficed for life, but, previously, almost everything else needed for a particular job could be picked up *in situ*. As people change jobs and jobs themselves change with great rapidity, such *ad hoc* learning is no longer sufficient. People need to re-immerse themselves in specialized communities to follow developments in specialized knowledge. Universities increasingly have to consider how they can support "life-long" learning to meet these needs. Perhaps, as Toffler suggested long ago, they might start to offer "learning contracts" to incoming students, committing colleges to their students for more than a standard four years.

As universities contemplate such changes, they need to find ways to reach people beyond the campus. Here, schools can draw on an inherent asset base generated in the daily round of seminars, colloquiums, lectures, and so forth. New means for capturing the transient activities of the classroom (live-boards, which capture the writings on a board for future reference, multimedia recordings, etc.) and for interactive dissemination (principally through Internet-like infrastructures) offer universities ways to provide a dynamic, responsive archive out of what formerly have been transient or broadcast practices.

Inevitably, capitalizing on these resources will require more than unedited dumps of classroom exchanges. To be useful, these exchanges will require the addition of different types of indexing and annotation, new and versatile search tools, and moderated channels for response. Here schools might develop links between students on campus (with time rather than money on their hands) and students off campus (with complementary resources). Students attending classes on campus might be able to index recordings in real time (these might be thought of as the multimedia equivalent of those exemplary class notes that classmates find so valuable today) and to respond to the issues raised by off-campus students through the interactive links.

In reaching out beyond the campus like this, universities are not simply expanding their fee base or extending their patronage. Communities of concepts don't emerge in the ivory tower alone. Valuable knowledge is created elsewhere in society, too. Consequently, in building better, interactive links between town and gown, between a field's on- and off-campus members, schools are serving their own needs, too. In the first place, they are also building links to expertise they lack themselves. And, perhaps most important of all, they are contributing to what Annalee Saxenian has called "regional advantage": the conventional science park of businesses fed from the university are, in fact, evolving into learning parks where universities and businesses feed one another. This process more firmly situates schools and their strengths within their regions rather than isolating them within their campuses.

FROM DELIVERY TO INTERACTIVITY

With such changes, conventional boundaries such as those between "town" and "gown" or students and alumni will start to blur as schools extend their reach across space and time. New technologies will be increasingly important for doing this. So far, "distance learning," which primarily involves delivering instruction to people off campus, has been the center of attention. As schools consider their options, we think it's important that they look beyond traditional paradigms of distance and delivery. A college's core competency, as we have attempted to say, involves a great deal more than simply delivering knowledge.

Our view is distinct from distance learning in several ways. First, distance teaching was developed with broadcast technology in mind. In the hands of institutions like the Open University (OU) in England, broadcast media have successfully allowed teachers to reach people who had little or no access to conventional schools. Questioning the privilege of the classroom more than the practice, however, such developments have only minimally altered the underlying delivery structure of pedagogy.

Second, when distance learning shifts education on-line and off campus, it can damagingly restrict the essential access to the authentic communities we discussed above. Students in dislocated, virtual campuses are unable to either engage fully with a range of communities, as undergraduates should, or to participate in particular ones, as graduates must.

Third, the focus on distance and delivery overlooks not only the needs of students, but all too often the strengths of new technologies, which are distinctive because they are interactive. Previous communications technologies—books, film, radio, television, telephones, video—have all supported distance and delivery, but they have primarily permitted only one-to-many or one-to-one communications. Knowledge communities, however, are built on more complex interactions, such as continuous conversation. Even in the technologically rich 20th century, such interactions have, for the most part, been possible only in face-to-face situations. The explosion of interactive and midcast (as opposed to broadcast or narrowcast distribution) technologies for the Internet argues that in the 21st century mediated communications will expand the possibility for rich, distal interactions—urging consideration of more than distance in distal education.

Already, innovative teachers and students are taking full advantage of the Internet to move from a paradigm of delivery to one of interactivity. We offer here a few examples of technologies and teachers that strike us as going in the right direction.

- *Newsgroups, usenets, bulletin boards, and listserv mail lists.* All these are based on the rudimentary software of electronic mail. E-mail has proved very useful in keeping teachers and students in touch with one another in one-to-one exchanges, but these groups or lists move beyond that by allowing all their members to address the group as a whole (in much the way someone asking a question in class addresses the whole class). Anyone who subscribes to a group or list can broadcast or midcast. Furthermore, many lists and groups capture the apparently ephemeral exchanges and comments of members in an archive that outlives the transient status of classroom questions. In sum, these systems essentially embrace both the features of many-to-many, real-time, conversation-like interaction and those of more enduring, written exchanges.

Such group interactions are particularly useful for auditors—"lurkers" as they are sometimes known on the Net. Like a good conversation or debate, group exchanges can be as illuminating for those who don't contribute as for those who do. And many lists have more silent partners than active ones. Evidence of the many lurkers haunting the virtual space often comes only when participants suggest taking an interesting discussion off-list. Then lurkers suddenly materialize to protest attempts to make a fruitful public discussion private.

- *Annotation systems.* Anyone who has lurked on a list knows that for every good conversation that gets going, there are a dozen false starts. For every useful contribution, there can be a dozen uninformed and highly opinionated ones that derail everyone. Often, conversational wheels merely spin or promising trains of thought get side-tracked. This is particularly true when too many participants are not well versed in the topic. Dan Huttenlocher, a professor in Cornell's computer science department, discovered all this when he created a list for informal undergraduate class discussions. He was disappointed to find how little it helped. "Particularly for undergraduates," he notes, "a list makes conversation easy, but focus difficult. Students don't need the opportunity to talk. What they need is something to talk about." Conversely, when he put problem sets on a class ftp server, Huttenlocher found this gave students a great deal to talk about, but no means for many-to-many conversation.

In response, with Jim Davis of the Xerox Design Research Institute at Cornell, Huttenlocher designed "CoNote," a World Wide Web annotation tool that allows students looking at a Web document both to post and to read questions and comments attached to that document. As a result, students can raise and discuss tricky issues, learn from others, discover they aren't the only ones stuck, and generally enter into lively debates about issues of importance to the class. Textual scholars have long known the importance of the interplay of text and commentary. This interplay can be traced back through the conventional footnotes and marginal notes to Talmudic commentaries. William Sherman has recently noted the importance of marginalia (or *adversaria* as they were called) to Renaissance science. Hypertext annotation systems like Huttenlocher's help to continue this robust interactivity between a text and its readers in new technological forms while extending the right to annotate publicly beyond a privileged few. (There are now several similar annotation systems in use on the World Wide Web. MIT Press, for example, uses a similar system with on-line texts of books, allowing readers to respond to authors.)

- *Shared on-line environments.* Nowhere on the Net has conversation become as lively as in MUDs and MOOs, shared on-line environments that allow all participating to see whatever anyone writes, though the participants may be continents apart. MUDs (Multi-User Dungeons) allow several players on computers connected by modems to play the game "Dungeons and Dragons" together. MOOs (object-oriented MUDS) remove the game goals, turning the dungeons into a computationally manipulable set of "rooms" where people can meet for on-line discussions and programming. MOOs have become the clubs and coffee-houses, pubs and cafes of the Internet.

  For courses that have difficulty finding enough live bodies on one campus, a MOO offers an interesting medium for interactive distal learning. James O'Donnell's graduate course on Boethius, conducted in the fall of 1994 for credit from the graduate school at the University of Pennsylvania, is an early example. Graduate medieval Latinists are few and usually far between, but Penn's LatinMOO allowed students from the United States and Asia to form a reasonable quorum. (The course on Boethius spanned some nine time zones.)

  Penn's LatinMoo was much more than a simple chat line. It comprised a "complex"—with a quadrangle, several classrooms, a Latin-only common room, and a virtual Coke machine around which people would gather to chat. O'Donnell opened the Boethius classroom to students enrolled in the class, while he made other parts of the MOO available for Latin students from his regular courses (including a "live" undergraduate class on Boethius) to get together more informally. To widen the conversation, O'Donnell combined other Net facilities with the MOO. In addition to putting the central text on a Web site with links to a commentary and other resources, he started a Boethius e-mail list that included all students in the MOO seminar and the live class, but essentially created space for virtual "auditors." This opened discussion to students and academics from around the world, while distinguishing levels of participation and access.

FROM DISTANCE TO OPEN

New on-line courses and new course technology emerge all the time. Our aim here has not been to attempt either a catalog or a survey. We offer these as examples of distal education that seem to us implicitly to go beyond issues of distance and to honor the interactive, communal character of learning and the emerging capabilities of the Net. In particular, they allow students to engage in what Dewey called "productive inquiry."

To some extent, addressing the needs of students in this way reflects the aspirations of what is called "open learning." Proponents of open learning seek to empower learners by breaking down barriers to education raised by conventional institutions. They wish to provide unhindered access to learning resources, so that technologically supported freedom of information may be turned into freedom of education for people pursuing their own learning needs. While such a shift responds better to the way people learn by facilitating interactivity and active engagement and inquiry rather than passive reception, even open learning underestimates some important roles institutions play.

First, as we have noted, a good deal of what an undergraduate diploma signifies comes from the way education socializes students, making them unreflectively familiar with the distinct mores of diverse communities. While open learning pursues access to information, it ignores the more important issues of access to communities.

Second, while open learning challenges the university's conventional role as gate-keeper to academic information, it simultaneously underestimates the importance of institutions representing educational achievement. As we argued earlier, it is the representation of experience that has exchange value in the job market. Employers who have proved generally reluctant to accept credentials from the university of life are unlikely to behave very differently with open learning on the Net.

Consequently, while the shift from distance to open learning is conceptually important, it fails to address both the communal and the institutional needs of learners. Institutional roles in providing access, oversight, and credentialing will remain important in the digital age. The institutional arrangements required by those roles, however, seem likely to change.

ALTERNATIVE CONFIGURATIONS

If we ignore, as some prefer, the way credentials provide both constraints on and resources for the higher education system—a valuable form of mis/representation as we described them—then it's possible to see the march toward, first, distance learning and, now, open learning as a fairly direct march of progress. With the development of various technologies, it can be claimed, students have slowly been able to take advantage of each new form of distance learning: the correspondence course, the broadcast-media course, and now Net courses. The future, as proponents of the electronic university assume, is simply to continue this progressive trend and move towards an "Electronic Worldwide University."

If, however, learning requires genuine participation, distance learning often provide its illusion only, while actually keeping students at a disempowering distance. This is a particular risk with use of the Net. As anyone who has sent e-mail to the White House, Congress, or even a newspaper knows, the Net can provide a powerful impression of interactivity and exchange while in practice denying both. Similar problems are likely to arise for on-line students. A distal learner, for example, may achieve access to public forums used by a campus class, but the campus community's private, off-line interactions will remain both inaccessible and invisible. Where Stanley Fish was once challenged by the question "Is there a text in this class?" the Net raises the challenge of discovering if there is "a class with this text?"

We suspect that, though Net interactions offer profoundly useful means to support and develop existing communities, they are not so good at helping a community to form or a newcomer to join. Dan Huttenlocher argues that from his experience there is an important synergy between his live classes and their on-line interactions that the on-line exchanges alone couldn't provide. "The Net isn't a good place to form communities," he claims, "though it's a very good place to keep them going." Clearly, someone with only on-line access to Huttenlocher's course material would not benefit from this synergy.

The experience of LatinMOO at first seems to challenge Huttenlocher's claim. A cadre of Boethius scholars did appear to form wholly on-line. Yet even here, on-line participation was significantly dependent on a deep base of off-line experiences. All the participants were graduate students, which by our earlier analysis makes them quite distinct from Huttenlocher's class. Graduate students have already been heavily socialized into the patterns of university and graduate work and behavior, whereas undergraduate classes have only started this difficult socializing process. Unlike Huttenlocher, O'Donnell didn't have to instill too many social conventions beyond those of MOOing itself, since participants had already picked up the niceties and the idiosyncrasies of scholarly behavior off-line. In short, O'Donnell's on-line class was inescapably enabled and enriched from the participant's background in off-line classes.

So for us, the idea of a progressive march toward open learning culminating in a future of virtual universities where all interaction is on-line is problematic. Furthermore, the accompanying whiggish story of a progressive march, a steady loosening of an age-old university grip on knowledge and access—though appealing—simply isn't true. Our reading of history is different and less relentlessly progressive. Indeed, we suspect that some earlier ways of organizing postsecondary education, though they might appear to have been superseded, could be useful in addressing problems raised but not answered by futuristic notions of a virtual, placeless university for isolated individuals.

The broad gate-keeping role universities now play is, in fact, a relatively recent development. For instance, the professions, which now rely so heavily on universities, previously relied much more on professional apprenticeship. In these areas as elsewhere, university dominion is a recent phenomenon, suggesting that institutional control is being centralized rather than diffused.

In 19th- and 20th-century Britain, for example, universities themselves oversaw much looser, more highly devolved arrangements. Students from Scotland to Singapore, for example, took courses and earned external degrees from the University of London, most without ever leaving home. Nor were these simply correspondence courses or early forms of distance teaching. The external degree importantly allowed students and teachers to form or join relatively autonomous local groups of like-minded participants thousands of miles from the degree-granting university. High schools opened their facilities to nearby students, particularly women, beyond school-leaving age, to allow local scholars to provide university-level courses in places without a university.

In this devolved system of higher education, pedagogy and control were widely distributed, involving both local and remote scholars and communities. This arrangement meant that students were neither dislocated from local networks nor trapped by the limitations of local resources. Local communities gave students opportunities for authentic access and membership while, from a distance, the university provided oversight, materials, standards, and credentials. Consequently, students could draw on the strengths of both the metropolis and the periphery. This type of arrangement significantly opened educational opportunities for rural women, the poor, and Third World residents who lacked access to universities, and it provided them with recognized and respected credentials.

For various reasons, the use of external degrees has diminished (though the University of London still administers some). Moreover, much of the "open" potential of the external system has given way to distance learning. Paradoxically, because it replaces local resources with metropolitan ones delivered from a distance, distance learning is more part of a trend toward centralization than devolution. Certainly learners have wrested some control from the academy, but, in other areas, the academy has increased its control. The single (and increasingly large) campus as the sole source—of faculty, disciplines, and colleagues—for matriculating students is the outcome of a 20th-century trend of concentration that has probably been as significant as the opposing triumphs of dispersal.

Any rethinking of resources for distal learning, it seems to us, needs to steer a path between the academy's centralizing tendencies and the optimistic faith that technologically mediated open learning offers a viable alternative. As we suggested above, to meet learners' needs for access to communities and credentials, institutions of higher education are more likely to be reconfigured than bypassed or abandoned.

The forces involved in the reconfiguration are too varied to make the outcome in any way predictable. Yet it seems unreasonable simply to shrug our shoulders at the ineffable character of the future. So, instead, in the following section, we suggest one way in which the current configuration, often thought of as a single and inseparable institutional unit, might be rethought. Our purpose is not to produce a new blueprint for "*the* idea of the university," but to undertake a thought experiment concerning the different pieces to be considered in reconfiguring higher education. With new technologies, we suspect, the components of the university, which once moved together, might develop along different trajectories on different time lines. We offer this sketch of a devolving university system as an intuition pump or discussion piece rather than a wish list or prognostication. It should be as useful to consider why it couldn't work as why it might.

REIMAGINING THE UNIVERSITY

Our discussion so far suggests that learners need three things from an institution of higher education:

- access to authentic communities of learning, exploration, and knowledge creation;
- resources to help them work in both distal and local communities; and
- widely accepted representations for work done.

If this is the case, then, along with the students themselves, there are three other crucial components of a college: faculty (drawn from communities of practice); facilities; and an institution able to provide formal, accepted representation of work done. At the moment, these four components are tightly woven together in particular colleges and their campuses. Distance education seeks to keep all but the students together. The history of the external degree, with its central credentialing but distal teaching, suggests that other configurations are possible. Moreover, as we've suggested, new, interactive technologies are starting to pick away at some previously invisible seams. Here, we pick a little further.

If these components are separable, degree-granting bodies (DGBs) might take up the degree-granting function. These would no doubt have to fight over students and faculty, just as colleges do now. DGBs could take on as many or as few students and faculty as they thought practical, becoming smaller than a liberal arts college or larger than an entire state system. They could set degree requirements and core courses as they saw fit. But a DGB would be essentially administrative, with little need to own much beyond its administrative competency and a building to house its (administrative) staff. Its loyalties might be to a locale or a region, or be national or international. Without the need for the massive capital investment that owning a campus and hiring a faculty requires, DGBs would be highly flexible, able to evolve to meet the needs of students, faculty, and the labor draft. Conversely, of course, they might be less resistant to unhealthy winds of change.

If a DGB could take on an independent status, faculty might also become more independent. Like doctors who contract to HMOs, they would need to find a DGB to sanction their teaching. But, also like doctors, they might find more than one DGB to do this. DGB sanction would allow students who study with a particular scholar to gain credit for work done toward a degree from the DGB. Scholars might contract individually or in teams. But, as distinct from the current system, they wouldn't be tied to one place. There is no reason for all the faculty of a DGB, or even all the members of a team, to be in the same place. Some could be on the East Coast, some on the West Coast, and some overseas. They might teach students from several DGBs on-line or in person, through tutorials, lectures, or seminars, or any combination.

In such an arrangement, fees would be likely to vary depending on the type of teaching offered—a lecture, a tutorial, a research seminar, a lab, or in-work training for graduate, undergraduate, or extension students. DGBs might pay a per capita fee to reward a teacher's ability to attract high-quality students to the DGB. Or, like 18th-century academics, scholars might collect a fee directly from the students they attract. (Adam Smith's Edinburgh lectures were paid for this way—he took a guinea per head and made £100 per annum; so were Hegel's lectures in Jena.) Or again, a DGB might pay for matriculating students while auditors could pay teachers directly. An option like this might help ensure that the structure and content of a course are not shaped by degree and exam requirements alone.

Research might be administered by a DGB or staffed and funded separately. For both teaching and research, faculty could find their own facilities. For some, these would be inevitably extensive, involving labs, equipment, and libraries. Others might need only a classroom. And yet others running small, local tutorial groups or on-line classes might need few facilities beyond an Internet link or a seminar room, which might be provided rather like branch libraries, dispersed across towns and cities.

Despite the loss of a tied academic administration and faculty, concrete facilities under such an arrangement would no doubt look very much like the campus of today. A particular campus would have to compete for faculty and students in the region, with the quality of its facilities a significant attractor. Both faculty and students using a particular facility might then come from several DGBs. The facility itself might thus become a regional magnet for staff, students, and DGBs. If this were the case, it would be in a city's or region's interest to maintain a high standard of facilities. Faculty and students wouldn't have to travel to their DGB, but they might want to travel to be close to superior facilities. On the other hand, they wouldn't be locked into one set of facilities. In well-endowed areas, some faculty and many students might use more than one facility. DGBs, faculty, and students might not use campus facilities at all. We would imagine, however, that given the needs for socialization, most DGBs and many faculty might insist that degree candidates spend a set amount of time on campus in groups rather than on-line individually. DGBs without such a requirement might well find their degrees rapidly falling in value and competitive worth.

Student choices would change significantly in any reconfiguration of this sort. More choices, of course, are likely to mean more complex decisions. The central choice would involve finding a suitable DGB. Perhaps a student would choose one that insists on conventional campus life—and one that has faculty on a particular campus. Or perhaps one that makes no campus demands, or one that includes certain faculty. Or the choice might be one that has faculty in the various regions a student expects to work in over the next few years: northern Scotland, Singapore, or San Francisco. A student also might choose a DGB whose degree in an area of interest is known to have a particularly high exchange value; or one that is prepared to validate certain kinds of in-work experience. But a student wouldn't be committed to working with the faculty of a single campus or a single region; furthermore, he or she might be able to work with local communities of excellence whose credentials are not accepted by universities under present arrangements.

In this way, a distributed system might allow much greater flexibility, employing local sites of professional excellence—research labs, hospitals, architects' offices, law firms, engineering offices, and the like—to offer mentoring programs that give students practical experience and course credits simultaneously. Regions that lack conventional academic facilities might start to attract students through the quality of mentors in the work force. Students in forestry, viticulture, mining, conservation, or ocean science would, for instance, be able to get credit for working with experts in the field, however far this might be from conventional academic centers.

Essentially, a student's university career in such a system would no longer be through a particular place, time, or preselected body of academics, but through a network principally of students' own making, yet shaped by a DGB and its faculty. Students could stay home or travel, mix on-line and off-line education, work in classes or with mentors, and take their own time. Their college careers wouldn't begin at age eighteen and end at age twenty-two.

Direct funding through fees wouldn't change much. DGBs would take tuition fees, while arrangements for faculty and facility per capita payments could be negotiated in a variety of ways, as we have suggested. (Of course, the extensive support provided by alumni to certain institutions might well ensure that these resisted all other pressures to reconfigure.) Subject to accreditation, private institutions could set up their own DGBs; states could set up their own. Some DGBs might try to be exclusive, others inclusive. Each would over time develop its particular reputation, attracting faculty and students through the exchange value of its degrees. Groups concerned about education in their fields—such as the AMA, MLA, or Computer Scientists for Social Responsibility—might try to establish themselves as DGBs. As we suggested earlier, degrees that reflect too much concentration, that represent too accurately the work involved, might well fall in value compared to those that mis/represent greater diversity. For in the end, the goal of a devolved system would be the education of students as capable of change on graduation as the world they encounter.

CONCLUSION

This sketch is not, of course, a road map for the future. Rather, it is something of a deliberate provocation intended to make the general point that the radical changes occurring in a university's environment— from the reconstitution of its student body to the reengineering of its technological infrastructure—will require quite different institutional arrangements from those found today. Distance learning, where much current interest lies, is, we believe, too deeply enmeshed within current arrangements to produce sufficiently radical change. Open learning, on the other hand, tends to ignore the strengths worth preserving in current arrangements. Without more thought to students and their practical needs, we fear that not only will these technologies be underexploited, but they may well reinforce the current limitations of our higher educational system.

4

The Responsibilities of Universities in the New Information Environment

STANLEY CHODOROW AND PETER LYMAN

The university is one of the most successful institutions of the Western world and, of course, is the victim of its success. It has become an avenue of social mobility, and, therefore, the people demand access to it beyond its capacity to provide high quality education. It has become an engine of economic growth, and so it is often seen as an economic, rather than an educational, enterprise. Yet for the university itself, perhaps the greatest consequence of success is that, in the new information environment, it may no longer be able to meet its responsibility to provide access to the information resources required for its work, the education of students and the production of knowledge. We will explore the origins and the future of this responsibility, which is now allocated principally to the library, as a purchaser of information for the university but which must inevitably involve other components of the university that purchase information. Ironically, the university, which was the first institution dedicated to production of knowledge as its principal function, has lost a clear understanding of its rights and duties in respect to academic information just when other institutions—polities, markets, and civil society itself—are being described in public discourse with academic-sounding phrases such as "the knowledge economy" and "the information society."

THE UNIVERSITY'S RESPONSIBILITY FOR INFORMATION

The university's responsibility for information resources is one of its original and enduring functions. In the beginning was the guild of teaching masters. The guild was the *universitas* (the medieval Latin word for "corporation"); the individual masters did the business of the guild, the making and selling of knowledge. The guild itself had several functions. It created and maintained a monopoly in the knowledge-making business by obtaining privileges from the authorities, principally the ecclesiastical authorities, and by regulating entry to the guild. It regulated the competition among the teaching masters of the guild, setting room rental charges and making other rules to manage the common business. Finally, because the masters fashioned knowledge on the basis of standard texts in each discipline—Justinian's *Corpus Juris Civilis* and Gratian's *Decretum* in law, Peter Lombard's *Sententiae* in theology, Galen in medicine, Ptolemy in astronomy, and so on—the guild managed the production of these texts for masters and students.

This last activity is the part of the original function of the university that concerns us, because here the institution's responsibility for the information used by faculty members and students begins. The basic principle of the medieval university—that the masters were independently responsible for carrying on the business, and the university was responsible only for the bare minimum of functions that enabled and ensured the stability of their business—created a balance of responsibility and authority between the corporation and the masters. Assigning the management of the production of textbooks to the university was not based on any fundamental principle but on practical considerations. Perhaps this is a clue to the origins of the enduring pragmatism that has been characteristic of the history of universities. Every master needed assurance that his students were working from the same text, for the production of knowledge in the middle ages was founded on the analysis of the meaning of words and phrases in the standard texts. To provide this assurance, the university contracted with the members of the scribners' guild for the production of books in each field, parceling out the quires to various shops and collecting, checking, and collating the segments to produce a consistent foundation for the work of the masters and their students.

This was the first stage of the university's responsibility for information resources. At each later stage, changes in organizational responsibility for information resources can be linked to a distinctive new mode of information: the medieval guild produced authoritative texts, ready for glossing; the early modern scientific society produced authoritative journals; and the modern learned society produces specialized disciplinary periodical and monographic literatures. And, we shall ask, what mode of organizational responsibility might be formed in respect to digital documents?

The foundation of university libraries, which have been the locus of the university's information responsibility in modern times, came much later. Early universities did not have libraries, and, only in the 14th century, when they built guildhalls, did the universities begin to acquire collections of books. For centuries, these collections grew slowly and haphazardly from the donations of faculty and other benefactors. Then, in the 19th century, the redefinition of the idea of the university as an instrument for social progress, and of scholarship understood as the production of specialized publication, led to a commitment, on principle, to the notion that the university had an obligation to collect and organize the information that its faculty and students needed for their work.

The 19th century was a revolutionary period in the history of higher education. The foundation of Friedrich-Wilhelm Univerität in Berlin (1809), the secularization of the English universities, symbolized by the foundation of London University (1825), and the proposal for a nonsectarian institution in Dublin (1845), and the passage of the Morrill Act (1862) in this country embodied the idea that research and education were useful to society.[1] This idea, anticipated as were so many other ideas by Benjamin Franklin,[2] gave the university a secular purpose. In a sense, this worldly purpose was a return to the purpose of medieval universities, even though those institutions had been part of the Church and their faculty and students had been in minor clerical orders, at least. Medieval scholars regarded their production of knowledge as practical— even theology was a practical field then, leading to employment in the

---

[1] Sir Robert Peel made the proposal for the institution in Dublin as a concession to the Irish. In 1834, there had already been legislation to admit Dissenters to the universities.

[2] In founding the school that became the University of Pennsylvania, Franklin enunciated the ideas that education should unite study of the theoretical ("ornamental" was his word) and the practical and that its purpose was to further the social welfare. These ideas reflected the Baconian notion that theoretical knowledge arose from and was tested by practical knowledge—that the two were inextricably entwined—and the Scottish idea that education should be for the common good. L. Benson and I. Harkavy make the argument that Franklin's idea stemmed from Bacon in "Progressing Beyond the Welfare State," *Universities and Community Schools* 2, no. 1-2, (1991): 2-28 Aberdeen. On the Scottish tradition and its influence on American education, see *The European and American university since 1800: historical and sociological essays*, edited by Sheldon Rothblatt and Bjorn Wittrock (Cambridge, Eng: Cambridge University Press, 1993). The first provost of the University of Pennsylvania was the Scot, William Smith, a graduate of the University of Aberdeen.

worldly Church—and their students, as the masters often rued, were as career-oriented as modern students. But in the late middle ages, the universities had come to be dominated by residential colleges and their purpose had been subordinated to the education—the intellectual and social polishing—of the elite classes. The first colleges in the New World were founded to educate the clergy, and they evolved, by the early 19th century, into finishing schools for the elite, consciously collegiate in imitation of Oxford and Cambridge. Then, the revolution occurred, leaving the small colleges intact in their role but changing the university profoundly. The revolution of the 19th century secularized and re-oriented the university. The foundation of London University broke the connection to the Church,[3] and Berlin introduced the idea of the research university,[4] but the greatest manifestation of these ideas was the land-grant university in the United States. In creating a theory of the university, the 19th century movements shifted the weight of the university's functions from the individual faculty toward the institution itself. While the faculty carried out the purposes of the university, it was the university as a whole that was responsible for the goals of the polities that founded them. One of the consequences of this shift was that the universities became increasingly responsible for the information used by faculty members and students in the achievement of these goals.

This shift of responsibility for information resources was very gradual, in part because the new emphasis on the corporate goals of the university did not affect the way the business of research and teaching was carried out. Individual faculty members remained, and remain today, the principal actors on the university's stage; they are largely independent entrepreneurs within the corporate structure of the institution. As a result, they continued to build personal libraries of substantial scholarly worth, relative to the resources available in the university library, until well into this century. Many of today's senior faculty members probably remem-

---

[3] John Cardinal Newman, the leading opponent of secularization, opposed the opening of the universities to Dissenters. A decade later, he became involved in a project to found a Catholic university in Dublin in reaction to the secularization of the universities in England and the proposal by Sir Robert Peel for a non-sectarian university in that city. Newman's famous work, *The Idea of the University* (Chicago: Loyola Press Reprint, 1987) resulted from the lectures he gave during two decades of debate on the role of religion in education.

[4] The idea of the research university, which by the middle of the century had spread throughout Germany, was transferred to the United States with the founding of The Johns Hopkins University in 1876.

ber mentors who owned a high proportion of the information they used in their work. In the post-World War II period, however, faculty began to expect that university libraries would have everything they needed. Libraries began to be ranked by size; universities began to be ranked, in part, by the size of their libraries. In our time, the universities are expected to acquire and manage nearly all of the information used by their faculties and students.

The revolution of purposes that took place in higher education during the nineteenth century also made the universities into the repositories of human knowledge and civilization. This was not, perhaps, the goal of any of the reformers, but it was the natural result of their intentions. Before the period of reform, no institution needed to claim, and none was regarded as being responsible for, all the intellectual disciplines. Libraries collected what their owners were interested in. However, the institution that would advance knowledge for the good of society would, by implication at least, make contributions across the whole range of disciplines, and its responsibility for information resources would cover all fields. And because the university-building movement of the 19th and 20th centuries was carried out by independent jurisdictions, every university was expected to have all of the culturally important information—that is, all of the information necessary for the advancement of useful knowledge of every kind. As we shall see, this consequence of the 19th century revolution also contributes to the dilemmas faced by today's librarians and university administrators.

By all measures, the 19th century revolution in higher education, which paralleled the industrial revolution and the rise of science and technology as a foundation of economic development, has been a great success. The universities have become great factories of knowledge and education and have contributed immeasurably to prosperity, especially in the developed world.

THE PRODUCTION OF KNOWLEDGE

The information crisis does not arise from administrative problems such as library funding. It derives from the historic evolution of the methods and content of the disciplines and the relation of the disciplines to universities. The disciplines transcend the boundaries of any particular university; the budgetary and administrative problems are only symptoms of disciplinary development. We have lost a sense of direction in balancing the role of universities as institutions responsible for managing the production of information and knowledge with the role of academic disciplines in governing its content. The multiple sources of disciplinary definitions have caused us to lose our sense of the boundaries between disciplines and produced the haphazard departmental structure of universities. The disciplinary organization of knowledge has been a basic feature of the modern university with its press imprint and research library from 1875, that is, from about the time that The Johns Hopkins University was founded—to about 1925.

In a special issue of *Poetics Today* dedicated to disciplinarity, David Shumway and Ellen Messer-Davidow describe scholarly disciplines as organizational strategies for the production of knowledge, originating with the medieval guild.[5] The system of education in the medieval universities was based on disciplines—the seven arts, law, medicine, and theology—but, in the late middle ages, the rise of the colleges within the universities reduced the influence of the disciplinary faculties. The disciplines then made a comeback in the 17th century, when they became institutionalized in the scientific societies for the study of nature, such as the Royal Society. These societies, through their scholarly publications, obtained a monopoly on the dissemination of authoritative new knowledge in their fields. The founding of the research university in the 19th century reunited the scholarly disciplines with the universities, which also founded presses that competed with the societies. The disciplines also became crucially important in the credentialing of new faculty members in the universities. Modern disciplinary societies are funded principally by memberships, but are also subsidized by universities through agreements such as donated editorial support, faculty gifts of copyright for published research, and higher journal subscription rates paid by libraries.

The academic department—which in principle has primary authority for hiring, promotion to tenure, and the curriculum—is where disciplines and the university meet. Thus, the character of a modern university is defined by the number and kinds of departments it supports, and, by extension, these independent components determine the nature and scope of its responsibility to support centrally such information resources as research libraries, computer centers, the network, and bookstores. In prac-

---

[5] David R. Shumway and Ellen Messer-Davidow, "Disciplinarity: An Introduction." *Poetics Today* 12:2 (Summer 1991)201-223.

tice, the responsibility for information is, however, defined in different ways by different types of institutions. For example, in the United States, private research universities typically offer fewer degree programs than public ones, but they provide far greater depth of library and information resources.

And yet, we must ask how complete the reunification of the university and the disciplines has been. In this interdisciplinary age, when a university creates a new academic program (such as environmental studies, neuroscience, cultural studies, or information science), does the program constitute a new discipline or profession? Moreover, in an information age, when new technology can become the basis for a new professional discipline or for the production of new kinds of knowledge, how should we understand the concept of a discipline, and how does it relate to the organization and responsibilities of the university in relation to society?

The present disciplinary structure was an invention of the late nineteenth century, organized around a dichotomy between the humanities and sciences, a relationship that C.P. Snow famously called "the two cultures," and by the invention of the social sciences, which occupy the ambiguous territory between. Immanuel Wallerstein argues that the traditional social science disciplines have become unable to manage their boundaries, and, in any case, do not map to the realities of the modern world.[6] Between 1900 and 1945, Wallerstein argues, history was organized as a discipline to study the past, while the present was the province of political science, economics, and sociology (corresponding to the western liberal separation between the polity, the market, and civil society). Nonmarket societies, he argues, were imperfectly divided into anthropology, for the study of primitive societies, and a discipline the 19th century called "world religion," for the study of areas of the world neither primitive nor organized around markets but that could be characterized generally by their religious culture.

By 1945, the worldwide reach of American power and global communication technologies made these intellectual boundaries (past/present, market/non-market, western/eastern) anachronistic. New transitional categories have evolved, but no comprehensive new scheme has been defined: comparative religion became "development," and then international and area studies; the humanities are evolving beyond na-

---

[6] Immanuel Wallerstein, "Open the Social Sciences." *Items: Social Science Research Council.* 50:1 (March 1996).

tional literatures through the development of cultural studies (overwhelming the humanities/social science boundary); science has spun off policy-oriented interdisciplinary fields focused on health, the environment, and other social problems. Interdisciplinary fields have not yet become disciplines, equal to or supplanting the traditional fields, and yet each is marked by new kinds of information that are not easily contained within the traditional disciplinary organizing systems of modern libraries.

Thus, Wallerstein has called for the reformulation of the disciplines in a principled manner and has created the Gulbenkian Commission on the Restructuring of the Social Sciences, rather in the manner of the Philosophes. In practice, nearly every research university is facing the proliferation of academic programs and, thus, new demands for information support. It is not the amount of information alone that is the problem, then, but the organization and management of information. Many of these new fields require new technologies and new library collections, and few have developed authoritative journals produced and organized by disciplinary societies; often these fields are using digital networks to invent new forms of scholarly communication. The research library is a microcosm of this problem—its catalogues organized by the Library of Congress classification system, which is based upon the nineteenth-century understanding of disciplinary order (the problem is imperfectly solved by computerized search engines based upon word matching). Research library costs are driven not only by commercial publishers but also by the necessity to support both old and new disciplinary paradigms (how often does a new program *replace* the literature of a traditional discipline?) and by the need to buy information internationally and catalog materials in dozens of languages. The computer center, initially responsible for the information infrastructure of the sciences and quantitative social sciences, now often provides support for information resources that are essentially private libraries, with no standards for the organization and archiving of data, no strategy for the preservation of data as technical standards evolve, and no public access. Many universities have created "information czars" to organize the management of information institution-wide, not recognizing that the crisis is as much academic as administrative in nature. The administration of information cannot proceed without clarifying the academic programs that define a university and the future of the disciplines that are its institutional partners.

are out there amidst thousands of bits of debris; useful resources disappear; sites migrate from one address to another. Librarians today are already extending their collection development procedures to the Web, mounting the results on the library homepage. At the moment, this effort is duplicative, as cataloging used to be. One looks to an organizational plan that distributes responsibility for the Web among libraries. But while duplication is a short-term problem, collection development on the Web will always be an iterative process. In addition to hunting for new sites, librarians have to make a sweep through already identified sites to ensure that they remain viable, reliable, stable in their organization, and resident at their listed address.

Collection development will increasingly shift toward what might be called continuous live action. This kind of collection development is the second stage of a change in the professional functions and responsibilities of librarians. Those bibliographers responsible for fields in which electronic resources are becoming dominant will spend the majority of their time assessing Web sites. Managing currently available information will become their principal function. Beyond that, they will participate in, perhaps lead, the effort to define what part of the information used by the disciplines they are responsible for will be preserved. The common view is that everything in the electronic medium can and will be preserved, because it takes up no space and the machines are relatively inexpensive. But all those who work with electronic information resources know that only some of the information can be archived, because archiving requires either printing it out or porting it from system to system as the electronic environment evolves. The technical problems of portage are not so difficult, but neither individual academic libraries nor the library system as a whole has yet designed a cost-effective way to manage technological change over the long term, especially when the term is measured in centuries.

Collecting and preserving information in electronic media are easy when compared with the problem of organizing the information. The rise of the library as the principal repository of information had the effect of creating a library profession that has both managed and organized information. The Age of the Great Library, roughly the last century, has been such an era of achievement because librarians worked out methods for managing information, so that users could find it efficiently. The systems of organization have been the most powerful tools in the knowledge-making business. As noted above, however, neither librarians nor computers can bring order to an infinitely expanding information universe.

The third stage of the change in the role of librarians will be to incorporate electronic information resources into a new, universal system of organization. Electronic information is generated everywhere on the planet and cannot be usefully conformed to the organizational program of any particular library. Today, we use the Web side by side with print materials, but as the Web resources grow, they will have to be integrated into a single information management system, into *collections*. Accomplishing that goal will be a huge task that will almost certainly fall to university-based librarians.

The Inflation in the Information Market

The inflation in journal prices and the vast increase in the number of journals published during the last two decades have been topics of continuing discussion by librarians and university administrators. This problem is another result of the 19th century revolution in higher education. The shift of weight from the individual faculty member to the university as a corporation has divided responsibility from authority in many aspects of the university's business. The responsibility for providing information resources was one of the most critical of those aspects.[9]

THE DIVISION BETWEEN AUTHORITY AND RESPONSIBILITY

Before the 19th century, the community of scholars constituted a single market in knowledge. The scholars made knowledge, and they bought knowledge. Not all scholars were on university faculties, and the university played almost no role in the market for research, either as maker or purchaser of knowledge. The function of the university, as a corporation, was to organize teaching.

This old market for knowledge maintained low prices. Scholars were (and are) most interested in the distribution, not the monetary value, of their work, and they were buying and selling to themselves. This was the

---

[9] See Chapter 6: P. Lyman and S. Chodorow, "The Future of Scholarly Communication," where a discussion of the immediate causes of library costs are discussed, while here we concentrate on its structural origins and the resulting strategic issues.

origin of the idea that scholarly communication is a gift culture—one in which information is a free good, freely exchanged, to sustain a sense of academic community. Once the responsibility for providing information shifted to the universities, however, the sellers and buyers were divided. Because scholars still had a greater interest in distribution of their ideas than in monetary gain from them, this division had little effect at first, but it has developed into a first-class problem for universities.

The first step in the development of this problem was the institution of tenure in the earlier part of this century. Tenure was (and is) the counterweight to the increased corporatism of the modern university. Tenure protects the academic freedom of faculty members and rests on two principles—first, that faculty members do the work of the university as individuals and need protection from interference in order to accomplish that work; and, second, that the university itself, under whatever pressures from outside or inside, might be a potential threat to its faculty's academic independence. Critics argue that this system of tenure has reduced the university's ability to manage the research enterprise to meet the goals set for it in the land-grant tradition. But tenure is the kind of balance between authority and responsibility that typifies the history of universities, functioning as a balance to the increasing corporate structure and function of the modern university to ensure the survival of the guild of teacher/scholars who carry on its business.[10] The somewhat peculiar organization of the government's support for research in the second half of the 20th century reflected this situation by making grants to universities for the work of the individual faculty members who had applied for the grants. The tension between the university and its faculty over the management of grants and, especially, over the recovery of the indirect costs of research, is a result of an institutional arrangement that places the burden of responsibility on the university while giving authority to do the work without interference to the faculty members.

This same division of responsibility and authority has now led to the inflationary spiral in the information market and the inability of the university to meet its responsibility. The rising tide of research and its obvious value to society have brought commercial publishers into the information market. Faculty members, having the authority to manage their research and distribute its results without constraint, have chosen to give

---

[10] See, for example, the special issue of the *American Behavioral Scientist,* "Tenure Matters: Rethinking Faculty Roles and Rewards." 4:5 (February 1998).

their copyrights to the commercial houses, which have sold the published results back to the universities at ever increasing prices. The publishers have also created new journals, fed by the enormous apparatus of faculty research, so that universities have not only to pay higher and higher prices but also to add more and more journals to their collections. The growth of the budget for serials has driven the monograph almost to extinction, reducing demand and raising prices for specialized works. It is increasingly difficult for universities both to supply their faculty members and students with the information they need and to meet the general obligation to be a repository of knowledge for the society.

The pricing mechanisms that are developing in the electronic environment greatly complicate this picture. Although it is not yet clear how the economics of electronic publishing will evolve, the possibility that users of information will be charged for each use raises further questions about both the university's ability to pay for information and the allocation of resources between printed and electronic materials.

One way to look at the inflationary crisis is as a function of a divided market. In modern universities, which collectively dominate the knowledge industry, the users and buyers of information participate in two different exchange systems, buying information from a market economy but using it within a gift economy. Information is far from a free good in the university, but it is free to the faculty and student users of information. Thus, there is no economic restraint on use within the university, while there is a strong one on the university's ability to purchase in the external market. The commercial publishers have exploited this consequence of the 19th century revolution by linking the two markets, becoming middlemen in the information market organization. The universities have not been able to fix the market system, because tenure and the tradition of faculty independence and authority on which it rests have deprived the institutions of leverage. If the universities managed their faculties the way industrial corporations control their employees, then the commercial publishers would not get the information rights that they now sell back to the universities at extraordinary prices.

So long as print was the only medium of serious scholarship, the universities and their faculties were locked in a frustrating cycle of price rises and subscription cancellations, while those faculty members and students dependent on monographs gasped for air. The new mixed environment in which electronic resources are as important as printed ones may create a break in this cycle. Faculties and students have direct access to electronic resources, and while the university purchases—or more accurately, licenses—some of these resources, the principal responsibilities of the university relative to the electronic environment are guidance and information management. Thus, the question arises whether in the electronic environment the university should give the majority of responsibility for the acquisition of information resources to its faculty and students. One way to end the debate over the library's budget—or, more broadly, over institutional expenditures—for information might be to allocate funding for information to the users. In its most extreme form, this distribution of funding for information would not specify that funds allocated to individuals should be spent for information—that is, members would decide what part of the funds allocated to them should be spent on information and what on other necessities. This radical notion is not a practical solution, in that libraries would likely become private goods once again, but it highlights the problem that universities are beginning to face. The university has a responsibility to provide information for the research and teaching activities of its faculty. It also has a larger responsibility to preserve knowledge for future generations. But in today's information environment, individual faculty members have increasing access to information outside the library, the traditional institutional component through which the university provided, managed, and preserved information. The university clearly has an obligation to help faculty members get access to those extraneous information resources; indeed, it has an interest in giving the help, which must be both financial and managerial in scope. Moreover, its larger responsibility to preserve knowledge requires it to maintain control over its information environment. A system that devolved responsibility for information from the institution to the individual faculty members or departments would produce a chaotic, uneven, and, ultimately, inadequate information resource for the long-term work of the university.

That one might entertain such a radical idea as distributing responsibility for information resources also signals the seriousness and apparent intractability of the problem faced by universities and their faculties. Many people think that the key to solving the problem lies in a change in the way intellectual property rights are managed. If faculty members kept their rights or assigned them to universities or reserved rights for their universities (or, more broadly for academic uses), then universities could continue to provide information for research and teaching according to the now traditional idea. But administrators have faced strong faculty opposition to any change in their university's intellectual property policies. Faculty members see the university's encroachment on their intellectual property rights as a threat to their ability under the tenure system to control the distribution of the products of their research. If, they argue, the freedom of inquiry is protected by tenure, then the freedom to use the results of inquiry, or to dispose of them as one will, is also protected. This widespread attitude does not hold much promise for a voluntary agreement between faculties and universities on the disposition of intellectual property rights, not because faculty members distrust the university but because they see the rights as essentially individual.

In the face of these problems, librarians and university administrators have begun to develop two strategies—consortial purchase and licensing of information resources and schemes to change the information market itself. Shared responsibility for the purchase of materials has already been developed for printed works, especially among libraries in systems or associations, such as the Committee on Institutional Cooperation (CIC) formed by the Big Ten and the University of Chicago, and the same idea is now being actively explored for electronic resources. This is a promising development, but it is unlikely to be a complete solution. Consortia reduce the market for information, which will very likely engender resistance from publishers and, at least initially, price increases. Resistance has already appeared in the form of package marketing, in which publishers refuse to sell the desired journals unless the buyer also purchases other ones. The answer to the price problem is certainly not in consortia. It must be in a new system of pricing that takes into account the new kinds of markets that are now emerging from information-on-demand practices and in the proposed replacement of copyright with contract law.

No pricing system will work, however, so long as responsibility and authority in the information market are split as they are now. The middlemen control the market because the producers and buyers cannot make a deal, even though the producers and buyers may be components of the same institution. The problem has not been solved by controlling demand—by reducing the growth of, or cutting, library budgets—although it might be addressed by limiting supply—by reducing faculty incentives to publish. Fundamentally, this problem arises from the self-contradictory nature of the modern university, which unites the ancient guild of teaching masters with the structure and obligations of a modern corporation. The only way to finesse the awkward situation that this du-ality has created—to avoid undermining the basic value of intellectual freedom that gives a faculty both its unique privileges and the means of doing its job—is for the university itself to enter the market as publisher, or to create opportunities for faculty and their learned societies to do so.

The second alternative—the creation of opportunities for faculty members and learned societies to compete successfully in the market—is being explored by the Association of American Universities (AAU) and the Council on Library and Information Resources (CLIR). The principle underlying this effort is that the process of review and editing, which are the most important added value offered by print journals, can be separated from the publication of articles. If that separation is effected, then publication can be done at low cost on the Web. The AAU is looking at the economics of such a system, while CLIR is studying the technical issues related to the preservation of published articles and the maintenance of their authority in the fluid medium of the Internet.

Both of these efforts seek to solve the inflationary crisis by creating an alternative market mechanism for scholarly publication. In both, the universities are trying to solve the problem without undermining the traditional position of a faculty and the privileges on which it rests.

CONCLUSION

The universities have a responsibility to provide information for their faculties and students and to preserve the intellectual and cultural heritage of society. Even if one could conceive of a university in which the institution gave up the first of these obligations, because it relates to the internal organization and budgetary constraints, the second one cannot be evaded, because it arises from the public function of the university. But no one now thinks that the university should shirk its responsibility to provide information resources to its faculty and students.

The division between the faculties and the universities that was produced by the 19th century revolution in higher education makes it virtually impossible for the institutions to meet their responsibilities. So long as the university does not control publication it will face the prospect of losing the war against inflation. But it cannot take control of the intellectual property produced by faculty members without depriving them of the academic freedom necessary for the production of knowledge.

Thus the problem has to be cast as an economic one. Thought of in this way, it could be resolved by federal legislation regulating the information market. The purpose of such regulation would be to protect the public good by ensuring easy—in other words, relatively inexpensive—access to information by academic institutions. The doctrines of Fair Use and First Sale in traditional copyright law are examples of such regulation. Library and university associations have been urging Congress to adopt a solution of this kind for networked information, so that scholarly communication in any medium would be available to faculty members and students.

The problem could also be resolved by a change in the information market that would bring faculties and universities together. As we have noted, the prospects for such a reconciliation are not good, if we are to rely on the voluntary and unified response of the faculty to the crisis. The faculty is too fractured by disciplines to unite on behalf of a solution that has the appearance, at least, of being a restriction on the members' independence and freedom. The answer must lie in market changes that the universities bring about by their own actions—first, by creating competitive non-profit publishers and, second, by changing the relationship between publication and the certification of the quality of faculty research. We believe that the solution to the problem lies principally in the second of these approaches. Once universities stop subcontracting with publishers for the evaluation of faculty research and find a more direct way to accomplish this task, they will be able to deal with the market. There is no doubt that universities will play a role in the publication of scholarship, but the form of that participation in the market is not yet clear, and it is not of crucial importance. What is important is that the universities reassert themselves in the market for information. Their future as centers of research and as institutions that teach the arts of research depends on it.

5

When Change Is the Only Constant: Liberal Education in the Age of Technology

SAMUEL R. WILLIAMSON

Life for a college president often resembles a series of Kafkaesque choices and activities. We live within an ever-shifting series of realities in which the only predictable constant is the inevitability of change.

Change, change, change, all around us. Each publication or media source or Internet message, whether academic or business or learned, speaks of it. The Internet has changed the way we communicate, and computers are finally breaking out of the science disciplines to make an impact in individual classrooms throughout the curriculum. In fact, the binary world has come to shape our entire political, and even intellectual, network—you are for or against, 0 or 1.

We form organizations to address this change. Committees on college campuses spend hours wrestling with the ramifications of change, and poor provosts everywhere have to find money to finance the ever-increasing costs of the high technology without which their colleges will fall behind in the competitive race for students and faculty members and key staff. Even the faculties are being challenged, as students arrive on campus with more skills and talents and demands for service than at any point in the past. And the cycle starts ever anew.

Where does all this leave the small liberal arts college or university? Is there a new paradigm of learning because of the technological revolution? If not, or if the answer to the question is as yet merely blurred, what are the major aspects of the new technology that affect our missions, our budgets, our faculties, and, most importantly, our ability to meet our standards of traditional excellence in the area of undergraduate liberal arts education?

INFORMATION, LEARNING, AND KNOWLEDGE

The questions lend themselves to answers both conventional and non-conventional. There is a continuing confusion about the nature of the paradigm shift that we are experiencing, if indeed it is a paradigm shift. What is happening is less a shift in learning and education than in communication and in the sharing, manipulation, and dissemination of information. We have managed to accelerate the degree to which information can be moved from one format to another, one place to another, and one discipline to another. But this change does not mean, for many, that learning itself has changed or that knowledge has actually increased.

On the other hand, some profound changes are taking place that do have consequences for modes of learning and the assimilation of skills. For centuries, liberal arts colleges have eschewed, and deliberately so, the storehouse-of-knowledge approach to undergraduate education. Instead, skills, concepts, and critical thinking have been our organizing principles. That others are just discovering the importance of these principles suggests much about the history of American higher education.

The new technologies do liberate us from the secretarial function—the literal transmission process for moving information—in research and in the classroom. Some might argue that this diminishes the role of the class and the lecturer, and, in one sense, it does. But, in another sense, it frees professors and allows them to focus on the class itself, to convert each class into its own tutorial, and to bring the human touch fully and firmly back into the educational experience. Thus, at the large research institution and at the liberal arts college, some profound changes are underway. Nor can we ignore the increasing influence of seeing the world in binary terms (whether personal or political) in which the choice is always 0 or 1, right or wrong, rather than among more subtle shades of gray.

The new technologies, moreover, make possible economies of effort that bring enhanced quality. Interactive simulations of experiments can now be run endlessly, and the student can observe the experiment ad infinitum and still have time to learn much. It is now possible to create situations in small liberal arts contexts that replicate much of what could be done in a major research laboratory. And, thanks to the Internet, a small college can have its students reading same-day editions of newspapers from around the world, an activity completely unthinkable even five years ago.

In our considerations, we must remember that undergraduate students are one species, adult learners another, and those thrown into industrial or governmental or military contexts yet others. The suggestion that there can be a common paradigm, or even a common format, for each of these learners should trigger cautionary signals, especially among those who have lived through more than one of the promised revolutions in American higher education. A failure to distinguish between these various categories of students will lead to false starts and invalid expectations.

For example, undergraduates profess a desire to learn, and their parents certainly concur. But the reality of practice is more jaded and fragmentary. Some students are naturally gifted learners, who would learn in any environment. But to extrapolate from these highly motivated students to the broader student body and to conclude that all students wish to be learners or that they can learn on their own with the assistance of the new pervasive technology is to assume too much. Many will want to learn, some will actually show the necessary initiative, and others will find the technology repellent to them. Put simply, the assumption that we can transform, and, therefore, will transform, all of higher education into a learning community remains to be proved. At the same time, for many of these students, the residential college provides a place for maturation and development that will convert them into learners. In fact, the advantages conferred by small residential programs have increasingly led some large state universities to create honors programs as a way to replicate the perceived advantages of the liberal arts college.

Where distance learning fits into these developments remains to be seen. It will certainly have an impact upon community colleges, and even large state universities, as students seek to reduce costs and avoid long periods of inconvenience to get their education. Whether it will initially change the small residential college or university is more problematic, for the residential experience itself (and not just the classroom experience) constitutes one of the major attractions of these institutions. But smaller colleges may well explore distance learning and the attendant approaches as a way to communicate with alumni, prospective students, and even far-flung faculty members away on research projects. The desire to remain in constant contact with alumni will be increasingly important for the private educational institution in the years ahead. No potential future benefactor can be left unattended.

COSTS, PRODUCTIVITY, AND QUALITY

Many information technology advocates mistakenly try to sell information technology on the basis of cost reduction. Thus far, the information technology revolution has seldom, if ever, led to cost savings. Rather, it has led to increased expectations from faculty members and students, to demands for ever more rapid shifts of equipment and software, and to an ever-mounting increase—almost Dilbert-like—of staff to support the effort. All of this has had a substantial impact upon increased costs.

Information technology has led to lower possible costs in three discrete areas: preventing institutions from entering fields (such as foreign-language instruction) that might be handled more effectively through consortia; helping to restrain the burgeoning costs of research periodicals and other library acquisitions; and reducing gradually the disproportionate amounts of time that college presidents and other administrators spend attending conferences, the purposes of which might ideally be achieved through computers and interactive video. But these are all marginal savings.

Major savings will not be forthcoming because to achieve them would tear apart the educational process itself: deep savings can be realized only through the reduction of faculty positions. Contrary to the belief of most faculty members, the real costs in the college derive not from administrative positions but from faculty positions. To reduce their number is to take away the very people who make the final difference in the educational process. This is not to defend outmoded ways of doing business, or disciplines that need redefinition, or even to defend that holiest of grails: low student–faculty ratios. But it is to suggest that teaching and educating are different from learning—if learning is defined as simply the acquisition of skills without their utilization, or if learning is seen only as the ability to pass certain standard sets of formalized examinations which themselves reflect a binary, and not always reflective, approach to the subject matter.

Can we enhance "productivity"? The very term makes faculty members shudder and calls into question all the leadership skills of an institution's hierarchy. Such gains are far more likely at the larger institutions, but we would all benefit by containing staff costs through the introduction of technologies that help with registration, record keeping, and the movement of administrative information from place to place.

QUALITY, CHANGE, AND ADMINISTRATIVE WORRIES

Should we continue to do business as we have done it in the past, adhering to the centuries-old practice of the professor, chalk, and the lecture mode? Not necessarily. To bolster productivity gains, we must encourage teachers to use technology to free up time that can be used to guide, to assist, to formulate, to challenge, to verify. They must use the technology to connect students with the world of intellect and reflection. Nowhere is this more important than at the undergraduate level, where these interactions with students form the heart of our educational mission and where the private liberal arts college has always made its major contribution. "Excellence," "quality," and "unique" pepper collegiate admission brochures and, indeed, much of the literature of higher education. But "quality" and added value, not cost savings and productivity per se, may be precisely the benefit technology brings to liberal arts education. Enhancing quality, as the Japanese auto industry reminded Detroit in the 1980s, sells a product. There is a far greater chance that enhanced quality will be present systematically in the small college and university.

Are we doing enough to assure the excellence of the curriculum? Are faculty members ready to change roles? And where will the changes lead? The answer to the first question must be "no." Older colleagues feel threatened, others remember how their disciplines were hurt in the wars to establish quantitative techniques in the 1960s, and still others are simply not interested. But there are subtle peer pressures that can often move the most obdurate: have faculty members conduct their business by e-mail; offer lucrative course-development grants; fund conference travel; fund travel to competitive institutions where faculty members might have an edge in what they do or attempt; provide technical support that can resolve even the most mundane problem; establish teaching centers that show how the technology can be harnessed, and staff them with senior figures who themselves have embraced the technology; make certain that presidents understand what is happening, if only to be cheerleaders for the operation from the sidelines. The net effect of this should be an enhanced quality of instruction and a deepening appreciation of qualitative improvements in the nature of instruction and in its outcomes. These new approaches should also allow more rapid assessment of their own utility.

But there will be a downside to the momentum: the already present drive among new and younger faculty members to associate more with their disciplines and their subject areas than with their colleges will increase through the use of e-mail and the Internet. If you are able to talk continually across the world to coworkers in the study of biology, how much time have you left to devote to more mundane duties, such as teaching students? Those who acquire the technological skills for teaching may spend more time acquiring them than on their disciplines and become effective technocrats but less accomplished professors.

For senior members of college and university administrations there are some cautionary lessons as well. Though reasons of efficiency and centralization may tempt them to appoint a single individual as omniscient czar for all computing and data-information technology on the campus, the action may be misguided. The rapid pace of change, coupled with heavy administrative duties, make it unlikely that any one person will be able to address every issue with the same degree of effectiveness or expertise. To be sure, such an individual may have opinions on every issue, but the opinions may be no more than that. A format that allows and prompts more internal debate, more adequate conversation about alternative approaches, and better use of all the experiences of an increasingly sophisticated faculty and staff will be more useful.

A senior administrator should also insist that projects have goals, an evaluative process, and clearly stated costs. Often, the initial investment will seem small and limited, so the project is undertaken and encounters far greater expenses and personnel costs than initially imagined. There is almost always a tendency to underrate the need for personnel to help the faculty and other less technically inclined support staff. Students can often assist in this regard and sometimes have more diplomatic skills than the older trainers and experts. But staff training and the issue of providing actual services often seem to be less well considered than the consideration of the manifold technical data that the hardware or software decision requires.

A final worry for senior administrators: how large a permanent staff should be assembled to help with the technology? The real trap here is clearly associated with faculty appointments. How do institutions assure a continuous influx of new ideas and new concepts? Can it be done with relatively permanent personnel, or is a more frequent turnover required than would be true for the faculty? It is certain that some appointments must have terminal features attached to them or the future flexibility of the entire enterprise will be endangered. And perhaps some privatization of functions should be considered. Though it may be difficult for the small, isolated college campus, such privatization is becoming more accessible with the development of an entire cottage industry of part-time and at-home employees whose own needs must also be serviced.

CONCLUSIONS

In the age of high technology, change for the sheer sake of change may become the order of the day for faculty members and staff members. They may press relentlessly ahead for every new piece of hardware or software, often without having learned to use their earlier models. And there is some danger that all the focus on technology and teaching could markedly reduce research and other scholarly activities. While some state legislators and former Secretary of Education William J. Bennett might applaud this total attention to teaching, it can only harm the academic enterprise in the long run. A "Mr. Chips" with a computer is still a "Mr. Chips," and an institution needs only so many of them. There must be a balance.

Liberal arts colleges have for a very long time focused their efforts on one kind of education, and they must continue to do so. Education at its best is not just training, not just learning, but the total experience of maturation, reflection, and intellectual, even spiritual, development. Residential settings provide this experience. The information technology revolution will help the small college retain its traditional distinctions and advantages, while conferring upon it many of the attributes of the larger research university. With access to worldwide stores of information and data, the student and the faculty member in the small rural college or the metropolitan small university will compete on an even footing with their colleagues across the spectrum of American higher education. And, given the nimbleness of the smaller units and their willingness to take risks, these colleges may well be able to use technology to enhance their educational quality far faster than large and potentially more cumbersome universities.

But the critical skills of liberal arts education will be essential in helping faculty members, administrators, and students put the new information explosion into perspective. For that reason, the liberal arts college and its curricular approach may be at a moment of genuine revival and prosperity. Liberal arts colleges have a role in the pluralism of American higher education. It is that role that has given them definable excellence in the past and is likely to do so for the foreseeable future.

6

The Future of Scholarly Communication

PETER LYMAN AND STANLEY CHODOROW

The system of scholarly communication governing the flow of information and knowledge within the academic community, and between higher education and the market economy surrounding it, has become unstable. The most obvious symptom of this instability is that the cost of scholarly journals has risen so rapidly and extraordinarily that every research library has canceled hundreds of subscriptions and can no longer collect what their local communities of users regard as necessary information resources. But there are deeper causes as well. In recent years, disciplines have continued to specialize and subdivide—thereby creating new journals at a rate far faster than any library can collect them—while the commercialization of scholarly publishing has continued to exert an upward pressure on the prices of individual serials. Because the system of scholarly communication is the foundation for progress in research and for teaching, it has to be said that the whole house of learning rests on an unstable foundation. Moreover, local institutions cannot respond effectively to the situation because "the library crisis" is a symptom of the breakdown of the whole traditional system of scholarly publishing.

In the meantime, scholars are finding the Internet to be an information resource and communications medium that can often serve as an informal substitute for the system of scholarly communication based on print. This is particularly true during the research phase of their work, although it is still the case that publication in print provides the authoritative evaluation necessary for professional advancement. Using computers and the Worldwide Web as they are, scholars are extending and intensifying scholarly discourse and creating new forms of scholarly communication. In many fields, the most important information used in the advancement of knowledge, although not yet necessarily advancement to promotion and tenure, is created by computers and available on the Web.

Yet it would be wrong to think that the development of electronic publishing and the "digital library" will solve the problems now apparent in the system of scholarly communication. The development of electronic media has not produced a replacement for the traditional system of scholarly communication; it has not changed the way we authenticate and evaluate research results; it has not become so efficient economically that it can challenge print publication. So far, what it has done is to increase the instability of the current system. It has undermined the copyright regime that has balanced property interests with educational needs in the past and created property interests for publishers analogous to those of the entertainment industry. The copyright system is being challenged, and may be replaced, by a contract regime optimized for multinational media conglomerates. Finally, the electronic medium remains too ephemeral for the preservation of knowledge, one of the most important goals of the current system of communication.

The future of scholarly communication depends on how universities, scholarly associations, publishers, the government, and scholars themselves deal with the current crisis. We will describe the elements of the current system, discuss the issues, the environmental factors, the fiscal crisis, and the technological change affecting it and then assess the possible futures of scholarly communication.

THE COMPONENTS OF THE CURRENT SYSTEM

The system of scholarly communication consists in the relationships among four components: faculty research and the system of academic evaluation, publishing, research libraries, and the intellectual property regime. Over the past century, this system has evolved into today's familiar pattern of academic discourse, as universities have become centers for research and as the government has become the principal supporter of research. Let us consider each component in turn.

Faculty Research and the Economy of Academic Merit

Institutional promotion and tenure criteria and federal research funding create incentives for scholars to publish (thereby expanding the supply and demand for journals), and to specialize (thereby creating journals and monographs with ever smaller markets and thus higher costs). Moreover, the faculty reward system in universities subsidizes publishers, both explicitly (page charges, manuscript preparation, the transfer of copyright) and implicitly (donated editorial work, subsidized research funding). As a result, there is a tacit, and, thus rarely discussed, conflict of interest between faculty authors, who select journals on the basis of scholarly prestige (in the hope that their records will impress deans, tenure committees, and colleagues), and their university libraries, which must then purchase these journals at any cost.

Publishers

University presses and disciplinary associations were founded to disseminate research in the original cycle of scholarly communication. The faculty produced the works to be published; nonprofit publishers organized the distribution of knowledge; the university libraries bought the published works at an artificially high price, as a subsidy for learned societies; and the faculty then used this literature as the foundation for further research and teaching. The publishers added value through quality control and distribution of printed information, but, equally important, they provided an independent authority for the evaluation of the research upon which the faculty promotion was based. However, over the past fifty years, as federal research funding has encouraged specialization, journal publishing has become commercialized, and some parts of the scientific and technical literature are now being monopolized by multinational publishing conglomerates.

Research Libraries

Libraries add value by organizing published information into collections (that is, into literatures) and by creating catalogs through which users can gain access to information. Libraries pay more for journals than individual subscribers do, originally, as noted, as a subsidy to support scholarly publishing. But this tradition now serves primarily to increase the profit margins of commercial publishing monopolies. Libraries cannot back out of the system because the dual use of scholarly publishing by universities in knowledge-making and in the promotion system has made the demand for journals inelastic. Thus, libraries cannot make rational decisions about journal subscriptions solely on the basis of the utility of the information published relative to its price.

Intellectual Property Law

While protecting the property rights of authors and publishers, copyright historically has given the educational uses of information a special status as a public good. Fair Use establishes special rights to copy information for nonprofit educational purposes, within several practical guidelines. Recently, however, the development of electronic commerce has been the occasion for a policy debate about whether copyright "subsidies" for education through Fair Use *of both digital and printed documents* should be ended. The debate has been fueled by the characteristics of digital publications, which are likely to be governed by licenses and contracts, not by copyright. Those contractual terms will exclude fair use (for example, copying for educational purposes) and the first-sale doctrine (for example, interlibrary sharing of collections).

CRITICAL ISSUES AFFECTING THE SYSTEM

There are two critical issues affecting the system of scholarly communication: the latent tension between the roles of universities as producers and consumers of knowledge and the introduction of new technologies.

The Production and Use of Knowledge

This issue is best illustrated by the way universities evaluate faculty members for promotion. A great deal of the weakness of universities as consumers of scholarly publications, particularly journals, stems directly from their practice of linking commercial publishing to the process of judging the quality of faculty research. In universities, the evaluation of quality relies on the quality of the presses or journals in which the work has appeared. The universities have, in effect, handed a major part of the evaluation process to publishers; it is difficult, then, for universities to argue that they can forgo purchasing and using the publications they have touted as important.

How can universities escape from this homemade dilemma? It is worth exploring two kinds of solutions to the problem.

First, institutions of higher education must begin a dialogue with their faculties about the criteria and methods of the system of promotion in the academic ranks, exploring changes in the way universities treat copyright, how faculty members are credited for editorial work, and the link between publication and the evaluation of the quality of published research.

Second, the leaders of higher education must look above institutional horizons to consider the future of higher education as a whole, as an earlier generation did in the first decades of the 20th century, when the present system of scholarly communication was invented. Yet, the prior task is to find a venue for this consideration.

Higher education is stratified into numerous market sectors within which competition rather than cooperation is the norm, so that there are few organizational contexts within which discussions of the future of higher education as a whole can occur. No association of institutions is broad-gauged enough to function as a forum. Foundations, notably The Andrew W. Mellon Foundation with its series of grants supporting the analysis of library costs and the creation of the Journal Storage Project (JSTOR), have begun this work by supporting studies and discussions of the whole system of scholarly communication.[1] We have to build on these projects.

The Effect of New Technology

The economic forces now changing the research library, which are the immediate concern of the Mellon Foundation projects, are symptoms of an information revolution that will ultimately affect every other aspect of the system of scholarly communication, research, and publishing, and possibly even the institutional forms of higher education. New technological tools have already created entire new forms of information and visualization in the sciences and the arts, although not yet in every academic discipline. Many of these new kinds of information cannot be reproduced in print formats, because they use new modes of gathering data, representing information, and communicating. The new modes will also change the methods and sites of teaching.[2] Similarly, the library of

---

[1] The Journal Storage Project is creating a national database of backfiles of scholarly journals as a common resource of the nation's research libraries, replacing local space costs with membership fees.

[2] The most important changes in the modes of instruction will be campus-based—that is, not in distance learning. See Stanley Chodorow, "Educators Must Take the Electronic Revolution Seriously," *Academic Medicine* 71 (1996): 221–26.

the future will reflect changes in publishing, as technology creates new modes of distribution. Finally, scholars, students, and the research libraries of the future will exist on the campuses of the future, virtual and real.

ENVIRONMENTAL FACTORS

Research libraries are only the first sector of the university to be transformed by market forces, because libraries mediate the boundary between information markets and the academic community, but they will not be the only aspects of the university to be changed. There is already debate over the introduction of business management principles into the administration of universities. The members of disciplines threatened by the commercialization of education have led the way in defending the traditional functions and organization of the research library. Here again, the library is a symbol of the university, as well as the part of the institution functionally responsible for the management of information.

The research library crisis reflects four fundamental changes in the political and economic environment for higher education. We find that these four factors are rarely linked to the crisis in the system of scholarly communication.

Electronic Publishing

Information technology has created the Net and the Web as extensions of the scientific culture of shared information, but today the commercialization of digital information is accelerating, contributing to the modern enclosure of the public domain. It is the commercial business model of digital publishing, not technology, that will fundamentally reshape the research library; on-line information itself is ultimately an evolutionary development in library collections. The technologies of electronic commerce are reshaping the network, creating transaction engines, digital cash, and new ways to protect, or control, intellectual property. As library acquisition budgets continue to be unable to keep up with either the information costs or the needs of faculty and students, the digital library may well take the form of a fee-for-service document-delivery business, shifting the cost of information to the consumer. We shall explore this scenario in the next section, but note here only that electronic publishing is a new paradigm for scholarly communication both because of its new technology, the network, and because of its business model which may bypass the library, linking the publisher directly to the consumer.

Information Policy

Federal policy is now focused on expanding intellectual property rights to promote investment in information markets and exploit the dominance of American media companies in international markets, rather than on the role of information access in public domains such as education and government. Given the acceptance of shrink-wrap licenses and encryption technologies, it is possible that in the electronic environment the consumption of information will be governed by contract rather than by copyright with its protections for educational Fair Use. The status of higher education as a public good was established by the Morrill Act's land-grant principle, which made education one of the main avenues to the constitutional goal of furthering progress by promoting the development of science and technology. The current attitude toward rights on the information highway, which reflects the needs of the entertainment and publishing industries, is changing the freeway into a toll road.

Commercial Competition

Higher education has had a near monopoly of accredited professional training, but, in the future, this monopoly may be broken by intense competition from the commercial sector. Taking note of Motorola University, Walter Massey comments that American industry spends more on training and educating its work force than colleges and universities combined spend on educating students.[3] The examples of the rapid growth of the University of Phoenix, a for-profit degree-granting institution with stock listed on the NASDAQ and the interest of Disney and other media conglomerates (which frequently own scholarly publishing houses as well) in "Edutainment" suggest that, at the very least, noncommercial education will lose its monopoly.[4] Scholarly activity and the system of

---

[3] Walter E. Massey, "Uncertainties in the Changing Academic Profession," *Daedalus* 126:4 (Fall 1997): 76.
[4] Arthur Levine, "How the Academic Profession is Changing," ibid., 16–18.

scholarly communication, with their hidden subsidies, high overhead costs, and indeterminate contribution to productivity, are likely to be perceived as liabilities in such a competition.

Privatization of Research

The university's attitude toward the intellectual property produced by faculty members is changing in response to the growth of an information economy driven by patent and copyright. While federal funding is still by far the largest source of external support, particularly in science and engineering, it is unlikely to grow as rapidly as in the past, if at all. In the meantime, industrial funding for research has been growing, raising troubling questions about the commercialization of the academic community, because industrial partnerships increase pressure on universities to participate in the economy in which information is proprietary. The principal challenge is to the system of scholarly communication that has been the infrastructure for research in this country. One effect of this challenge is that universities are beginning to think about whether it is possible to make a claim on the intellectual property that has traditionally been regarded as the private property of the faculty member. Such a claim would bring copyright into line with the evolving treatment of rights based on patents, but the claim would be made in the interest of controlling costs rather than securing revenue.

THE FISCAL CRISIS OF THE RESEARCH LIBRARY

The changes in scholarly communication and in libraries being wrought by new technologies come on top of economic changes that have been the talk of librarians and academic administrators since the late 1980s. A 1992 study of 24 American research libraries commissioned by the Mellon Foundation[5] describes the decline of research libraries, not in absolute terms but relative to their mission to maintain a comprehensive record of published research.

Moreover, library collections and technologies are capital investments that require recurring maintenance support—for example, for items such

---

[5] Anthony M. Cummings, Marcia L. Witte, William G. Bowen, Laura O. Lazarus and Richard H. Ekman, *University Libraries and Scholarly Communication* (Washington D.C.: The Association of Research Libraries, 1992).

as space, reshelving, and preservation.[6] The growth of digital collections will not solve this problem, because printed materials remain the largest and most important segment of the information environment and because digitally stored data also will require substantial efforts and costs for preservation and continuous access.

Aside from the general problem of the capital investment necessary to maintain the library, the Mellon study describes three primary dimensions of the fiscal crisis of the research library.

The Rising Price of Information

The general price index in the United States increased by an average annual rate of 6.1 % between 1963 and 1990, while the price of books increased an average annual rate of 7.2%, and the price of serials (journals plus other serial publications) increased 11.3% annually. Since 1970, the price of books has risen at about the average inflation rate, but the price of science, medical, business, and technology journals increased by 13.5% a year on average. The consequence, as Brian Hawkins points out, is that between 1981 and 1995 budgets for collections at 89 research libraries increased by an average of 82% in real dollars (corrected for inflation) yet lost 38% of their buying power.[7]

Growth in the Amount of Information

The scholar's sense of an "information explosion" is well justified. The Association of Research Libraries has estimated that by 1991 there was a total of 118,500 serials being published. Over 70,000 of these titles were new since 1971. Fields with the largest federal funding grew the fastest and produced the largest increases in price. Increasing prices

---

[6] Maintenance costs include preservation, because books and journals published between about 1850 and 1970 were printed on acidic paper that is disintegrating. On the problems, methods, and costs of preservation, see the papers published by the Commission on Preservation and Access. See especially the documentary films *Slow Fires* (on paper preservation) Washington, D.C., Council on Library Resources, 1987 and *Into the Future* (on digital preservation) Washington, D.C., Commission on Preservation and Access, 1997. Both films were written and produced by Terry Sanders and American Film Foundation.

[7] Brian Hawkins, "The Unsustainability of the Traditional Library and the Threat to Higher Education." Aspen Meadows, Colo: The Aspen Institute, (October 18 1996), 2. See also, Brian Hawkins, "Creating the Library of the Future: Incrementalism Won't Get Us There!" *The Serials Librarian* 3/4 (1994): 24.

reflect growth in the amount of information published in a field, because new journals tend to be highly specialized and appeal to much smaller markets.

New Technologies

Collections have averaged between 33% and 35% of research library budgets since 1963, while salaries have decreased from 62% to 52%, and operating expenditures have increased from 6% to 14%, reflecting the expense of new technologies. Libraries first invested in technology in response to the information explosion—to automate technical services for managing collections (the acquisitions, circulation, and cataloguing functions)—and, subsequently, to support new collections that are technology based (ranging from slides to microfilm to machine-readable data files to CD-ROMs to networked information).[8] Observing that staffing costs declined as a percent of the total budget as automation technology was installed, the Mellon study concludes that technology may make library operations more efficient, and certainly changes the way basic library functions are managed. But there is an equally important consequence. The automation of the catalogue has changed the way scholars and students use the library—indeed, use information—and the way, as a result, they conduct their research and pursue learning.

The Mellon Report presents this development as a *fiscal* crisis, implying that it can be solved.[9] But Hawkins argues that collection budgets are not sustainable given the rate of increase of journal prices, making this a process of irreversible change. How, then, can the library be managed during this transitional phase, in which the vulnerabilities of the old system are more apparent than the possibilities of a new, as yet undefined, system? Academic administrators might focus their dialogue with librarians around two issues:

---

[8] See Malcolm Getz, John J. Siegfried, Kathryn H. Anderson, "Adoption of Innovations in Higher Education." *The Quarterly Review of Economics and Finance*, 37: 3 (Fall 1997): 605–31.

[9] The Mellon Report observes that, between 1980 and 1990, the library budget as a percent of educational and general expenses (E&G) fell every year but one (ending at 3.08% in 1990) thus supporting the interpretation that the fiscal crisis of libraries is caused by a legitmation crisis within universities. However, the growth in E&G expense may reflect factors other than academic activity requiring library support, such as student services and administrative requirements imposed by federal and state regulation.

- When should information use be subsidized? The use of information by faculty members and students is subsidized, not free; the word "free" used in relation to libraries only encourages unrealistic expectations. Today, some information appears to be free to users (library collections) but some is not (course readings, personal libraries, copies made for personal use). Between these categories, there is emerging a new world of information commodities, such as document delivery and electronic data. Where should the boundary between subsidized and fee-for-service information be drawn?
- How can the quality of library services be measured? The quality of research libraries has historically been measured by budget inputs (the size of collections and personnel budgets). How can the quality of the library be measured by the impact of library services on the quality of teaching and research? How can the quality of such services as the way the library provides access to information, the reference functions, and teaching be measured?

TECHNOLOGY AND SCHOLARLY COMMUNICATION

Aside from its current effects on the library and the flow of information, how will information technology reshape scholarly communication and publishing? In this section we shall attempt only to describe the dynamics of this transitional moment as it may shape our management choices in the short term. In the next section we will explore an alternative future.

A prototype of the future of scholarly communication already exists: it is the Internet, which uses electronic mail for discussion, the World Wide Web for distribution of papers, and myriad experimental digital environments for specialized forms of representation of knowledge and communication. This infrastructure began as a medium of research of use to the military and has been largely supported by the government. The primary concern, then, is how to finance it as a stable and affordable communication system that can support high-quality information for research, teaching, and learning across all fields.

It is the future of scholarly publication, the electronic marketplace for information and its link to the authentication of the quality of research, that is problematic. Because of their origins, the Internet and the Web technologies are optimized for free access to technical information. But the future of networked communication will be shaped by the requirements of electronic commerce, with greater attention to the security of information, the auditing of transactions, digital cash management, and the creation and protection of new forms of intellectual property.

Given that printing, inventory maintenance, and the distribution of paper are estimated to be half of the cost of publishing, it is distinctly possible that electronic publishing will replace paper as the primary medium for scholarly articles. But a new medium will probably imply new formats for scholarship as well and, perhaps, new content. Information products may evolve from the journal subscription to the individual article delivered on demand and perhaps to the paragraph delivered from a subscription to a database. A system based on these trends would make information a service more than a commodity, a kind of utility, one that would bill the consumer directly for information consumed. The library's role as intermediary between publisher and consumer might well disappear in the document delivery scenario.

The proliferation of bibliographic citation databases has made scholars aware of articles that are not available in the library, particularly since journal price increases have forced libraries to reduce the number of subscriptions, creating a market for the delivery of documents at the article level. Just as Hollywood resisted videotape before discovering a lucrative new rental market, so publishers have resisted document delivery. Today, however, copyright revenue from course packets and document delivery has created new income streams for publishers.

Publishers are likely to prefer today's subscription model for two reasons: it is predictable, and it is favorable to publishers, because it pays for information before it is received and provides income for published information even if the information is not used. Document delivery favors the consumer, in that one pays only for information that is specifically requested. A third possibility, that information will be licensed by subject, creating searchable databases that include articles from many journals and publishers, would make the search the unit of knowledge. In such a system, time-on-screen might determine price. All of these scenarios would affect the pricing of information and change the universities' budgets for information in fundamental ways, not to speak of the change in the role of the library and librarians.

Document delivery might also change the way the quality of publications is evaluated. Today, personnel committees, deans, and provosts rely on the quality of journals and presses to help them assess the quality of a faculty member's contribution to knowledge. Tomorrow, the number of requests for an article or monograph might become an additional indicator of significance, rather like the way the number of citations functions as a measure of value in some disciplines today.

In transferring the cost of library materials from the university's library budget to the user, document delivery raises fundamental equity issues for higher education. Should higher education subsidize all the information needs of all faculty members and students, or should the demand for information be moderated like a market, by shifting some costs to the consumer? If some faculty members have information budgets in their grants, while others are in fields in which extramural funding is not available, how should the university allocate its information budget? Equally important, because information products are unique and have unique value for research in various fields, this system would sustain the monopoly of information purveyors without the counterbalance of the Fair Use policy under the copyright law. While it is not clear what the pricing system for information would be under such a system, the potential is there for a radical change in the universities' budget systems.

One thing is already clear about this emerging information market, however. It makes possible the assemblage of a comprehensive record about the way individuals consume information. As such, it has created a valuable new business, based on close electronic surveillance of consumers' behavior. The capacity of this business also has obvious political uses that challenge traditional notions of privacy and academic freedom in this country.

Academic leaders and librarians have also explored the possibility of removing scholarly communication from the commercial sector by creating new nonprofit scholarly presses; or by recreating Fair Use by limiting the transfer of unlimited copyright from faculty authors to publishers; or by separating the evaluation of the quality of research from publication.[10]

THE FUTURE OF SCHOLARSHIP

Thus far, our exploration has focused on the future of the institutions that have managed scholarship for the past century, rather than on the

---

[10] See Chapter 4, S. Chodorow and P. Lyman, "The Responsibilities of Universities in the New Information Environment" in B. Hawkins and P. Battin, eds, *The Mirage of Continuity: Reconfiguring Academic Information Resources in the 21ˢᵗ Century* (1998). The Stanford Library's "High-Wire Press" is the leading prototype of a new University-based publishing system (*http://www.gu.edu.au/alib/highwire/highwire.html*). But, also see OCLC's new role as distributor of digital journals.

needs of scholars as they are now evolving. Yet only an understanding of the future needs of scholars can provide a reliable agenda for reinventing the system of scholarly communication. In conclusion, let us engage in a thought experiment to explore how the Web must be perfected if it is to become an infrastructure for scholarly communication.

The Future of the Author

In the age of digital networks, information is flowing as it did in the age before authors and, eventually, their publishers, became particular about the ownership of their work. In the Middle Ages, works of literature—history, theology, law, medicine, and literature in the strict sense—grew and changed from writer to writer. The great glosses on the Bible and on the foundational texts of law, medicine, theology, and philosophy were composite works, put together from the works of many teachers and scholars. The glosses eventually achieved a standard, or vulgate, state, but they evolved for a long period before doing so. All of these kinds of medieval works and documents grew organically from generation to generation. What was significant about them was not who wrote them but what they contained.

Electronic works possess the same kind of fluidity and imply the same de-emphasis of authorship—this in an age in which ownership of ideas can create international trade crises and lead publishing houses to fight the electronic revolution with all their might. The invention of the author has been a useful legal fiction with which to trace the ownership of particular expressions of ideas as property; for ideas themselves cannot be owned, and it has never been a simple matter to trace the lineage of scholarly ideas.

A work of scholarship mounted on the Internet will belong to the community of scholars it serves. Scholar-users will add to the work, annotate it, correct it, and share it with their students and colleagues. All the really important works of scholarship, the works we commonly call research tools, will quickly evolve into new fields and subspecialties in the hands of scholars.

This imagined world is already becoming a fact in many fields, yet print is still the official record of scholarship. Digital publications are not yet linked to the economy of academic merit and prestige, the criteria and procedures for the distribution of promotion and tenure. How will the individual contributions of scholars be recognized or attributed? How will we reward or judge scholars for the purposes of promotion within the cursus honorum of the academy? The experience with print media tells us that we should do what we can to prevent the economy of academic merit from being linked to commercial publication in the digital world.

What is a Publication?

The imagined world is one in which the electronic medium has radically changed the nature of "publication." In the fluid world of the electron, the body of scholarship in a field may become a continuous stream, the later work modifying the older and all of it available to the reader in a single database or a series of linked databases. In such a world, scholarship would progress in a perennial electronic conference or bulletin board. Contributions and debates would occur on the Internet and be continuous.

The future world of scholarship we are envisioning is one in which collaboration will become the norm, even in fields now the province of sole practitioners. It is also one in which the information used by the teams of scholars will be in liquid form. The electronic format encourages constant change—addition, subtraction, alteration—and its organization is fundamentally different from the one used in printed materials. When scholars create information resources directly on the Internet, they use a variety of new organizational methods and expect the materials to grow and change constantly, perhaps even to be given a completely new organizational form if someone develops a better way to present the data. We can expect many scholars to resist such fluidity in their information resources, because it will relegate the traditional footnote—to which some of us are inordinately attached—to the dustbin. In the long run, however, the tradition of citation will not be able to hinder the evolution of our methods for managing information. Some future edition of the *Chicago Manual of Style* will provide models of citation very different from the ones we use now.

One consequence of this process will be that the usefulness of scholarship may decline more rapidly than it does now. Medieval historians can use many works published in the 16th and 17th century; they contain valuable information and insights. The value of a work rests on the amount and accuracy of its citations of sources. In the fluid, electronic world of the future, the information base will evolve and its history will become murky.

When the authority of a work is difficult or, in some fields, impossible to establish, old publications will lose their meaning. One wonders how our successors at the end of the 21st century will learn the history of their scholarly disciplines—or will scholarly disciplines themselves be transformed, becoming global and transnational, as the sciences already have, and requiring new cosmopolitan intellectual foundations?

The Future of Editorial Authority

But there are some problems in this picture. First, a persistent dissenter from the way the majority of scholars are approaching an issue will remain a constant presence in the discussion, perhaps hindering its flow. Today, a dissenter publishes his or her views, which can be taken seriously or ignored as the community of scholars wishes. In the electronic environment, the community will find it difficult to ignore the gadfly. This is not an unmitigated good thing. The gadfly is often not right, and what is interesting and stimulating in the dissenter's view is almost always absorbed by the other members of the community long before the dissenter himself is ready to move on to other issues. Who will be the editors of the electronic dialogue?

Preservation of Digital Knowledge

All fields go through periods of stagnation, and one of the ways to overcome them is to retrace the debates to find a new starting point. In the ever-changing electronic environment, the older work disappears into the newer, and the stages of scholarly thought are obscured.[11] This may be a significant defect of the electronic environment. Moreover, it is becoming clear that the preservation of electronic resources involves migration from one "platform" to another, and that implies continued use. Who will use up space and effort keeping a database alive unless it remains in use? We have not found a good storage technique for electronic sources, as we did for writings when we discovered parchment and figured out how to bind folios into codices.

---

[11] All of us have noted the change in the meaning of "draft" in our writing on the computer. The distinct draft is now an artificial stage of composition, and often we simply do not leave a record of the development of our ideas as we rewrite, rearrange, and reprint our work.

What is an Electronic Literature?

As you can see, this picture of the future predicts changes in the form and, probably, the essence of scholarly discourse. The intellectual process we have used for centuries rests both on the means of communication and on the methods of scholarly discourse, so a change in the former will probably alter the process as a whole in significant ways. We predict, or perhaps can already observe in many disciplines, a revolution in the tools or methods of discourse. Today, the medium of exchange is the printed book or article, but the rapid growth of electronic exchanges among scholars in all fields points to the vision we have sketched of the future. If what we have imagined were to be realized, one can see the problems of collection, management, and citation of information. Who will collect the stream of scholarship presented in the electronic medium? How will it be broken up into pieces that can be cited and found with sufficient certainty?

Notwithstanding the present dominance of printed media, much of the most important information being produced by today's research activity is transmitted in the electronic medium. This trend creates great problems for scholars:

- How does a scholar cite information retrieved from the Internet? The problem is not that the resource has no address (the URL address will do, if it has been archived in a manner that guarantees its survival into the future) but that there are no chapters or pages in many of the resources. People are not only mounting books and articles on the Internet; they are also putting up original sources in true database format.
- How does a scholar know whether an electronic resource found on the Internet is sound, that is, contains reliable, up-to-date information?
- Assuming that the reader has the equipment and knowledge, how does he or she know whether the cited electronic source is the one to which the author referred? The address might be correct, the title or description might be fine, but the data might have been altered by addition, subtraction, emendation, and such since its original citation. The owner or maintainer of a database might change the principles of its collection or the features of its presentation, both of which would complicate use and citation.
- How will new people enter a field, bringing new insights and related information to bear on important scientific or scholarly questions when the sources of information "float," as they do on the Internet? The active participants in a field will know about the migration of ideas, but those who come afterward, in particular those who enter the field from laboratories or academic programs that are not in the mainstream of research in the field, will have problems tracing the citations in earlier publications to the origi-

nal source. There is not yet an easy-to-use reference work to track such re-locations. The great, fixed classifications of the modern library are equal-opportunity sources for seekers of knowledge. The Internet is not, in its current form, a stable environment that can sustain scholarship over a long time and a wide arena of scholars.

What is the Digital Research Library?

These questions are not the only ones raised by the use of new electronic resources in scholarship. The successful growth of knowledge requires a confidence in the ability of scholars to attain a nearly complete control of the existing body of information in a field. Each contributor to the field strives for completeness. Although none ever achieves this goal, the scholars in a field collectively possess the knowledge necessary for judging the significance of discoveries. Here, again, we must recognize that our confidence that we have mastered the relevant information in our fields has traditionally rested on our confidence in libraries and librarians.

CONCLUSION

We believe that administrators and librarians should try to anticipate changes in scholarly discourse in their discussions of the current crisis in the system of scholarly communication and information management. These changes will cause some additional headaches for the managers of information and, particularly, for those responsible for the academic reward system, but they also hold out promise for a return to an information environment in which the progressive diminution of the domain necessary for a thriving system of scholarly communication can be reversed. The future of scholarly research and of teaching depends on the reestablishment of that public domain.

7

Camel Drivers and Gatecrashers: Quality Control in the Digital Research Library

DOUGLAS GREENBERG

It is said that Abdul Kassem Ismael, the scholarly Grand Vizier of Persia in the tenth century, had a library of 117,000 volumes. He was an avid reader and truly a lover of books. On his many travels as a warrior and statesman, he could not bear to part with his beloved books. Wherever he went, they were carried about by 400 camels trained to walk in alphabetical order. His camel drivers thus became librarians who could put their hands instantly on any book for which their master asked.

Until very recently, perhaps no one had devised a better scheme for the staffing and organization of a library than Abdul Kassem Ismael. Certainly no one had devised a more portable system! Of course, Ismael's system worked in part because the library had only one user making demands on the staff, enough camels to carry the collection, and enough camel drivers to care for the camels and serve the needs of the Grand Vizier. The modern library does not have these luxuries, especially in this country, where access to information is something akin to a constitutional right, and where no major library has enough staff or space to care for its collections. Access to information is at least a theoretical prop for democratic politics and social equality in the United States. Providing it is a social good of undoubted value.

Because we cannot tolerate the elitist structure of Ismael's system, and because we have so much more information to care for and distribute than he did, we have begun to attempt to democratize access through electronic technology. As Ismael's library grew, he bought more camels and hired more camel driver-librarians. Until recently, we have done pretty much the same thing. But today, we hear interminably, we are about to move to the era of the digital library, a new beast of burden that will finally and fundamentally transform Ismael's system, making vastly more information available with no increase in staff. We will create the universal library, as transparently usable in Perth as in Persia. In which case it would probably be a good idea first to figure out just what a digital library actually is.

Despite the extensive, mind-numbing discussions of and work on the creation of the digital library in individual libraries, on campuses, and nationally through such efforts as the Digital Library Federation, very little has been said (or done) to specify what it signifies to use the adjective "digital" to modify the noun "library." The term "digital library" may even be an oxymoron: that is, if a library is a library, it is not digital; if a library is digital, it is not a library. We have not thought as systematically as we should about the characteristics of the print library and how and whether they can, or should be, duplicated, transformed, or abandoned in a digital world. Digital library projects abound, but they are disparate, even contradictory, in their aims, and they are also blissfully unbothered by the unintended consequences that they presage. As the wag said: "If you don't know where you are going, any road will take you there." That is precisely our situation in the transition from the print to the digital library. Because we do not know where we are going (but want to get there very quickly), the application of digital technologies sometimes becomes an end in itself.

As an exercise in nostalgia if nothing else, I propose to describe some of the characteristics of the book and the library, and then do the same thing for the electronic environment and, before then, suggesting some of the potential dangers of failing to heed the differences and some of the advantages of recognizing them.

We begin with some preliminary descriptions. The book and the library embody order, linearity, knowledge as sequence, information as a hierarchy of value, predefined relationships among disparate data, and an emphasis on the physical reality of information embodied in the printed page and three-dimensional objects. The Web page and the Internet embody disorder, circularity, knowledge as consequence, information as equality of value, relationships among data created on the fly, and an emphasis on the electronic reality of information embodied in magnetically encoded media and digital transmission mechanisms.

Thought and creativity are more frequently analogous to the Web page and the Internet: stream of consciousness, unlikely connections, imagined and created relationships all transmitted electrically across the synapse. Most of what we know, on the other hand, was originally created and organized in the linear, hierarchical, and physical world of the book and the library. We are accustomed to suppressing many of our instinctive ways of thinking, which I believe actually lack the organizational specificity of the book and the library, relying as they do on intuition, experience, and instinct.

We have learned to accommodate our impulse toward discursive thought to the inflexible categories and order we have imposed on information, but we have done so for reasons that are more logistical than anything else: we have needed, as Abdul Kassem Ismael did, a systematic mechanism for locating static print information. Our most pressing problem of the moment is that we are trying to create new pathways of access to static materials created in the culture of the book and the library, but we are using the Web and the Internet, which are inherently dynamic. As we move increasingly from digitized information created in the world of print to truly digital information, we will have to wrestle with a new problem: how to devise dynamic mechanisms for locating information that is itself dynamic as to both content and location.

The modern research library is a marvel of the human genius for organization, structure, and order, as well as for creating the tools through which that order can be understood and navigated. As complex as our libraries and library systems can sometimes be, we have only embellished Abdul Kassem Ismael's model. We begin with a question and proceed systematically from a road map to take us to a library building through its doors to an On-line Public Access Catalogue (OPAC) or other catalogue that will identify and locate the precise item or items in the library that will help us answer our question. Floor plans of the library's interior will take us to the exact shelf location where that item resides. If the item is a book, a table of contents and an index will give us two different ways to discover whether the answer is within its covers. The existence of page numbers permits us to go to a relatively small block of text and scan it for our answer. At each point along the way, we follow a route through a series of boxes within boxes until we find the tiniest box in which (we hope) our answer will be found.

Another attribute of the library, less commented upon than its hierarchical structure, is its incorporation of many mechanisms to assure the reliability of the information it contains. Just as the user proceeds to the building, to the catalogue, to the floor, to the shelf, to the book, to the page, there are entry points for printed information along the way and hurdles of trustworthiness that must be surmounted before entry is granted. Nothing gets into the library unless some reliable person makes a judgment that it belongs there. Nothing gets into the "E" section of the Library of Congress cataloging scheme unless someone makes a judgment that it belongs there. Nothing gets published in the first place unless several people make a judgment that it is worthwhile and reliable (scholarly work, for example, must pass muster with peer reviewers and publishers). Libraries, in turn, make judgments based on experience about the reliability of publishers. Authors themselves are also gatekeepers, and they provide others with the opportunity to check their reliability through the use of (sometimes fallible) bibliographies and footnotes.[1]

In other words, the structure and physical organization of a research library guarantee that if there is information within its walls to be found on topics we can define narrowly, we will find it within a reasonable amount of time. In addition and equally important, the elaborate structure of gatekeeping in the research library, which includes peer review and many other mechanisms for the assurance of reliability, provides a reasonable guarantee that the page in the book on the shelf on the floor in the library that contains what we are looking for, has the stamp of approval of numerous referees of different kinds whose judgment can be trusted.

Moreover, there is a close relationship between the library's physical and organizational structure and its gatekeeping function. Each level of the structure contains another check on the quality of the information within. The construction of the hierarchy that the library supports is thus not only a way to provide access to information that follows a rational road map, but a way to be certain that nothing gets into the library that does not belong there. And the library is dependent upon external others (publishers and scholars primarily) to make that happen.

The elegant, hierarchical, and logical simplicity of this scheme has served humankind very well—at least since Alexandria, to say nothing of 10th century Persia. And it is likely to do so for a long time to come. The physical library will not be disappearing anytime soon. But emerging modes for the creation, storage, and transmission of knowledge and information, as well as for access to it, threaten to establish an alternative to the library that is both more and less than a "virtual duplicate" of the

---

[1] See Anthony Grafton, *The Footnote: A Curious History* (Cambridge, Mass.: Harvard University Press, 1997).

physical structure of the library and that embodies a very different sense of what knowledge is and how it should be organized, accessed, and communicated.

Compare the structure and reliability of the research library and the printed book to the structure and reliability of the Internet and the Web page. The Internet has no organizational hierarchy of containers of information that proceeds smoothly and sequentially downward from the vast storehouse to the single page. On the Internet, we go directly from a first point of access to the individual page. We may make a stop at a search engine or two, but by comparison to the hierarchical structure of the library, the Internet's structure is flat. It depends not at all upon the structured arrangement of knowledge.

Arguably, it subverts all structured knowledge by assigning the same significance to a page of trivia assembled by a high school student as it does to a page of data on the solar system assembled from the Hubble Telescope. Furthermore, the information on the Internet is dynamic. It is constantly changing, and it is easily changed both by its creator and by others. This is as true of data from the Hubble Telescope as it is of a high school student's Web page. New data will supercede the old on the Internet. This is part of its power. But the text of the first printing of *Moby Dick* in a rare book library will never change. Indeed, its location—if we mean by location its place in a sequence of other books on a shelf—will never change either. Print information is as static and as stable as the medium on which it appears (provided it is acid-free!). Electronic information can be as ephemeral, as changeable, and as dynamic as the media on which *it* is stored.

If the key to the library's power is its rigid, counterintuitive arrangement of static information in a comprehensible and hierarchical structure, the key to the Internet's power is its flexible arrangement of dynamic information that permits the human mind literally to jump from one thing to another and back again with no more than stream of consciousness as a guide. It is anybody's guess which of these systems is better adapted to human creativity and curiosity.

What is certain, however, is that the connection in the library between its structure and the reliability of the information it contains is not duplicated on the Internet. Indeed, just as the library and Internet are opposites on the matter of hierarchy and organization, so too are they opposites on the matter of gatekeeping and reliability. None of the mechanisms that assure the reliability of the information we find on a page in a university press book in the "E" section of my local research library pertain to information I find on the Internet.

How did the information get into the library? Through multiple gatekeepers right down to the page level. How does it get onto the Internet? Without any gatekeeping whatsoever and with no time lag between creation, publication, and access, all of which are separate processes of quality control in the print world. The existence of the multiple gates and gatekeepers of the print world thus makes the structure of information in the library possible, and the structure permits and empowers the organization of the gatekeeping function. On the Internet, neither structure nor gatekeeping exist.

This relationship between gatekeeping and organizational structure has a direct consequence for access in both environments. Although we have been ever more clever about finding aids and access tools in the print library, the organizational and gatekeeping functionaries of the print world slow our access to information. We need to consult road maps, campus maps, OPACS, library floor plans, shelves, tables of contents and indexes, and individual pages. We may even, *in extremis*, have to speak with a librarian or two. And we must do these things in sequence; removing a random book from a random shelf on a random floor of a random library and consulting a random page is not likely to help us much. On the Internet, we can move more quickly, and sequence is meaningless. The increased speed is thrilling, but since neither we nor the information we are pursuing has passed through any tests of trustworthiness and reliability, we may wind up with information that we discover to be useless or, worse, information we believe to be trustworthy that is actually not information at all but actually the product of fabrication or imagination.

The gatekeeping function of the print world is vital to the entire scholarly enterprise. All the participants in the scholarly community both depend upon it and exercise it. Publishers are gatekeepers when they choose to publish some work and not others. They benefit from gatekeeping when they identify peer reviewers whose *bona fides* has been established by others. Libraries, in turn, benefit from the work of the publishers and establish their own standards simply to keep their customers. We would be very skeptical about libraries if we thought that they put anything on their shelves that happened to be dropped on their doorsteps. Scholars require effective gatekeeping from publishers and libraries in order to do their work, but, in their work as peer reviewers of manuscripts and in outside tenure and promotion reviews, they also serve as gatekeepers.

Universities similarly benefit from the work of the publishers, libraries, and scholars (and, significantly, they frequently fund the whole process through library budgets, university press subventions, and faculty salaries and research support). What is more, they participate crucially as gatekeepers themselves when they hire and fire faculty. We trust the best universities to hire faculty whose work can be relied upon. Indeed, that is in some sense the most salient characteristic of a great university: its faculty produce scholarship that is utterly credible from the collections of libraries whose integrity is flawless.

The differences between the library and the Internet are made even more complicated by the fact that, as noted earlier, there are really two kinds of material going up on the Net these days: digital information that exists only in that form and digit*ized* information that originated in the world of print. The reliability of both is suspect in the digital world because their provenance is difficult to trace and easy to fabricate. Moreover, the most trustworthy material produced in the world of print is ironically the *least* likely to find its way into digital form. Copyright restrictions and the desire of rights holders to protect their intellectual property have thus far caused many holders of rights to existing peer-reviewed information (scholarly journals are only one example) to hesitate about providing digital access to their material.

Nature abhors a vacuum, and digital material created for the Net or digitized material that is not peer reviewed is far more likely to appear on computer monitors these days than scholarly material of the highest quality and reliability.[2] Students, never inclined to be concerned about these sorts of issues in any event, are likely to think that the boundary between the Net and the Library is transparent or nonexistent. Indiscriminate use of unsubstantiated data—and the lack of quality gatekeeping on the Net to distinguish it from reliable data—can threaten the very standards of scholarship and meticulousness that are at the core of the modern humanities and social sciences. At the very least, the quality of undergraduate education in the arts and sciences is threatened. The social catastrophes that a paranoid might predict as a consequence of all this are probably best left undiscussed here.

---

[2] Projects like Journal Storage Project (JSTOR) and others are, of course, encouraging exceptions to this generalization.

Of course, the undependability of electronic information is not the only difference between the Internet and the library. True digital information will exist in new forms and formats and combinations of forms and formats that do not exist at all in the material world of the library and the book. We have not yet learned how knowledge created in these new forms and formats will be used, much less what sorts of retrieval mechanisms we will have to create for them.

The emergence of genuine multimedia resources, including fully searchable audio and video archives, combined with the possibility of seamlessly integrating images, sound, and motion with text, means not only that the digital library will be very different than the traditional library, but also that the scholarly work we create from research conducted "in" the digital library will be characterized by a multiplicity of media and formats. New kinds of information resources will, it is not too much to say, dictate the creation of new forms of knowledge and new ways of communicating it.[3] We are only at the beginning of knowing what those new forms of scholarship will be like and what the tools will be to help people find and use that information and knowledge.

The implications of all this—not only for research collections as collections and for research as the acquisition of new knowledge—are pro-

---

[3] At earlier stages in the development of these new technologies I tried to explore some of the implications of this sort of scholarship. See "Get Out of the Way If You Can't Lend a Hand: The Changing Character of Scholarship, Technology, and the Significance of Special Collections," Sul H. Lee, ed., *The Role and Future of Special Collections in Research Libraries* (NewYork:The Haworth Press, 1993), 83–98; *The Journal of Library Administration* 1 (1993): 83–98; *Biblion* (Fall, 1993): 5–18 [published simultaneously], "Technology and Its Discontents: Some Problems and Possibilities for the Humanist in the Virtual University," Proceedings of the Conference on Changes in Scholarly Communication Patterns: Australia and the Electronic Library (Consultative Committee of the Australian Academies of Humanities, Science, Social Sciences, and Technological Sciences and Engineering, Canberra, Australia, 1993): 131–146, and "Return to the Valley of the Dolls: Reflections on Changing Lanes Along the Information Superhighway," *Biblion* (Autumn, 1996): 3–16. An ironic sidelight to this series of publications was that they involved a conceit about what the shape of scholarly work on the novelist, Jacqueline Susann, would be like when true multimedia research became possible. In a case of life imitating art, Peter Graham of the Rutgers University Library recently sent me an e-mail from the SHARP-L listserve run by the Society for the History of Authorship. It reads, in part: "I am working on an ever expanding project that has brought me to a place where I need to do some serious work on Metalious' *Peyton Place*." I cannot foreswear suggesting of Grace Metalious as Truman Capote did famously of Jacqueline Susan that the notion of Metalious as a serious writer is an oxymoron. See also Douglas Greenberg, "Technophobia, Papyrophylia, and the Real Thing: Psychoneurotic Barriers to Technological Innovation in Cultural Institutions," *Association of Computing Machinery Newsletter*, Special Interest Group on University Computing Support (February 1997).

found. The very meaning of what a research collection is must change almost unrecognizably to accommodate new forms of research materials, new mechanisms of organization, new kinds of access points and finding aids, and, subsequently, new forms of scholarly communication.

Meanwhile, we must continue to pursue the preservation of the print record and electronic access to it. We must also urgently consider the preservation questions of the digital age. The recent film produced by the Commission on Preservation and Access, *Into the Future*, treats some of these questions superficially, but the implications of digital technology for current standards, policies, and procedures of preservation and conservation have not attracted truly thoughtful consideration in either the library or archival communities. Instead of focusing merely on the brief half-life of electronic information and the frailty of magnetic media, we also ought to be framing policies and procedures for ensuring that electronic materials are retained in pristine and original condition and are not changed by "gatecrashers" from the Internet. The "indeterminacy of the text" to which literary theorists point in the print world, is, in the digital environment an almost overwhelming reality.

Just as we still do not allow pens into the rare book room of the library, we must assure ourselves that we have done all we can to keep the electronic graffiti artists and doodlers away from the electronic primary resources and digital scholarship. This will be easier said than done since we will not want to defeat one of the Internet's most alluring characteristics: its capacity to provide unfettered access to basic knowledge for anyone who needs it. Firewall technologies, digital signatures, and the like have begun to provide this sort of security in the commercial world. Digital libraries and digital librarians will need to apply the same sorts of technologies with a ruthlessness equal to that of commercial enterprises.

If we address these problems, they are soluble. In the meantime, the digital library marches on, with or without attention to these caveats. And it does contain within it some truly transformative possibilities that do not threaten the liberal arts tradition at all. Indeed, they promise to enliven and reinforce that tradition.

A less threatening, even promising, aspect of technologically based research collections involves the blurring of distinctions that are embedded in our system of scholarly and educational work but are more logistical than logical. We have tended, for example, to distinguish between library materials that are used for research and those that are used for instruction. Large universities that own significant collections of primary resources frequently separate them from the teaching collections of the library; they may even have undergraduate libraries with a core collection of secondary and printed primary materials. The real stuff of scholarly research is invaluable and fragile and, quite sensibly, protected from the sometimes overeager hands and highlighters of undergraduates.

This is a perfectly reasonable way to protect research collections, but no one should ever have believed that such protection served an educational purpose. Anyone who has taught undergraduates knows, in fact, that primary sources are the very best way to engage them in the scholarly enterprise. The new technologies permit us to digitize and make accessible to undergraduates powerfully educational collections of primary sources without endangering them (either the undergraduates or the sources). And, since such digitization can be undertaken by colleges and universities themselves, their authenticity can be assured (if it can also be protected).

The tendency of the Internet and analogous technologies to substitute unstructured information for structured information is similarly a potential benefit to both scholarly research and undergraduate education. The capacity to undertake full text and key word searches of vast bodies of information on the Internet is a powerful tool for research, as is the ability to "click" from place to place on the Internet, without returning repeatedly to catalogues, shelving schemes, library floor plans, and book stacks. Moreover, the imminent ubiquity of images, video, and audio that are also searchable is thrilling from an instructional and research perspective.[4] The potential dangers of having students and colleagues using materials that have not been properly vetted and authenticated should not prevent us from exploiting these technologies, provided that we do so with care and a due regard for the traditions of the academy.

Another aspect of the same blurring of distinctions has to do with the creation of databases or Websites of selections of primary source materials rather than making the materials themselves completely available

---

[4] An early example is the Oyez Oyez Oyez Website *(http://court.it-services.nwu.edu/oyez/)* at Northwestern University which permits access to oral arguments of the Supreme Court over the Internet. The Chicago Historical Society plans a comparable site that will include 9,000 hours of interviews conducted by Studs Terkel on WFMT in Chicago and, when the technology permits, 4 million feet of WGN news film. The Historical Society is also considering what mechanisms it will need to employ to protect its intellectual property rights, assure scholarly and educational access, and establish the authenticity of the material.

electronically. This is not only a matter of reducing the expense involved in digitizing a complete archival collection; it is also a way to impose intellectual structure in the electronic environment. Databases and well-crafted Websites, like libraries and good scholarly books, actually work against the natural tendency of the Net to flatten information and remove hierarchies of meaning. They simultaneously can permit research of a very high order and educational experiences that are as valuable for elementary and junior high school students as for undergraduates and senior citizens.[5]

The Internet thus promises to enrich at least as much as it promises to threaten traditional academic culture. Nonetheless, the nomenclature to which we are accustomed, itself an artifact of the world of print, is likely to need revision, even replacement. The distinction between education and research, as we have seen, is already blurring. Similarly, distinctions between collections and the scholarship they support, between collections and exhibitions, between scholarship and exhibitions, between documents and artifacts, between texts and objects are all likely to get very murky indeed as technology allows us to reformat, reorganize, and redefine the materials of our cultural life.

Imagine, for example, side-by-side on your screen, the score of a great work of music and a performance of it. Or a transcript of a great political speech juxtaposed to a video recording of its delivery and a newspaper account. Or a 360° view of a great piece of sculpture accompanied by a recording of a great actor reading from the sculptor's diary, and a scan of the diary itself in a third window. Remarkably, none of these are quite the technological wonder that they would have been just a few years ago: the technology exists, and the mechanisms of access are becoming increasingly inexpensive and available.

One can even imagine that a new, digital form of scholarship will emerge very much sooner than we expect. If our resources are no longer confined to the printed page, why should our scholarship be? Indeed, digital scholarship derived from digitized or digital resources should command the creation of a new kind of digital footnote that provides

---

[5] The superb work of Professor Edward Ayres and his colleagues at the University of Virginia in the Valley of the Shadow Project *(http://jefferson.village.virginia.edu/vshadow2/)* exemplifies this sort of work, as does the collaboration between Northwestern University, Professor Carl Smith of Northwestern, and the Chicago Historical Society, "The Great Chicago Fire and the Web of Memory" *(http://www.chicagohistory.org/fire/).*

hotlinks to the sources in the same way that print footnotes do. One might even argue that such "hypernotes" will provide a more effective method of authenticating scholarly citations than print since it will be possible to follow links to the notes without leaving one's desk. A search of the original sources for a piece of multimedia scholarship will immediately and easily provide verification of the quality of the author's research—more immediately and more easily than do print footnotes (which are only occasionally checked by readers). Provided that we can build sufficient safeguards of authenticity into our systems of distribution and scholarly communication, therefore, the promise of the Internet to create not only digital libraries but digital scholarship and digital classrooms is very powerful indeed.

In the end, it is all a matter of quality control. Both Abdul Kassem Ismael's camel drivers and our gatekeepers safeguard the integrity and reliability of the libraries they protect in order assure users that they can count upon the information they find there. The digital library thus far lacks its full complement of camel drivers and gatekeepers. Our friend the Grand Vizier Abdul Kassem Ismael would surely be astounded—both by what the digital library threatens and by what it promises—astounded, that is, if, in fact, he ever existed. I discovered his story on the Internet.

8

The Changing Scholarly Requirements for Information Resources

SUSAN HOCKEY

Much "hype" continues to surround the use of electronic resources and information technology, at least in those disciplines that have not traditionally made substantial use of computers. This essay concentrates on the use of information technologies by scholars in the humanities, but the comments are also applicable to other disciplines, as well as to the development of digital libraries for other disciplines. We can all imagine a kind of utopia where every scholar has desktop access to all the information that he or she needs. In reality, we are a very long way from this vision, both in terms of what information is converted to electronic form and in our understanding of how to create, deliver, and manipulate that electronic information to serve a wide range of scholarly needs in a cost-effective way.

On the face of it, the current picture of humanities electronic resources, particularly those resources available via a Web interface, looks promising. Electronic catalogues and bibliographies have made it very much easier to locate items and, in some cases, to obtain them by electronic ordering. Collections of electronic texts offer a wide range of materials in different languages and genres. New electronic journals seem to be appearing every day. Increasingly, material is being made available in image, audio, or video format.

Although massive amounts of information are now available, much of it can only be searched and manipulated in very simple ways. It is perhaps significant that the creators of these collections of material often choose to call them "archives." They provide the user with a mass of information, but not much in the way of navigation tools to help contextualize that information and to put what have been called the "intellectual frameworks" around it. Extracting knowledge from the information is difficult, but that knowledge is crucial to the critical thinking and interpretation that are the essence of scholarship in the humanities.

A principal concern is the need to create ways of storing and encoding electronic information to help us extract knowledge and to develop better tools for manipulating that knowledge. There are two primary questions that need to be answered with respect to research needs: 1) How can we build high quality multipurpose electronic resources that will last into the future? and 2) What do scholars actually want to do with these resources?

Different communities have different perspectives on the use of electronic resources. Some groups see the main function as access or delivery. An electronic representation of an object will be delivered to a user who is then assumed to use it in the same way, more or less, as the physical object from which the representation is made would be used. An enhancement of this activity is hypertextual delivery, where it is possible to navigate through the object or collections of objects in a nonlinear fashion, but with the same overall function of looking at or reading the object.

Other groups are much more concerned with the processing and analysis of material. They want to find instances of features within electronic objects and to count, sort, and otherwise manipulate those features for the purposes of studying the style of an author, of analyzing the variant readings in a text, or of carrying out some form of linguistic analysis. Given the time and expense involved in creating electronic resources, it is important that the resources can serve many users. Consequently, technical choices must be driven by scholarly and intellectual concerns as well as by cost. To realize the promise of electronic resources for enhanced and transformed scholarly research in the humanities will require substantial financial and intellectual investment. This essay provides an overview of the complex interaction between scholarly requirements and technical choices and points to accompanying advantages and disadvantages.

CD-ROMS

All too many projects begin by saying that they are going to produce a CD-ROM. They then choose some software, often because the software is able to display nonstandard characters that they need, or because the salesperson has demonstrated some attractive graphics. The project then begins to create the electronic resources in the proprietary format required by the software. To people less experienced with computing, this route would seem the obvious one to take. Unfortunately, at the moment, there also seems to be a lot of pressure to produce CD-ROMs, making this format an easy initial choice. The quick "show and tell" prototype built in this way also looks good when an institution wants to impress the Board of Governors or to promote its electronic wares more generally. But electronic products that contain very little data defeat their own purpose. The user needs to begin the long haul of compiling sufficient electronic information to make the product useful. However, more often than not, by the time the user has enough material for any serious work, the software vendor has gone out of business, or the interface is outmoded. A lot of money has been spent compiling electronic information that is unusable by any other software. The information is lost forever, and the project is dead.

Most published papers about these tools are written by the producers. If they want to develop the product further, they may admit that it has a few shortcomings. Otherwise they tend to give the impression that the product is God's gift to scholarship and that it is being very widely used. In reality, with a few exceptions such as the Oxford English Dictionary CD-ROM, sales of CD-ROMs in the humanities are poor. Furthermore, and in contrast to a book, the sale of which does not normally lead to further dialogue between purchaser and publisher, once an electronic product is on the market or is being used by different groups, the producer or publisher has to provide ongoing technical support by employing expensive computer personnel. The multitude of CD-ROM formats is also a serious, and expensive, problem for libraries, which have to provide the technical staff to support a wide range of different products.

ELECTRONIC TEXT

Electronic text, which is defined here as a transcription of text letter by letter, is a revealing example of the complex interaction of scholarly requirements and technical choices. Our understanding of both the potential and the complexity of electronic text is based on more years of experience than we have had with almost all other formats of electronic information. (Digital images will be discussed briefly later.) When scholars first began to create electronic representations of textual sources, it was soon found necessary to insert additional information or *markup* into the text in order to carry out sensible word searches. For example, a

search for the word "enter" in Shakespeare would retrieve very many oc-
currences of stage directions containing "enter," as well as the word "enter" within the text. Or, even worse, when Roman numerals are used for
act and scene numbers, a search for "I" would find all instances of "Act
I" and "Scene I" as well as the personal pronoun "I". A computer program cannot distinguish between these characters without information
to help it, but it is surprising how many existing electronic versions of
Shakespeare do not meet even these basic needs.

There is no way to identify something as an act number or stage direction when it is encoded directly in the World Wide Web's Hyper Text
Markup Language (HTML). This problem is not restricted to Shakespeare and Renaissance drama. HTML also has no way to identify the
author of a work, a title, a chapter number, a source of a quotation, or
almost any other component of a document that scholars might want to
cite. These are simple requirements when compared with some complex
humanities texts, which might include multiple alphabets and languages,
marginalia and other notes, variant readings, and other types of critical
apparatus.

Early efforts to insert markup usually concentrated on attempting to
reproduce the printed page as closely as possible, but encoding information with typographic markup does not help very much, even though
very many electronic documents now begin their life on word processors
in this form. Typographic markup is ambiguous for any computer processing other than printing. Something in italics could be the title of a
work, a foreign word, or an emphasized word. The real advantage of
electronic information over print is its searchability, but searching titles
when they can only be identified as italics is not very satisfactory. In an
attempt to make electronic texts more searchable, different projects developed their own way of encoding features of interest within their texts,
but were then faced with more problems when they wanted to exchange
material. Given the time and costs involved in creating a good electronic
text, it makes sense to use a common format and one that can handle all
the different scholarly needs. It also makes sense for that format not to
be dependent on any one kind of computer or computer program.

Hyper Text Markup Language (HTML)

The World Wide Web markup language, HTML, is technically an application of Standard Generalized Markup Language (SGML), but its set of
encoding tags is very limited. The tags appear to have been designed

solely for interpretation and display by Web browsers. The HTML tags are a curious mixture; mostly they do not describe the information within the document but simply indicate what it is to look like on a screen. Even those tags that do indicate a component of a document, for example <blockquote>, provide little to help the user search for the component. Hypertext linking in HTML is also weak. It is only possible to link to a complete document or to a point within that document, whereas it is often a section of text within the second document that is of interest. HTML has introduced many people to the concept of structured markup, but its limitations are now being recognized in many quarters. In autumn 1996, under the auspices of the World Wide Web Consortium, a new project began to create a cutdown version of SGML that would run directly on the Web. Version 1.0 of the Extensible Markup Language (XML), which emerged from the project, was adopted in December 1997, and support for it is expected to appear in the next generation of Web browsers. In XML, users can create their own sets of tags to match the needs of their documents and can use a style-sheet mechanism to determine how those tags will be interpreted by software.

Digital Images and Optical Character Recognition (OCR)

At present, a good many digital library projects seem to be favoring digital images over text. It is easy to see the advantages from the perspective of the producer of information. Images are cheaper to create, even though they occupy much larger amounts of computer storage. There also appears less understanding, in some quarters, that a digital image is a surrogate for an object. Because of the technical choices made when the image is created, the surrogate is, in fact, an interpretation of the object. Somebody else may make different technical choices leading to a different interpretation. From the user's perspective, images provide access to material but do not make that material very usable. It is much more difficult to read from a screen, especially when the screen resolution is not high enough to display the whole page at once. Invariably, users attempt to print the documents and often end up wasting many hours fixing problems with their printers, as well as incurring extra costs in printer consumables. Optical character recognition (OCR) only works effectively with very clean printed texts. Even then, a text that has been scanned by an OCR program needs more work to insert markup to make it processable. OCR yields a typographic representation of a text, which, as we have seen, is ambiguous. Computer software that will automatically analyze a digital image and provide enough information about it for humanities applications is a long way off. Therefore, textual information has to be associated with the images to make them useful. Early imaging projects stored this information in proprietary database formats and then found that it would not migrate from one computer to another.

Standard Generalized Markup Language (SGML)

The Standard Generalized Markup Language (SGML) is generally acknowledged to be the best solution to the problems described above. Developed in the 1980s, SGML allows the creator of an electronic text to define the features of interest within the text and to encode those features through a standard format that can be used on many different computers. SGML looks rather like HTML—in fact HTML is a very simple version of SGML—but it is very much richer in the way it is used to identify and describe features within a text. SGML can be used to encode names of authors, titles, quotations, and so on, but it can also encode linguistic analysis (morphology or syntax, for example), literary, historical, or other critical interpretations—in fact, whatever features the compiler of a text thinks are important. From a scholarly point of view, SGML enables the creator of an electronic text to build a model that corresponds to the structure of the original text and, moreover, to add his or her interpretation to that structure and to allow for other possible conflicting interpretations of the same material. This feature is in contrast to other encoding schemes or data structures, which require the electronic text to fit an existing predefined model, almost always leading to simplification and consequent loss of information at the time the electronic resource is being created. SGML has one other big advantage. A text in SGML format is also plain ASCII code. It can easily move from one computer to another and will thus outlast the computer on which it has been created. The same text can be used by many different programs for different purposes. SGML is, therefore, a way of ensuring that the investment in the data is maintained for the future.

DOCUMENT TYPE DEFINITIONS

It is not particularly easy to get started with SGML. Defining the model of the text can be a lengthy process, but it must be done thoroughly if any serious scholarship is to be based on the text. Fortunately, a number of text models, technically identified as Document Type Definitions (DTDs) in SGML, have already been created, and compilers of electronic texts can download these from the Internet. For the humanities, the most important of these models is the one developed by the Text Encoding Initiative (TEI), the result of seven years' work by over a hundred volunteers, coordinated by a Steering Committee representing the three major text analysis scholarly associations, and by two editors who put together the final TEI Guidelines and DTDs. The TEI received substantial funding from the National Endowment for the Humanities, the Commission of the European Union, and The Andrew W. Mellon Foundation. No doubt these funding agencies had seen how much time earlier projects had spent in deciding how to encode their texts and also how much time can be lost in converting from one proprietary encoding scheme to another. Another widely used SGML DTD is the Encoded Archival Description for finding aids. This was originally developed at Berkeley and is now maintained by the Library of Congress. Other DTDs exist for journals, monographs, and reference works.

METADATA

Structural and coding problems and the difficulties of finding information on the Web have led to much recent interest in metadata, or data about the data. The MARC record used by library catalogues is probably still the most widely used metadata format, but it was designed in the 1960s as an electronic representation of the card catalogue to help users find physical objects such as books. Users would accept the books and then do whatever they have always done with them. Various attempts have been made to use MARC records to catalogue electronic information, adding, for example, a field to identify the Web address of an item. However, these additions do not appear to provide adequate descriptions of the electronic properties of the information. Users will want to know what encoding scheme has been employed for an electronic text, or what enhancement has been done to a digital image. In the future, this information is more likely to be used by a computer program that operates on the electronic object. It seems sensible to store it in a machine-independent way that is meaningful to both computer programs and human beings.

The TEI was one of the earliest adopters of SGML for metadata. Before the TEI, very many electronic texts existed about which very little was known. In some cases, it was not even clear which language the text was in. There was no way of identifying the source from which the text was transcribed or of noting which features had been encoded within it or what changes had been made to the text. All of this information is, of course, crucial for any scholarly use of the text. The TEI defined an electronic text file header, which includes bibliographic information about the text, details of the principles governing the transcription of the text, and a revision history noting what changes were made to the text, when they were made, and by whom. The advantage of using SGML for this function is that the metadata is in the same syntax as the text itself and can thus be processed by the same computer programs.

RETRIEVAL SYSTEMS

We have seen that SGML can handle the complexities of source text well, but there must also be a means of processing those complexities to deliver what scholars need. In recent years more software has become available for working with SGML. The OpenText search engine was originally developed for the Oxford English Dictionary, one of the very early modified academic applications of SGML markup. OpenText is being used by many digital library projects, including JSTOR, which was initiated by The Andrew W. Mellon Foundation, the Humanities Text Initiative at the University of Michigan, and Chadwyck-Healey's Literature Online (Lion). With an appropriate Web-client, it can function as an easy-to-use and very fast retrieval program, but it is weak in hypertext linking. The OpenText software, because of the way it works, also requires institutional technical support. It cannot run on an individual's personal computer.

Approximately thirty institutions to date have been recipients of a suite of software under the Higher Education Grant Program operated by INSO Corporation (formerly Electronic Book Technologies (EBT). INSO's Dynatext provides a model of an electronic book that allows users simply to read the book, or to follow links to pop-up annotations, images, or other sections of text. Navigation is aided by a table of contents in a separate window. Although INSO's major customers are companies such as airlines and semiconductor manufacturers, which have massive amounts of technical documentation that must be kept up to date, the software works reasonably well for many humanities projects. Notable applications in the humanities include the CD-ROMs of

Chaucer, Johnson's Dictionary, and other texts being published by Cambridge University Press, and the CD-ROM versions of Chadwyck-Healey's electronic textbases. The concentration on the book model is a weakness of Dynatext. It can carry out sophisticated searches, but examining the results of these searches can be very clumsy unless additional programs are written on top of it.

OpenText, EBT, and almost all other retrieval programs carry out a search in a very crude way by simply looking for a sequence of letters. When a text is encoded in SGML, the program can use the markup to refine the search to some extent, but it is unable to separate homographs, to apply lemmatization (putting words under their dictionary headings) or any other kind of linguistic analysis, or to search for concepts, a feature of interest to most users. Current research in computational linguistics is addressing these problems by attempting to build electronic dictionaries or lexical databases from which retrieval programs can derive more information about the properties of words. These dictionaries store linguistic information as well as common co-occurrences of words. For example, if a program could use such a dictionary to detect that the word "bow" was a noun and that it co-occurred with other words connected with ships, "bow" could be assumed to be the front of the ship, not something tied with ribbon or used to shoot an arrow, or a verb meaning to bend over. These dictionary-based analysis programs are still experimental and are not widely available. Neither are they completely successful, but there is a continuing effort to enhance the dictionaries by using various statistical analyses to study usages of words within large text corpora.

CONCLUSION

In conclusion, despite the impression given in this essay, there are enormous benefits to be gained from working with electronic resources. It is clear that they make possible research that never could have been contemplated before. When used sensibly, computer programs can also provide a much more accurate picture than can humans, who invariably make mistakes. It is critically important that the current activities continue but with less emphasis on short-term goals and a greater recognition of work that leads to better and longer-lasting electronic resources. It has taken a long time to realize that the investment is really in the data. We need to concentrate on preserving and enhancing that investment for future users. Serious evaluation of electronic resources, particularly from the users' perspective, is especially needed. Such an evaluation involves not only detailed review of all the scholarship that would be present in a traditional publication, but critical assessment of how the electronic medium is being used to deliver and manipulate the information. A meaningful evaluation needs to be conducted by individuals who have a good understanding of both the intellectual and the technical implications. Unfortunately, there are very few such individuals at present. More training and education for both the producers and the consumers of electronic resources are needed to produce the expertise to assess existing resources and to guide the creation of better resources for the future.

Section 3

Challenges in Implementation

9

The Unsustainability of the Traditional Library and the Threat to Higher Education

BRIAN L. HAWKINS

Libraries are at the very center of those characteristics that define a society. Benjamin Franklin, understanding that free and open access to recorded knowledge is the intellectual foundation of a democratic society and free market economy, created the first public library in Philadelphia at the turn of the 19th century.

At the turn of the 20th century, Andrew Carnegie of Pittsburgh created Carnegie Libraries in communities across the country—public libraries that gave ordinary citizens the access to knowledge and the benefits of scientific research previously enjoyed only by the elite. The Carnegie Libraries grew into the system of school libraries, public libraries, and research libraries that generations of immigrants would use as a road to upward mobility, inventors would use to create new businesses, and teachers and students would use to pursue their scholarly endeavors.

But as the beginning of the 21st century approaches, the very survival of our libraries is seriously threatened. While the electronic superhighway promises vast amounts of information available in an almost ubiquitous fashion, economic and technological forces are narrowing our citizens' access to information. School libraries are closing all over the country, public libraries are cutting hours, and research libraries are cutting subscriptions to journals and library materials at an alarming rate.

As great as the economic threats to libraries are, however, perhaps the greater threat is the perception that technology will solve these problems, and that all someone has to do is search the World Wide Web for any information one needs. A vast amount of "information" is indeed available on the Web today, but it is not a coherent collection of information. In addition, the amount of scholarly, intellectual, and aesthetic information is truly minimal, and access to the Web is anything but egalitarian. These are a few of the concerns that must be communicated clearly and articulately to our college presidents and provosts.

It is not surprising that people have come to believe that the digital library is already well toward completion. We see television commercials suggesting that a student in Italy completed a doctoral dissertation by using digital resources via the library at the University of Indiana. What people fail to realize is that these important experiments are enormously costly, not systematic, and are not sustainable without special philanthropic and corporate support. Digitization of library materials is not happening *en masse*, nor is it likely to with each institution continuing to act independently. Contrary to apparent popular opinion, we are not making significant strides in making library materials available electronically, and our current efforts are best characterized as experimental, episodic, and uncoordinated. In the meantime, we are rapidly losing financial capacity to support traditional library collections.

At a series of meetings held in 1994, chief academic officers and librarians from many of our greatest institutions of higher education gathered to share their thoughts on the future of research libraries. Most envision a future with universal access, by students and faculty, to information in all possible media via a single, multifunction workstation. This vision is shared by our universities' technology leaders, as well as by many faculty who anticipate new and exciting methods of instruction allowing students to integrate the knowledge of the ages. These conferences, however, also found another commonality—*"that of not having any plan or vision on how we might achieve this dream and get from here to there!"*[1]

Academic leaders, librarians, and technologists all seem to be waiting for the information revolution to arrive, apparently believing it is just around the corner because they keep hearing about it on television and reading about it in the press. We will not see this wonderful future, however, unless we focus on how to create it. If we do not begin immediately, our libraries, our educational institutions, and, indeed, the very intellectual fiber of our broader society could be in jeopardy.

For the last two decades, librarians have warned us of the "slow fires" within the walls of our libraries—the acid within the paper destroying

---

[1] Richard M. Dougherty and Carol Hughes, *Preferred Futures for Libraries: A Summary of Six Workshops with University Provosts and Library Directors* (Mountain View, Calif.: The Research Libraries Group, Inc., 1991), 14.

the books that represent the intellectual and cultural history of our civilization. Despite the seriousness of this problem, it is minor when compared with the potentially crippling economic threats to the ability of our libraries to store and preserve information. There have been cries of warning regarding the erosion of our libraries' ability to acquire information due to inflationary trends, but the full impact does not seem to have been fully recognized.

In the 15-year period from 1981 to 1995, the library acquisition budgets of eighty-nine of the nation's finest schools nearly tripled, and in real dollars increased by an average of 82% when corrected for inflation, using the Consumer Price Index (CPI). These increases may seem impressive, and they represent major commitments on the part of these universities, but the reality is that the average library in this elite group of libraries lost 38% of its buying power during this period, as shown in Figure 9-1.[2] In those 15 years, the inflation rate for acquisitions was consistently in the mid-teens. Although the costs of books and monographs did not rise quite as fast, the cost of some serials—especially those in the sciences—increased over 20% a year. If these trends continue, by the year 2030 the acquisitions budgets of our finest libraries will have only 20% of the buying power they had just 50 years earlier.

This problem is universal in scope, but the solution has been relegated largely to research institutions because historically they have developed the largest, most complex and oldest collections. The eighty-nine schools that were analyzed represent nearly 40% of all library acquisitions among the more than 3,200 colleges and universities in this country. The research universities of this country have assumed a major societal role in creating, preserving, and organizing the world's knowledge and have been funded through student tuition, through formula-funding at public institutions, and through endowed book funds. Our great universities are losing their library buying power, and none of these historical sources of revenue can keep up with the increases in cost.

As dire as these projections may be, it should be recognized that they

---

[2] The data provided annually by the Association of Research Libraries were analyzed, focusing on the eighty-nine ARL schools in the United States, which reported data from 1980 and 1995. Sources: Kenneth L. Stubbs and Robert E. Molyneux, *Research Library Statistics 1907–08 Through 1987–88* (Washington, D.C.: Association of Research Libraries, 1990). Kenneth L. Stubbs, *ARL Statistics 1988–89 Through 1990–91* (Washington, D.C.: Association of Research Libraries, 1992). Electronic data from *http://arl.cni.org/stats/Statistics/stat.html*

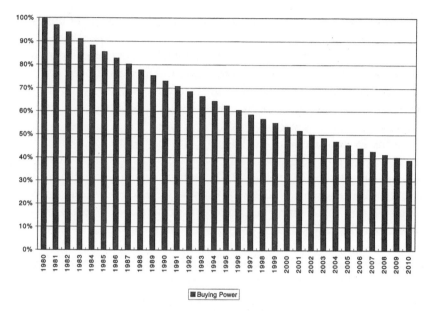

Figure 9-1. Library Buying Power: 1980–2010

are based on the precarious assumption that library acquisition budgets will increase an average of 8% compounded per year as they have for the past 15 years. This amount is nearly three times inflation and nearly twice the amount of total increases in the cost of higher education. With the pressures on higher education to cut costs even more, the problem of sustaining our libraries is probably even worse than just predicted. Recognizing that there is no way for the old paradigm to work, we must address these problems immediately. A recent Mellon Foundation report reached the same conclusion:

The rapidly rising prices of materials, the continued increase in the number of items available for purchase, the fact that university libraries seem to be acquiring a declining share of the world's output, the impracticality of continuing to build large, costly, warehouse-type structures to shelve printed materials, thus replicating collections that exist elsewhere—these and other developments cause one to ask whether established practices, which are already eroding, can be continued for very much longer.[3]

---

[3] Anthony M. Cummings, Marcia L. White, William G. Bowen, Laura O. Lazarus, and Richard H. Ekman, *University Libraries and Scholarly Communication* (Washington, D.C.: The Association of Research Libraries for the Andrew W. Mellon Foundation, 1992).

Libraries clearly will not scale into the 21st century using the current model. We must develop a new paradigm that meets the economic parameters of our institutions, and yet still supports the traditional values of libraries and scholarship. While the economic problems are significant, we should not focus on this dilemma solely as a financial problem. The problem of long-term access to information and the extent to which the scholarly record is being lost should worry anyone concerned about the future of the university. Traditionally, libraries collect only about 6% of all information that is published. Without intervention, even this amount of preservation is in serious jeopardy.

There are three basic contributors to the total cost of a library: purchase or acquisition costs, personnel costs, and space costs, each of which needs to be explored to fully appreciate why the traditional library cannot be sustained as it has in the past.

PURCHASE COSTS

Librarians and others concerned about the library collections in colleges and universities have focused on acquisition costs. The extraordinary impact of inflationary increases in the 1980s and 1990s, especially on scientific, technical, and medical journals, has been well documented and was illustrated in Figure 9-1 showing library buying power. Acquisition budgets have outstripped inflation significantly but have fallen far short of the increase in total acquisition costs of materials as shown in Figure 9-2 as increasing at 12% compounded. The earlier chart showing the decrease in buying power was the result of an earlier analysis based on data from 1981 through 1991. In looking at Figure 9-2, however, one sees that the gap between the 12% increase in materials cost and the average increase in the Association of Research Libraries (ARL) acquisitions budgets increases at a faster rate beginning in 1990, as the slope of the line for ARL acquisition budgets begin to flatten out.

This reduction in the increase of ARL budgets reflects the broader economic pressures facing higher education. Throughout the 1990s, our universities have been pressured to control costs and increase accountability. The average increase in the average total library budget and the average acquisition budget declined dramatically during the five-year period from 1991 to 1995, as is shown in Table 9-1. If the average library acquisition budget is maintained at the levels of the last five years, then the degradation in the ability to acquire information speeds up. If simi-

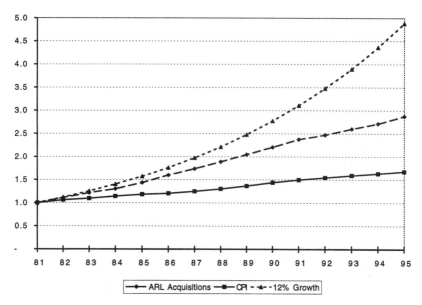

Figure 9-2. Growth in ARL Acquisition Budgets, Inflation, and Acquisition Costs

lar levels are maintained in the future, the projection made earlier—that buying power in 2030 will be just 20 percent of that in 1981—appears overly optimistic. The 20 percent level would be reached much sooner—23 years earlier—in 2007.

Exacerbating the effects of this declining growth in purchasing power is the rapidly increasing rate of available information. Many experts believe the information explosion is well under way, with information doubling every two to three years. The amount of published information that is available and desirable for a library may be increasing at a lesser rate, but information growth is a real issue in the acquisition of library materials. If information is doubling every four years, then there is a compounding impact of inflation and information growth. In 1981, it was es-

Table 9-1.
Average Increases in Total Library Budgets and Acquisition Budgets by Five Year Segments

	1981–1985	1986–1990	1991–1995
Total Budget	9.25%	7.52%	4.1%
Acquisitions	9.67%	8.98%	5.4%

$\mathcal{B}\upsilon\gamma\prime\mathcal{N}\mathcal{G}$

Library Borrowing Power: 1980 - 2010

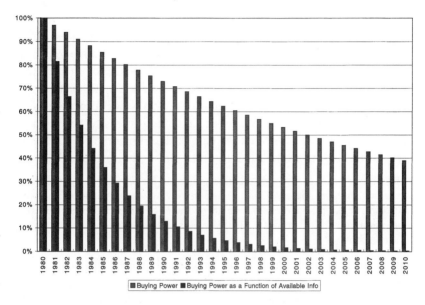

Figure 9-3. Loss in Buying Power and the Exponential Growth of Information

timated that about 6% of the then available information was collected. When taken in combination, as shown in Figure 9-3, the decrease in budgets due to inflation and the projected increase in total information suggests that the available budgets in 2001 will only be able to purchase 2% of what they had twenty years before. This implies that collections will be archiving something of the order of one-tenth of 1% of the available information.

PERSONNEL COSTS

Much of the current concern about library costs focuses on the initial acquisition of materials. This is a significant problem, but there are other less apparent costs as well. The costs of catalogers, reference librarians, and other personnel are substantial, averaging about twice the annual cost of acquisitions in the typical research library in the United States. However, without these talented support and service providers, a library would only be a warehouse, and not a vital part of the academic infrastructure.

Strides have been made to develop cooperative and sharing arrangements to keep support costs down, and such solutions should continue to be pursued. However, none of these approaches have substantively reduced costs. Rather, they have mitigated against losing services in the face of reduced budgets. While it is necessary to further collaborate and cooperate in leveraging specialist talents of catalogers, and other professionals, the two-to-one nature of support costs to actual acquisitions reflects the labor intensive nature of libraries. This is not surprising as libraries have long been known for their commitments to service and support of students and faculty. Pelikan, in describing the role of the library in meeting the broad missions of the University, suggests that:

> As the volume of scholarly helps increases, the need for professional guidance in the use of such helps increases with it; and that professional guidance can come only from subject bibliographers who are sensitive and thoroughly trained and whom research scholars recognize as their peers and colleagues in the raising up of future scholars.[4]

Despite the obvious importance of reference librarians, it is unlikely we will see the employment of such professionals increase proportionately with the growth of patrons, much less proportionately with the growth of information. In fact, the percentage of budgets spent on operations decreased from an average of over 67% of the typical library budget to about 63%, as shown in Figure 9-4.

This decrease has two causes. The first is the effort to keep up with the inflationary spiral of costs associated with acquisitions. This is seen in Figure 9-5, which shows the percentage increase in total budget and the two elements that comprise this total—acquisitions and operations. The rate of operational increases is clearly smaller. The second reason for the decrease is that the last five years of this period have been characterized by significant reductions in university budgets, and the support staffs of libraries were not exempted from these reductions. While information was growing, and attempts to reengineer the support structures of our universities were under way, the ratios changed only slightly. Although the trend is in the "right" direction in leveraging available resources, Pelikan and others would argue it is in the wrong direction in support of scholarship.

---

[4] Jaroslav Pelikan, *The Idea of the University: A Reexamination* (New Haven, Conn.: Yale University Press, 1992), 115.

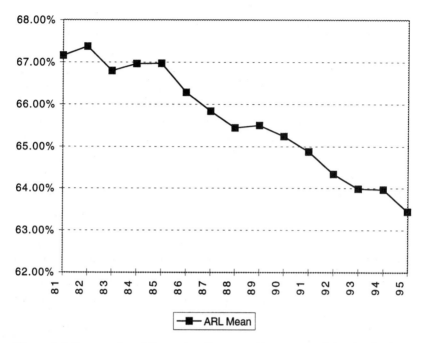

Figure 9-4. Personnel and Operating Costs as a Percentage of the Total Library Budget

As the information explosion continues, and as more and more information is available, everyone will need more help finding, sorting, and filtering the available materials. The number of users, the amount of information, and the costs of a labor-intensive model clearly make the current model unfeasible and unscalable.

While libraries may be able to share or pool technical support services, it is unlikely they can significantly increase the efficiency of personnel who support users directly. A "virtual reference librarian" supporting many users on a network may gain some leverage someday, but the increasing numbers of users coupled with the current lack of resources are a growing concern in the short term.

It is unreasonable to expect any significant transformation soon in the way libraries assist their users to sort and select information because the issues of "filtering" become greater as the amount of available information increases. Some place high hope in the ongoing development of "agents" or "knowbots" to electronically filter through the increasing

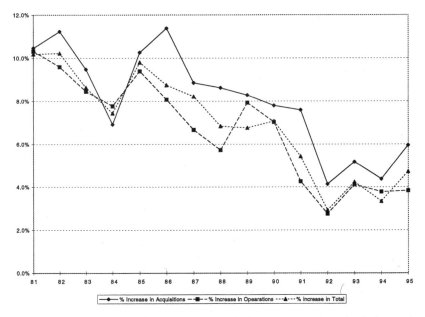

Figure 9-5. Annual Percentage Increases in the Average ARL Total Library Budget, Acquisition Budget and Operational Budget

mass of available information, selecting the precise information that matches a person's individual profile of interests and preferences. While dreams of these "digital aliens" are intriguing, a prudent planner should expect increases—not decreases—in the human capital needed to help people navigate the network, at least in the near term. In this environment of increased access and availability of networked information, eliminating unnecessary and irrelevant information will prove to be a larger challenge than finding it.

SPACE COSTS

While the problems associated with the acquisition of new information are alarming, focusing on this set of costs masks the magnitude of the real problem. If we proceed with the library model as we have known it, the costs associated with storing and archiving the information will bankrupt our institutions of higher education.

This problem was clearly identified 20 years ago, but our institutions failed to heed the warnings.[5] If one assumes that new building costs are approximately $170 per square foot, then the cost of physically housing a single volume approaches $20, which would correspond with the $10 to $12 cost identified in 1982 if inflation is factored in.[6] (This figure was recently corroborated in another study.[7]) In addition to the physical cost of constructing this space, it costs Brown University approximately $1 per volume per year for maintenance of the library building, counting expenses such as heat, light, air control and custodial service.

Looking at the experience at Brown University, building construction in the last three decades would be in excess of $60,000,000 in today's dollars. In addition, the maintenance costs of library facilities at Brown exceed $2,000,000 per year. Often these associated costs of housing and maintaining our library collections are ignored because space costs often are not reflected in line items that appear in the library budget. Regardless of where they appear, however, these annual costs—plus the capital costs of new construction—need to be understood if one is to appreciate the level of crisis associated with continuing our current library traditions.

The problem is apparent if we look at library construction in combination with the size of the total library collection. Figure 9-6 graphs the size of the Brown University library collection. The black bars represent the construction of a new library or opening a new dedicated facility.

The three libraries built at Brown since 1961 reflect an addition of over 200,000 square feet of space and a very large proportion of all new construction that occurred at the University in the past three decades. With the information explosion occurring in the exponential fashion already described, the cost of physically housing these materials will become astronomical.

This problem is duplicated to some greater or lesser degree on every campus in the United States, as well as on campuses around the world. This is especially disturbing when one takes into consideration the conventional wisdom that only 10% of the collection is heavily used, while 90% of the collection is used infrequently, and the vast majority of the

---

[5] Daniel Gore, *Farewell to Alexandria: Solutions to Space, Growth, and Performance Problems of Libraries* (Westport, Conn.: Greenwood Press, 1976).

[6] Philip D. Leighton, and David C. Weber. *Planning Academic and Research Library Buildings* (Chicago: American Library Association, 1986), 124.

[7] Malcolm Getz, *Storing Information in Academic Libraries*. Unpublished manuscript, Dept. of Economics and Business Administration (Nashville, Tenn.: Vanderbilt University, 1994).

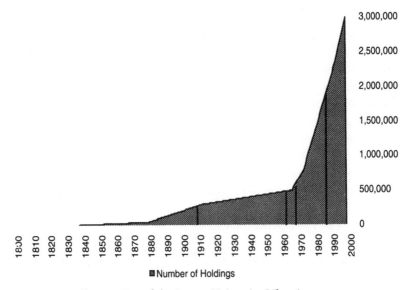

Figure 9-6. Collection Size of the Brown University Libraries

collection never circulates. To be sure, circulation does not directly correlate with use or with the value that access to these materials might have. Access to information, no matter how often it circulates, is a strongly held value that is part of the fundamental mission of a library—especially a research library. Still, the old model of access cannot be sustained, and should not be duplicated by scores of other institutions.

In keeping with the "efficiency" value of the corporate world of the past decade, libraries have been criticized for not adopting a "just-in-time" model of information (vis-à-vis the industrial manufacturing model), but instead maintaining a "just-in-case" philosophy. While this parallel phraseology is perhaps clever in the criticism of the failure to achieve efficiency, what is missed is that the archival and stewardship roles of the library are essential to the enhancement of knowledge and cannot be judged solely by a criterion of efficiency. Certainly the efficiency of the archival function can—and should be—enhanced, but the archiving of important information is extremely important to scholarship and to our society "just-in-case" it might be needed by scholars and practitioners in years to come.

It is abundantly clear, with the dramatic decrease in the price performance curve of electronic information storage, that reductions in the cost of storing information could be achieved if electronic storage were the accepted medium for archiving scholarly information. Not only would electronic storage be far cheaper, it would also eliminate the present duplication. Information could be available in a very few defined locations on the network, and yet accessible to users internationally, at all times and places that the network was available. This aspect of the cost of scholarly information is the most easily dealt with. It draws upon a solution that requires no new innovation and which attains the needed increases in efficiency.

Moving toward a cooperative strategy of electronic storage will not only reduce problems associated with physical space, but will also address the critical problems of preservation of print materials that libraries are facing. The decaying materials, which are being destroyed by the acid-based paper upon which they were printed, must be either treated, copied, or stored on an alternative medium if they are to be saved. Movement of many of our library resources to an electronic medium would solve multiple problems, although in all likelihood, new and unanticipated challenges will emerge associated with this new paradigm.

FUTURE DIRECTIONS IN SUPPORTING LIBRARIES

Clearly, in the current economic context with unprecedented pressures on higher education to slow the increase in tuition, dramatic increases in library budgets are unreasonable to expect. However, if the solution to making up this gap is not adding money at an exponential rate, then what can be done? The following steps should be considered as part of a broad strategy.

Enlist Faculty Support for a New Paradigm

At present, our colleges and universities subsidize and pay the costs of research. The faculty then give this intellectual property away to professional organizations and profit-making publishers, only to have the colleges and universities buy this material back at ever increasing prices. In the long term, this model will devastate the scholarly publication paradigm. Part of the solution is to have professional organizations and other nonprofit organizations become their own publishers and distributors of their materials electronically over the network. If scholars become their own publishers and if these materials are contributed to a "commons," then a sustainable model begins to emerge.[8] The most fundamental change that must occur is the way in which rights are given to publishers for the academic information generated within the higher education community. This basic premise is not new, but it is becoming of greater and greater importance, and is well summarized in the Mellon Report.

Alternatives to current copyright management can be imagined. For example, universities could claim joint ownership of scholarly writings with the faculty they pay to produce them, then prohibit unconditional assignment to third parties, thus becoming important players in the publishing business themselves. Or universities could request that faculty members first submit manuscripts to publishers whose pricing policies are more consonant with larger educational objectives. Another possibility is that university-negotiated licenses grant unlimited copying to libraries and individual scholars and specify said permission in the copyright statement. All these proposals are extensions of the broader idea under current discussion, that universities should reclaim some responsibility for disseminating the results of faculty scholarship.[9]

The authors of the Mellon report go further to suggest that in an electronic world at least some of the functions of publishers could be avoided if the faculty editorial and review efforts become part of the "circle of gifts" that fuel such an enterprise. Just the act of giving limited permissions, and retaining the copyright, preserves the right to freely disseminate information and begins to address this massive problem. An active effort must be mounted to stop current practices of giving away exclusive rights to the developments that come from our institutions of higher education.

To enlist the support of faculty, we must educate them about these issues and advocate their support to publish with those groups who are most consonant with the broader set of academic values. Recently, at the University of Wisconsin, a faculty resolution was passed, urging faculty members to:

. . . consider publishing work with publishers whose interests are sympathetic to the academic enterprise. University presses and scholarly societies offer avenues for the dissemination of information that remain under the control of the academic community. The University should continue to support and encourage

---

[8] Ann Okerson, "The Missing Model: A 'Circle of Gifts,'" *Serials Review* 8:1–2 (1992).

[9] Anthony M. Cummings, Marcia L. White, William G. Bowen, Laura O. Lazarus, and Richard H. Ekman, *University Libraries and Scholarly Communication*. (Washington, D.C.: The Association of Research Libraries for the Andrew W. Mellon Foundation, 1992).

those institutions whose function is to make the results of research available on a nonprofit basis.[10]

Of all of the suggestions made here, this change in the scholarly communication paradigm is the singular most essential change in creating a sustainable model for research libraries.

Develop a New Paradigm

What is needed is a collection of information, in many formats, stored electronically in locations throughout the world, but organized, collected and shared via a central networked organization. It would be a library that draws upon a myriad of resources that already exist, and supplemented with donations and purchases of intellectual property through a radically new business model that could reverse—or at least slow—the devastating economic decline destroying our great libraries.

Much of the private and public sector has been challenged to reengineer practices that were designed for the industrial age, but which are ineffective and cumbersome as we make the transition into an information age. Libraries are no exception. Our industrial age libraries are not scaleable into the next century, into an information age. If one believes that the intellectual and information legacy of our civilization must be preserved, then a revolutionary solution is in order. However, as suggested by Harvard's librarian, technology alone will not solve this problem:

The greatest challenge facing library leaders in the next decade is not to implement new technology, it is to implement new entrepreneurially oriented management structures and cultures in our ailing industrial age libraries.[11]

A commonly discussed solution to these problems is to move to an electronic model where information *access*—rather than ownership—is the defining characteristic of a quality library. Because of the "shareable" nature of information as described by Harlan Cleveland,[12] existing

---

[10] University Library Committee Report, University of Wisconsin-Madison, Faculty Document 1214a, May 6, 1996.

[11] Richard De Gennaro, "Technology and Access: The Research Library in Transition," in *Organizing a Research Agenda: Information Studies for the '90's* (Halifax, Nova Scotia: 1990).

[12] Harlan Cleveland, "Information as a Resource," *The Futurist* 16 (December 1982): 34–9.

library resources could be leveraged if the same access to information were assured and the abundant duplication of purchases that characterizes the present system were eliminated. This access model has been widely accepted as the future to which institutions should aspire. It suggests economies of scale in buying the rights to use information *as needed*, rather than purchasing it with the notion that someone might someday have use for it.

How does one define a collection policy in an electronic environment? Historically, a college or university defined its collections as a function of the academic programs that it offered. In this nonduplicative world, a new business model needs to be found that looks at information from a broader and more centralized approach. Such a model is described in some detail elsewhere,[13] and this or some other more centralized and less fractionated solution is critical. But while a more centralized effort is

ingle entity for a number of rea-
n the philosophy underpinning
, which may be the embryo of

increasingly represented in digital
d provide broad access to those re-
fordable. The concept of building a
n to meet this growing need. How-
to serve as the repository for the na-
if we posit a system of independent,
o manage to standards of broad ac-
ut also positing a level of collective
ion aims to define, promote and en-
ans for the nation's digital libraries
derate" in the national interest the

ssential to capture the existing strengths of our nation's greatest libraries and yet to move to a more centralized and common solution, which is so essential if we are to renew and reinvent the American library tradition for the high technology society of the 21st century.

---

13 Brian L. Hawkins, "Creating the Library of the Future: Incrementalism Won't Get Us There!" *The Serials Librarian* 24:3/4 (1994): 17–47.

14 "Building the National Digital Library: A Federated Approach." Report of the Planning Task Force, National Digital Library Federation, Council of Library Resources, 1996. (*http://www.clir.org/diglib/dlfptfrpt.html*)

Use Electronic Distribution

Distribution of information over the network is one of the keys to cost reduction. The work that has been done so far, however, suggests that the savings in paper, binding, mail distribution, and so on, do not appear to be as great as one imagines. There are still labor intensive processes of editorial review and peer review, copy editing, and production preparation embedded in the process. While some advocates suggest that some of these functions can be reduced or eliminated in an electronic world, clearly the quality of scholarly publication would change. Professionals in specific fields must be the judge as to whether these changes would be deleterious. The added value of these processes, however, will certainly come under greater scrutiny. Although current work suggests that the savings inherent in electronic distribution might be only 35%, these analyses fail to consider the "downstream" costs of support and storage, which will be discussed shortly.

Distributing information over the network fundamentally changes the library model. In the model that has been operative since Alexandria, scholars have been required to go to the library, and its resources were limited to those who could get there, while the new library is brought to the scholar. This more egalitarian access has the strong potential of increasing the volume of information—or at least the volume of scholarly "products"—being generated in a scholarly publishing environment.

Lobby for Appropriate Copyright Policy

Further changes in copyright law as it applies to the electronic world must be explored. Many aspects of information in an electronic world need review, including the concept of fair use, the contributions and availability of information in the public domain, and the need to balance personal gain and societal cost. As national and global information infrastructures are being established, it is imperative that public policy issues be carefully discussed. We must assure that the newly created laws, regulations, and other restrictions keep the public interest and the availability of general information clearly in focus.

Explore New Sources of Revenue

No library has ever been "free" in that there were no costs associated with it, but in an ideal world there would be no charges directly assessed to the patron or end user. While this principle makes it very difficult to define a feasible business plan, it is essential to creating the kind of egalitarian and democratic academic environment to which we must aspire. The very nature of the democratic process assumes a free flow of information, an informed populace, and an environment in which the marketplace of ideas determines truth. This basic premise is central to Jeffersonian democracy, and there is no reason to move away from the model of the free library just because the economics of a paper environment are becoming untenable, or because we shift the medium on which we store our words.

The costs of most of the world's great libraries have been borne by tuition paid by students, gifts from philanthropists, taxes paid by citizens, or a combination of all three. As has already been suggested, the ability to enhance or even sustain the revenues from these sources is questionable. Furthermore, many users of these library resources have never "paid" for this free access. If we are able to move away from the model of the self-contained library, with various stakeholders contributing to a "commons" that is available electronically, then a new model for revenues might emerge. In such an environment, the burden of financing libraries could be shared among institutions of higher education, public libraries, K–12 systems, corporations, the federal government, international partners, and philanthropic groups. It is important to involve all stakeholders in this process—and to avoid a pay-per-view model of libraries—to maintain the traditional values that are so important to our educational systems, and our society at large. These values have the potential of being endangered if commercial interests drive this new paradigm.

ACADEMIC OPPORTUNITIES

This paper has focused on the economic crisis facing the traditional library and possible solutions. It should be stressed, however, that these proposed changes also offer exciting new academic opportunities that should not be overlooked in the attempt to address the economic problems.

New Types of Scholarship

There are many advantages to having information available in an electronic format, and it could change the nature of scholarship. Electronic distribution allows for the integration of information as well as its retrieval. With the availability of electronic information, software can assist the user in locating information more easily, information can be integrated and connected to related concepts, and compound documents incorporating text, pictures, video, and sound can allow for multimedia environments that create new educational horizons. The recognition that the amount of information in our society is becoming overwhelming, and that we need new tools to navigate this information is not new. More than 50 years ago, Vannevar Bush, Franklin Roosevelt's science adviser, stated:

> The difficulty seems to be not so much that we publish unduly in view of the extent and variety of present-day interests, but rather that publication has extended far beyond our present ability to make real use of the record. The summation of human experience is being expanded at a prodigious rate, and the means we use for threading through the consequent maze to the momentarily important item is the same as was used in the days of square-rigged ships.[15]

Today's technology gives us many tools to navigate this morass of information, many of them based upon Bush's concept of facilitating the reader in working his or her way through this process. While much of the technology and software needed to help people navigate through large amounts of information has been developed, there has not been corresponding movement in making the informational resources of our society available in an electronic format.

With an electronic library, a whole new dimension of scholarship and education will emerge. Text stored electronically permits scholars to quickly search enormous amounts of information and to ask new questions that would have been impossible to address with text in printed form. This "new information" will undoubtedly include hypertextual materials, with finding aids embedded in the text. It will include compound documents including images, data sets, graphics, and other multimedia materials, which have the potential of profoundly affecting the ways in which students are educated and in which scholarship is shared.

More Integrative Approaches to Thinking

The vast amounts of information that we encounter can be bewildering. The information explosion is causing greater and greater difficulty in

---

[15] Vannevar Bush "As We May Think," *Atlantic Monthly* 176:1 (July 1945): 101–08.

keeping up with material in one's field, much less learning how different areas of scholarship intersect and affect one another. While our scholarship is becoming more specialized, it is making the process of integrative learning—one of the key goals of a liberally educated person—even more difficult. Marshall McLuhan, the communication philosopher, suggested that as the new medium of television and global telecommunications emerged, we would become a "global village." Instead, with electronic networks and with greater emphasis on specialization, we face the danger of allowing thousands of tiny global villages to emerge, none of which is particularly connected to the others. We need to create educational environments that are interdisciplinary in nature, and which show how concepts link to other areas—to the architectural influences, the musical trends, or the political themes that are associated with some historical period or phenomenon.

These "linkages" can be embedded into information that is stored electronically, thus allowing a person to peruse these related topics, not with the commitment of months in the stacks of a great library, but with the push of a button. This "linking" software is critical if we are to prepare liberally educated persons who must cope with lateral integration of information as well as vertical specialization. However, it takes the availability of electronic information, and specialized software, to make this dream come true and to address the concerns expressed by Harlan Cleveland.

It is an open secret that the modern university is not well suited to the task of educating people for the get-it-all-together function. The university's self-image, its organization, and its reward systems all tilt against breadth.[16]

The more we learn, ironically, the less tied together is our learning. It's not situation-as-a-whole thinking, it's the separation of specialized kinds of knowledge . . .[17]

More Opportunity in Support of Life Long Learning

It is ever more clear that education cannot be something that is accomplished exclusively at the front end of one's life. Learning must be a life-long process, and the opportunities to pursue education must be ever

---

[16] Harlan Cleveland, *The Knowledge Executive: Leadership in an Information Society.* (New York: Truman Talley Books, 1985), 191.
[17] Ibid., 195.

more available wherever a person might be. Whether that distance is measured in physical miles or psychological miles—in the north woods of Maine, for example, or the long mile from the New York Public Library to a tenement in Brooklyn—if we don't try and create an information infrastructure that is technically and electronically available to everyone, we will miss an important opportunity to improve our society.

With an electronic library, a person's rural or metropolitan residence would not affect his or her ability to access the scholarly works, new scientific advances, or artistic performances stored in such an entity. This resource would mitigate the further polarization in our society of those who have books in one's home and those who do not.

Both the processing and the uses of information are undergoing an unprecedented technological revolution. Not only are machines now able to deal with many kinds of information at high speed and in large quantities, but it is also possible to manipulate these quantities so as to benefit from them in new ways. This is perhaps nowhere truer than in the field of education. One can predict that in a few more years millions of schoolchildren will have access to what Philip of Macedon's son Alexander enjoyed as a royal prerogative: the services of a tutor as well-informed and as responsive as Aristotle.[18]

While this description of the availability of information and intellectual challenge described by Patrick Suppes in 1967 was perhaps premature, it is now in the realm of possibility. The technological advances have been dramatic, but the provision of electronic information has not progressed much since he wrote this over a quarter of a century ago.

CONCLUSION

It is clear that the current unit of analysis—the campus library—cannot survive in the existing environment. The leveraging of our library resources is clearly called for, with the best solution being at the largest system-level possible—an international group of cooperating libraries. While associations of campuses, consortia, and other groupings will alleviate the problem, the best solution is found when no system or national boundaries are limiting factors, but where information is maximally available. This principle is already shown to be the case in one of the few present examples of information that is available across virtually all existing boundaries.

---

[18] Patrick Suppes, "The Uses of Computers in Higher Education." *Scientific American* 215 (September 1966): 207.

For the sake of science, the knowledge base of molecular biology should be a public, international electronic library, supported by all for the benefit of all. No one organization or nation should control this type of information for public gain. Another reason for public ownership, especially of scientific knowledge, is that database and knowledge management is of such magnitude that individuals and their organizations cannot be expected to bear this burden as they have in the past.[19]

This illustrates the intellectual advantages as well as the economic advantages of a broader system. While there may be a sense of nostalgia for the self-contained library on campus, it is a luxury that is no longer affordable economically or intellectually if our libraries and educational systems are to survive.

It is fine to suggest that the solution to the problems of the library rest in looking across system boundaries, but the competitive instincts of our campus cultures currently work against this. Status is conferred upon an academic institution for having more volumes in its library than that of a competing institution. We rank the "best" libraries as a function of the total number of holdings, rather than the appropriateness of the collection in service of curricula, the quality of services, or other qualitative measures. Part of the reason higher education finds itself in this difficult situation with respect to its libraries is a long and unproductive history of competition rather than cooperation. The new electronic library would be a major step in reversing these tendencies and overcoming some of the inherent difficulties identified by Patricia Battin several years ago.

Commitment to new cooperative inter-institutional mechanisms for sharing infrastructure costs—such as networks, print collections, and database development and access—in the recognition that continuing to view information technologies and services as a bargaining chip in the competition for students and faculty, is in the end, a counterproductive strategy for higher education. If the scholarly world is to maintain control of and access to its knowledge, both new and old, new cooperative ventures must be organized for the management of knowledge itself, rather than the ownership of formats.[20]

Part of what keeps us focused on the smaller unit-of-analysis—the campus—is the tendency of our institutions to use the size of the campus li-

---

[19] Nina W. Matheson, "Strategic Management: Knowledge as a National Resource." Paper presented at the Medical Librarians Association Annual Meeting, New Orleans, Louisiana, May 1988.

[20] Patricia Battin, "New Ways of Thinking about Financing Information Services," in *Organizing and Managing Information Resources on Campus*, ed. Brian L. Hawkins, (Washington, D.C.: EDUCOM, 1989), 382.

brary as a competitive factor. They fall into the trap of "bigger is better." As long as we continue to rank libraries on the basis of the total number of holdings, we reinforce the suboptimization of information resources. It is only when the available access to information is ubiquitous that we can gain the economies of scale and the universal intellectual opportunities that are necessary. "Bigger is better" is not particularly meaningful in an electronic age, and it is also an entirely relative statement when the unit-of-analysis is that of a given institution or set of institutions. We can no longer afford this competitive stance; it not only fails in terms of cost-effectiveness, it is ultimately destructive.

The economic problems that have been ascribed to libraries in this paper apply equally well to the basic structures of our educational institutions. The old models are breaking down. Trying to "go it alone," emphasizing independence over interdependence with our sister institutions, is not a principle that will succeed or endure much longer.

In his classic treatise on "The Idea of the University," the 19th century theologian John Henry Newman suggested that the library is the embalming of dead genius and that teaching was "the endowment of living (genius)."[21] In his reexamination of Newman's work, Jaroslav Pelikan emphasizes the interdependence of teaching and learning and the essential role that libraries play in facilitating these educational functions:

A university that would, in its enthusiasm for "living genius" or in its eagerness for "development" and "looking forward," neglect its vocation as a repository for "the oracles of the world's wisdom" and for the tradition would lose not only the past but the present and the future as well.[22]

This living layer of teaching is built upon the top of past genius. In a coral reef, one finds a delicate, vital, living layer of coral polyps, grounded on the top of the calcium-based remnants of millions of previously living animals. To destroy or allow the erosion of the foundation of these stone-like structures will in turn cause the demise of the living reef. So, too, the destruction or erosion of our libraries has a vital relationship to teaching and learning, which in itself is the very basis of the vitality of society.

---

[21] John Henry Newman, *The Idea of the University Defined and Illustrated: I. In Nine Discourses Delivered to the Catholics of Dublin (1852); II. In occasional Lectures and Essays Addressed to the Members of the Catholic University (1858)*. Edited with introduction and notes by I. T. Ker. (Oxford: Clarendon: 1976).

[22] Jaroslav Pelikan, *The Idea of the University: A Reexamination* (New Haven, Conn.: Yale University Press,: 1992), 112.

A reef also exemplifies the importance of looking at the right unit-of-analysis. When examining the ecosystem of the reef, it makes little sense to study a given cell, a particular coral polyp, or even a marvelous coral head. While each of these subunits may be of special interest, or particularly beautiful, none can survive in isolation if the ecosystem is under attack. It is the entire reef structure and ecosystem working together that provides the necessary structure, protection, nutrient base, and latticework that supports a much grander set of life forms. There is a richness of life on a coral reef, teeming with plant and animal life, all intermeshed with, and supported by, and dependent on the dead remnants of centuries of previous generations of coral. These other animal and plant habitats are dependent on the coral structure of the past, and their destruction would result in the system collapse of many of these interdependent life forms.

If we look at the idea of the university, with its multiple functions, the "living genius" of teaching cannot live if we allow the "embalmed" genius of the library—this stone-like structure which reflects the accumulated information of the centuries—to be destroyed. Not only will the educational system be irreparably harmed, the impact on related systems and other dependent systems will also be felt, as Pelikan suggests when he states:

> The dynamic interrelation of research with teaching, and of both with the acquisition, preservation, and circulation of documents and artifacts, applies to galleries, museums, and above all to libraries.[23]

As we enter an age of information, we must be vigilant in the preservation of the "embalmed genius" of the past in order to allow for the exciting "living genius" of teaching and research that are possible in a new electronic world. Preserving the "embalmed genius" is also essential if our society is to prevent the collapse of our system of higher education. Our success in saving the concept of the library will depend upon how quickly, thoroughly, and responsively we decide to react.

We must heed the warning signs and come up with new models for the 21st century, not try to sustain our old structures for their own sake. As Patricia Battin suggested several years ago,

> The persistent and futile attempt to finance contemporary information services from the conceptual and financial perspectives developed for a pretechnological

---

[23] Ibid., 113.

age can only frustrate our aspirations and surely dilute the quality of research and instruction in our society.[24]

The library of the future will be less a place where information is kept than a portal through which students and faculty will access the vast information resources of the world. This new library needs to bring together scholars and information resources without necessarily bringing either one to a physical building with a card catalog and books. The scholar may be at home or in her laboratory or in her classroom and the information may be in Kyoto or Bologña or on the surface of the moon. The library of the future will have the daunting task of helping scholars discover what relevant information exists, anywhere in the world and in a variety of formats and media. The library of the future will be about access and knowledge-management, not about ownership. The hurdles that will be faced in creating this new electronic environment will most likely come from our unwillingness to break from our competitive tendencies, our parochialism in glorifying the past, and our unwillingness to accept the inevitability of change. Almost 150 years ago, Henry David Thoreau suggested that "Books are the treasured wealth of the world— The fit inheritance of generations and nations."[25] It is yet to be determined whether our society is committed to making this inheritance a reality in the age of information.

---

[24] Patricia Battin, "New Ways of Thinking about Financing Information Services," in *Organizing and Managing Information Resources on Campus*, ed. Brian L. Hawkins, (Washington, D.C.: EDUCOM, 1989), 382.
[25] Henry David Thoreau, *Walden* (Salt Lake City: Gibbs M. Smith, Inc. 1981): 93.

10

Managing Academic Information Resources in the Future

RICHARD N. KATZ

Academic information resources remain the life blood of the academic institution, and the library, or academic information center, remains the scholarly, social, and cultural center of the campus. The delivery of such resources over networks is changing profoundly the culture, economics, and practices of colleges and universities. The evolving shift from a primarily print-based model of delivering academic information resources to one that is network-based demands the attention of senior campus leaders. Changes in the ways academic information resources are stored, accessed, and distributed will alter the social and economic relationships among key campus constituents, could raise the costs of these resources tremendously, and could even threaten the relatively free flow of academic information. The transformation from predominantly print-based information resources, owned and financed by the campus, to a hybrid environment of print and networked multimedia resources will require a new conception of the flow of academic information within the campus, among institutions, and between higher education and the commercial sector. It will fall upon campus leaders to develop appropriate strategies, management practices, and financial investments to support that new conception.

The preparation of robust academic information resources for network delivery will be expensive, and the responsibility for these activities is likely to move from individual institutions to university consortia, learned societies, and commercial enterprises. Campus librarians as mediators of campus demand, arbiters of information's long-term value, and contributors to the culture of the institution will continue to play an active role in new collaborative relationships with technologists, faculty members, and a variety of commercial providers. Networked delivery of academic informa-

154

tion resources will demand a complex technical infrastructure, making possible a sophisticated commerce in these resources. Commercial providers are well organized politically to exploit the capabilities of this infrastructure and are seeking to change intellectual property laws in ways that will pose serious threats to the academic enterprise.

The creation of an environment for electronic commerce in academic information resources will depend on the ability of institutions to identify both the members of their communities and their rights and privileges. Campus technologists must develop the services that will enforce these policies.

This chapter addresses how academic resources will be managed in the emerging networked information environment. A set of aggressive, and arguable, environmental assumptions are presented, followed by a discussion of potential management models that address such policy issues as rights management, quality assurance, physical and intellectual control, storage, protection, and distribution. Recommendations are offered to help campus leaders with the academic information resources management challenges that lie ahead.

WHAT ARE THE UNDERLYING ASSUMPTIONS?

Seven aggressive assumptions underlie the premise that academic information resources must be reconfigured in the first significant way since the opening of the Alexandrian Library. These assumptions are presented as absolutes for the purposes of stimulating debate and encouraging institutional leaders to seize the opportunity to shape the future of higher education in a technological society.

- *The primary form of academic information resources will be digital.* Today, the vast majority of published academic information resources can be found, in some stage of their production cycle, in digital form. While the digital version is treated often as a perishable by-product of the eventual final print product, this circumstance will change in the future. Reasons for today's continued reliance on print media include ergonomic and economic familiarity and a lack of well-established management practices for capturing or archiving digital content.[1] Progress in video display technology,

---

[1] In fact, while the primary forms for storing and delivering academic information resources will be digital, paper is likely to continue to dominate as the medium of choice for using such resources. In academic disciplines in which the visual interplay between the scholar and the recorded information is key (e.g. history, anthropology, art history), paper, parchment, clay, and canvas will continue to be central to scholarship.

rising environmental sensitivities, ease of distribution, and improvements in methods of protecting electronic information property rights will conspire against the printed word as the predominant carrier of scholarly information, in favor of the electronic, digital word.[2]

- *The sources of academic information will continue to increase in number and complexity.* Until the invention of the computer, academic information resources came to college and university libraries in a limited number of forms, from a relatively limited number of sources. The number of such sources is now rising exponentially and will reach soon an inflection point in its growth curve, or move to another and more sharply-sloped growth curve. Rapid breakthroughs in fields such as remote sensing, nanotechnology, and computational chemistry are producing literal rivers of information for eventual academic research and other uses.[3] Within existing management models, information from instrumentation sources (particle detectors, chemical robots, remote sensors, etc.) is managed within research groups. As miniaturization technologies continue to improve, and, as the costs of specialized (and wireless communicating) processors continue to fall, new streams of data from packages, utility meters, parking meters, and other sources will become torrents of potential academic information resources to be managed.[4]

- *The use of academic information resources will continue to rise and diversify.* Rapid increases in global literacy will fuel new demand for academic information resources. If and when network-based access to these resources becomes cheaper (on a life-cycle and opportunity-cost basis) than access to printed resources through college and university libraries, demand for academic information resources will rise. This phenomenon is already apparent with resources such as MedLine and other medical information resources that are used, through universities, by members of the public at large. It is likely that the rise in use of these resources will occur initially and most strikingly among university-educated consumers; in rural areas of the developed world not served by academic centers, and in those developing nations with fast-rising rates of literacy. The lack of a large "installed base" of traditional print-based libraries will promote further a rise in the use of such academic information resources over networks in the developing world.

---

[2] Columbia University Professor Eli Noam argues even more aggressively that the printed book is likely to disappear, except in its recreational form. See E. Noam, plenary address delivered at EDUCOM, October 29, 1997.

[3] See, for example, Zina Moukheiber, "A Hail of Silver Bullets," in *Forbes*, (January 26, 1998): 76–81. Moukheiber describes the emerging field of robochemistry that combines computer miniaturization techniques with genomics to screen millions of chemical compounds for pharmacological efficacy. A new class of information resource managers, bioinfomaticians, is growing fast to develop strategies and tools to manage the volume of research information in these areas of research.

[4] See John Gage, "Technology, Change and Opportunity in Higher Education," plenary remarks delivered at the 1997 Annual Conference of CAUSE, the Association for Managing and Using Information Resources in Higher Education, December 3, 1997.

- *From a technical standpoint, access to digital academic information re-sources can soon be ubiquitous.* Subject to existing limitations of access based on literacy and legal barriers, the technical and economic barriers to ubiquitous access to academic information resources will be removed in the near future. A variety of near-term technical innovations, such as NetTV, network computers, cable modems, and improved caching and compression techniques, will make moderate-to-high quality access to network-based academic information resources *technically* accessible to virtually all who want them. Certainly, anyone with access to a television, a cable TV and/or telephone connection, and an Internet access account can become a network-based consumer of academic information resources. It is likely that technical access to digital academic information will be superior to access in today's print-and-store context which, despite widespread interlibrary document delivery systems, depends on geographic access to an academic information center.

- *The users of academic information resources will be increasingly mobile.* The geographic moorings of the typical faculty of a U.S. research university are already loose. Joint appointments are common, as are multiple laboratories, international speaking obligations, and sabbatical leaves. The promise of distributed learning models will reduce, for some activities, the centrality of the campus as the place where teaching, learning, and research are conducted.

- *The network's ability to decentralize technical power is changing the political economy of academic information resources.* If desktop publishing has made it easier for authors to create attractive information resources, the World Wide Web is making it easier for authors to deliver such resources globally.[5] Electronic courseware authoring software is adding multimedia capabilities to this mix. The value added by traditional academic publishers will be questioned by increasing numbers of authors. Technologically sophisticated authors will have the potential and desire to by-pass traditional publishers (or to demand increased economic rents from them), thereby posing new challenges for institutions, particularly as the boundaries between book and course become fuzzy. In the longer run, deficiencies in areas such as information maintenance and quality control will likely cause a return to network-based scholarly publishing by commercial enterprises.

- *Driven by technology and economics, the organizational focus of managing key academic information resources will shift.* Institutionally based academic information centers continue to be organized on the Alexandrian model under the assumption that the centralized collection, management,

---

[5] See Patricia Battin, "New Ways of Thinking about Financing Information Technology," in Hawkins, ed., *Organizing and Managing Information Resources on Campus*, (Washington, D.C.: EDUCOM, 1989), 369. Battin observes that "[Information technology] makes possible an unprecedented decentralization of technical power to individual option while at the same time it requires a globally coordinated infrastructure to permit effective individual exercise of that power."

and care of physical resources will best assure the protection of scarce tangible assets from the physical risk of fire, theft, or flood. This methodological emphasis will likely continue at institutions with incomplete or insufficient technical infrastructures, and among institutions with significant holdings of information artifacts constituting the nation's intellectual heritage. The evolution of new economic mechanisms for recovering and/or subsidizing the costs of electronic access, storage, and delivery will encourage the development of new management models for the particular institutional mix of resources. Commercial providers are likely to assume new roles in the management and delivery of networked information resources.

WHAT ARE THE POLICY IMPLICATIONS IF THESE ASSUMPTIONS ARE CORRECT?

The changes posed by a possible dramatic shift towards the network-based delivery of academic information resources are profound. Campus leaders must anticipate such possible policy implications and begin to organize the campus and its financial and human resources to capitalize on new opportunities and to mitigate new risks. Some of the policy implications include:

- Academic information resources in the future will become increasingly interactive, and they will add a further premium to the relative value of the electronic word. Thus, there will be an increasing need to invest heavily in networks and networked information, and in the preparation of the professoriate for facilitating student learning in a networked context.
- As research collaborations continue to transcend the boundaries of campus and country, the management of the information amassed by them will become increasingly a matter of consortial concern.
- Managers of academic information resources will be confronted by a rising tide of increasingly complex compound "documents" and will need new skills and technical resources to manage resources of this kind. Users of academic information resources will need increasingly sophisticated tool kits to manipulate source data, perform simulations, render numerical data visually, and so forth. These managers will need to support electronic infrastructures that mitigate some of the fragmenting tendencies that increased faculty, student, and staff mobility will create. Much of the focus of academic information resources management will likely shift to concern over how to build and maintain learning-centered community networks to address social and cultural aspects of the student learning and socialization processes.[6] Included in this activity will be difficult and divisive efforts to define the boundaries of the electronic campus community. Choices about

---

[6] Brendan A. Rapple, with commentaries by Joanne R. Euster, Susan Perry, and Jim Schmidt, "The Electronic Library: New Roles for Librarians," in *CAUSE/EFFECT*, 20:1 (Spring 1997): 45–51.

the nature of these boundaries will have significant policy and economic impacts.

- Media-enriched "books" will become hard to distinguish from multimedia "courses" and the pricing and licensing of these materials will be problematic. The issues surrounding the ownership and management of rights to intellectual property will grow increasingly complex in this environment. In select markets (business, general education, language instruction), traditional publishers will endeavor to retain their current dominant positions by investing heavily in the licensing and high-end production of the work of academic super stars. The scale of these investments and the quality of the resulting resources will be unprecedented. Software companies and segments of the entertainment industry will continue to enter this market.[7] Campus leaders will have to craft new understandings with their faculty regarding the ownership of faculty course materials, or face the prospect of witnessing campus "courses" being delivered over networks by commercial third parties. Such practices will stimulate an important policy debate about the relative academic and economic value of campus-based degrees.
- The differential rates of increased use among academic trading partners will create issues related to the economic balance of trade between academic information (net) importers and exporters.
- The continued explosion in the volume of academic information resources will necessitate advances and investments in search engineering, information description (metadata standards), and customer education and support.
- As institutional network infrastructures mature, and as the costs of storing electronic media continue to decline, the storage and dissemination of multiple electronic copies will proliferate. Attention will shift, for many, away from the creation of comprehensive institutional collections and toward the creation of collection confederations that regulate and guide distributed collection development strategy, and inter-enterprise commerce in academic information resources.[8] Institutional collection strategy and policy

---

[7] It is forecast that the size of the overall market for information "content" (e.g., information resources) will rise to $550–600 billion by the late 1990s. The market for information content will rise faster than that of the technical infrastructure across which this content will flow. Numerous studies indicate, for example, that distance education is one of the most highly valued network services sought by consumers. See, for example, Dwight Allen, H. William Ebeling, and Lawrence Scott, *Perspectives on the Convergence of Communications, Information, Retailing, and Entertainment: Speeding Toward the Interactive Multimedia Age,* (Private paper distributed by Deloitte and Touche, 1995): 31.

[8] This shift is already well underway. See, for example, Jeffrey R. Young, "In the New Model of the Research Library, Unused Books are Out, Computers are In," in *The Chronicle of Higher Education,* (October 17 1997): A27. See also Donald N. Langenberg, "Information Technology and the University: Integration Strategies for the 21st Century," in *Journal of the American Society for Information Science* 45 (June 1994): 324. Langenberg argues that "...increasingly, new and unanticipated alliances, aided by open, campuswide dialogue on the role of information technology, will greatly advance the integration process. Moreover, not only will this collaboration be institution-wide, it will in some cases also be inter-institutional."

will be mediated by collaborative agreements for electronic collections, and by institutional academic priorities for special collections of archival materials, ephemera, and physical artifacts. In the longer term, the role of academic confederations may shift to the coordination of collection development and rights management, while the custodianship of academic information resources may shift to centralized commercial sites. Centralized electronic repositories will facilitate security, backup, disaster recovery, and archival management of academic information resources and will exploit more effectively the economies of scale associated with the management of mass electronic storage and retrieval. Commercial interests will likely dominate the mass storage environment, under contract with combinations of: (1) individual authors; (2) commercial academic publishers; (3)university presses; (4) academic learned societies; (5) commercial software and/or entertainment firms; and (6) college and university federations.

WHO WILL MANAGE ACADEMIC INFORMATION RESOURCES?

Managing academic information resources in the future will require significant changes in economic, technical, legal and behavioral areas. It is important to consider the issue of where, and by whom, academic information resources will be managed in future decades if the seven environment assumptions are correct. The network-based model of academic information delivery will change the political economy of academic information resources management, and the changing relative influence of those involved in management activities will affect the nature of the resulting economic, technical, legal, and behavioral solutions.

The emergence of the network as a significant, and eventually dominant, delivery vehicle for academic information resources will create considerable economic opportunity for many. The diversity of institution priorities, historical investments, and levels of technological readiness suggests that there can be no monolithic solutions. The management roles and responsibilities (e.g., management models) associated with academic information resources will be supplemented by new management models.

Figure 10-1 describes the dominant practice in higher education. In this scenario, faculty members and other academic authors write up the results of their research and convey the publication rights to either commercial or university publishers in exchange for recognition (e.g. tenure, promotion, job mobility) and, when suggested, money. Publishers add value to manuscripts by screening them and providing editorial services. Publishers are then responsible for the production of print and electronic

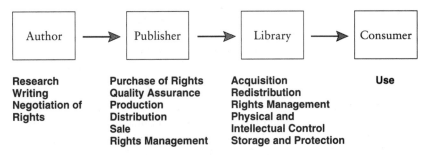

Figure 10-1. Institution-Publisher Centric Model

publications, for their marketing, sale, order fulfillment and distribution, and for the allocation of economic rents between themselves and the contributing authors.

The consumers of the resulting publications—notably academic libraries—acquire, through current copyright law, the legal rights to disseminate the materials acquired by the institution. Limited copying rights for educational purposes are permitted under the fair use conditions of the law.

Figure 10-2 describes a content creation and management model wherein authors—in Marxian terms—take back the means of production. In this scenario, authors—enabled by technology—bypass both the commercial publishing sector and the academic information center and conduct commerce directly with end consumers over the network. These authors retain full rights to their intellectual property and employ a variety of push technologies (listservs, e-mail, pointcast) and pull technologies (Websites, search engines, metatags) to attract consumers.

Figure 10-2. Author-Centric Model

There are many who believe that network technologies will enable such a fully distributed and decentralized marketplace. To a large extent, the devolution of many of the activities associated with the academic information "value chain" is occurring as a result of the eased "self publishing" capabilities fostered by the World Wide Web. The author-centric model, like much of today's Web environment is a frontier, lacking in the business rules, quality controls, bibliographic values, and management practices that make it possible for those who acquire information to differentiate the quality of available information. In this frontier environment, there is an illusion that information is free of cost. Rather, authors who self-publish on the Web are rarely able to monitor the use of their intellectual property or to recover the costs of creating, producing, or distributing this property. Universities that serve thousands of Web pages are similarly unable to recover the costs of their extra-institutional commerce. Finally, the consumers of undifferentiated information are unable to capture or recover the costs of the time they have invested in finding needles in haystacks. In sum, the author-centric model of academic information commerce, while appealing in a romantic, frontier-libertarian sense, is a model unsupported by a needed management infrastructure and is probably not scaleable. A world in which everyone can create a document, save it as an HTML file, post this file to a Web site, and broadcast the document's whereabouts via electronic mailing lists is likely to be one in which information content is substantially devalued. Such a world satisfies authors' need to say something, without addressing students' or researchers' needs to know something. The collection development librarian and the publisher as mediators of market demand and supply are missing from this model. The consequence of this model is likely to be an open Web frontier populated by second-class information and littered by abandoned, disused, and non-maintained sites.

The consortium model (Fig. 10-3) recognizes the unique scale economies that derive from the assumption that the academic resources to be managed in the near future will be electronic. In general, those aspects of managing the storage and retrieval of physical artifacts (books, periodicals, etc.) benefit in limited ways from scale. With the exception of mass—and typically offsite—storage, the costs of accessioning artifacts, marking them for physical control, shelving them, storing them, and retrieving them are relatively constant across collection size. This is true because the dominant drivers of the costs of physical custodianship are labor and space. In fact, it is likely that diseconomies of scale exist in

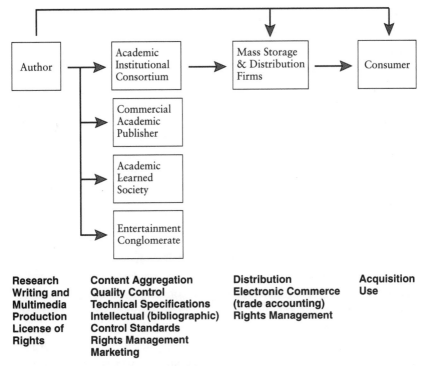

Research | Content Aggregation | Distribution | Acquisition
Writing and | Quality Control | Electronic Commerce | Use
Multimedia | Technical Specifications | (trade accounting) |
Production | Intellectual (bibliographic) | Rights Management |
License of | Control Standards | |
Rights | Rights Management | |
| Marketing | |

Figure 10-3. The Consortium Model

this area of academic information management if one assumes that the largest collections (Library of Congress, Harvard, Berkeley, UCLA) are maintained in geographies characterized by high costs of land, labor, and facilities.[9]

In electronic form, academic information resources enjoy the scale economies demonstrated by electronic mass storage generally, including scale economies of disk storage, systems management, and operations management. For this reason, the management of electronic academic information resources is likely to become highly centralized and, in all

---

[9] Even large regional library storage facilities that have been established for the purpose of lowering the unit cost of managing academic information resources may suffer diseconomies of scale, if the entire economic costs of this management strategy were accounted for. Such costs would necessarily include the cost of patrons' incremental time to retrieve resources from such facilities, as opposed to the institutions' cost of storage and retrieval.

probability, commercialized. Firms like IBM and EDS currently manage huge data repositories under contract with a variety of public and private organizations and are likely to displace the roles of traditional distributors, government agencies, and academic libraries in storing and distributing information resources. Of equal importance, centralized and commercialized organizations may become the early developers and managers of the commercial infrastructure that will be necessary to monitor the global "trade" in information resources, and to account for trade balances between suppliers and consumers. This activity will become of central importance as licensing agreements and pay-per-view pricing replace the current dominant pricing model of library acquisition and Fair Use regulation.[10]

While it is probable that commercial organizations will come to dominate the distribution and rights accounting for academic information resources, it is unlikely that they will vertically integrate other activities, currently performed by university and commercial academic publishers, related to quality assurance. The likely concentration of responsibility for electronic storage and distribution suggests strongly the need for concentration in activities related to production and selection (i.e., peer review). This environment is likely to be dominated by a mix of existing and evolving entities, notably commercial publishers, scientific and learned societies, and consortia of colleges and universities. It is also likely that, as the boundaries that currently distinguish books from multimedia courses diminish, creative (talent) agencies and film studios will compete with traditional publishers to place star-quality faculty under contract. It is also possible that as concentration of key activities occurs, faculty writers/producers of academic information resources will form production guilds (like United Artists) to protect and maximize their intellectual property rights.[11]

---

[10] See David Brodwin and David Kline, "Post Web World," *Upside*, (February 1998). Brodwin and Kline argue that ". . . while pundits pronounced the arrival of a new disintermediated information environment, where upstart publishers could market their wares directly to customers, . . .what's happened is the recognition that content must be reintermediated with value-added services to cut through information overload and increase information's usefulness." The authors conclude that in a post-Web world, "the power of size, brand clout and reintermediated content is greater than ever."

[11] It should be noted that colleges and universities need not be passive in the course of these forecasted changes. Agile institutions will, indeed, craft new partnerships with their faculty to accomplish shared purposes. However, in cases where campus policies and practices change slowly and in a context of competing objectives, commercial operations will have the resources and political will to outpace many of our institutions.

Importantly, in this scenario, the role of the individual academic institution is small and must, therefore, be leveraged. In the case of virtually all institutions, the ability of individual colleges and universities to influence the rights regarding either the sale or use of academic information resources is likely to be limited. This likelihood underscores the importance of the role to be played by the academic consortium.[12] Consortia for the purposes of vetting and publishing academic information resources or for licensing the use of such materials are likely to be increasingly important mediators of supply and demand in this kind of concentrating market environment. Few colleges and universities will have either the marketplace strength (brand name recognition) or the production scale to succeed in such a market. The roles of the institutional university press, as a supplier of academic information resources, and of the institutional university library, as a consumer of academic information resources, will likely undergo significant change in the next 5–10 years.

It is important to note that while the consortium model is likely to be the emergent model of academic information resource management, the technology underlying this model will also support other models. The creators of academic information resources, in this technical environment, will be able to produce academic information resources independently and either distribute such material independently (self-publish via the Web) or deposit them with distributors in a variation of the academic vanity press. Materials deposited in the latter fashion will enjoy the benefits of distributors' storage management practices and electronic accounting infrastructure, but not the cachet or imprimatur (e.g., branding) of the academic or commercial publisher.

WHAT MUST BE DONE? RECOMMENDED ACTIONS

The discussion of who will manage academic information resources in the future leads naturally to recommendations about what must be done to assure the effective management of these resources. If the proposed model of marketplace concentration is realized, college and university

---

[12] This forecast, while dire, does not depart in significant ways from the current environment. Currently, most faculty members are free to contract independently with publishers for the sale of their writings. Further, academic libraries purchase (or not) the rights to make available materials written, in some cases, by their institutions' own faculty.

leaders will need to guide campus strategies and investments in a number of key areas.

Set the Course

Campus leaders must craft a vision and finance sustainable strategies to support the increasing numbers of community members who will seek remote access to academic information resources.[13] The vision of a robust environment in which information resources and scholarly discourse are exchanged over networks will likely change forever the information management economics and practices of colleges or universities. Institutions that are technologically and organizationally adept will be able to provide members of their communities with access to rich collections available currently to large and elite research universities.

Ironically, those institutions that have delivered their academic missions by amassing such collections may find their flexibility impaired by the need to finance the costs of space, new print publications, and document preservation. These institutions must anticipate continued rising collection costs. Costs of acquisition will continue to rise at rates greatly in excess of inflation as the publishers of academic information resources shift their attention to electronic media and reduce the quantities of print editions. Such institutions will also witness the erosion of their onsite patronage, as traditional seekers of printed academic information resources acquire these materials instead over networks at their homes, offices, or other convenient locations. Importantly, institutions that choose to remain preeminent print repositories cannot eschew the new costs of electronic delivery. Indeed, the size and prestige of such institutions will likely cause them to pursue a strategy of seeking preeminence in both domains. Institutions pursuing such a strategy will see total campus information resources management costs rise.

A second strategic choice for institutions is that of increasing specialization. In this vein, institutions may opt to continue to acquire and manage print-based academic information resources of specialized natures to support the academic programs based on such resources. Institutions

---

[13] Richard N. Katz, "Technology Enriched Teaching and Learning: A Business Planning Perspective," in *Reinventing the University: Managing and Financing Institutions of Higher Education*, eds. Johnson and Kidwell (New York: John Wiley & Sons, 1997), 33–56.

choosing this strategy will manifest their academic objectives in part by collecting print materials, photographs, ephemera, or other artifacts in select areas. This choice may be a wise and economically accessible one for institutions that have already achieved recognition in specific collection areas. This strategy also suggests major investment in a technical infrastructure, but It has the advantage of focusing institutional investments in resources that are not electronic. Such a strategy also makes it possible to support changing scholarly needs as information technology influences the course of instruction and research in particular areas.

A third choice is to make the major institutional commitment to network based academic information resources necessary to become a global supplier of such resources. Institutions of this kind are associated with economically viable university press operations, and they have financial resources and reputations to acquire ownership rights to important academic information resources. These colleges and universities will find themselves in an extraordinarily competitive global marketplace, with competitors from the publishing and entertainment industries and from a variety of consortia and cooperatives. This option is probably available only to institutions of sufficient intellectual appeal to attract the attention of would-be contributing authors. Academic institutions will have to compete financially to acquire global rights to sought-after material. The success of this strategy will depend on preferred access to scholars who publish, editorial talent, and a superior information delivery infrastructure.

The fourth strategy for colleges and universities will be to prepare a technical and human environment that encourages members of the institution's community to use academic information resources through distributed virtual environments developed by those institutions. Such institutions will be, for the most part, consumers of academic information resources and will likely leverage their purchasing influence through membership in a variety of consortia or buyers' collectives. Institutional investments, under this strategy, should shift away from the collection of print publications, and toward the acquisition of electronic information resources through consortia. In addition, significant effort and investment should go toward the development of institutionally unique virtual environments. These environments, unlike the Web of today, must recapture the community member's *sense of place* in the way that the campus and library foster a learning community. Today's higher education Web sites, except for institutional logos and artwork, largely fail to promote a sense of place sufficient to foster loyalty. As "surfing" is not a community-building activity, campuses will have to investigate and implement technologies that encourage loyalty to their virtual environments. Such technologies must be organized to foster interaction, for interactivity is the primary source of learning, community building, and, ultimately, loyalty. Traditionally, the campus library has been a major center of campus life, and not merely a warehouse of books.

The mandate, under this last strategy, to construct robust distributed virtual environments is economic. The network will allow its users to acquire information from a variety of sources. Successful institutions will leverage their information acquisition expenditures through site licensing, pooled purchasing, and other arrangements. If the virtual environments that provide the gateway to these materials are not compelling, members of the community will continue to demand access to traditional print collections at increasing costs for maintaining both print collections and an underused technology infrastructure. Conversely, those campuses that develop the best virtual environments to support access to electronic information resources are likely to attract the attention of donors, prospective students, alumni, grantors, and others.

Invest in Campus Networking

Dr. William Graves makes the point that a campus intranet, linked to the Internet and based on open Internet standards, can provide:

- a method for enhancing the reach, timeliness, and effectiveness of human communication in every aspect of the institutional mission;
- a learning infrastructure to increase the quality of student and faculty academic work, and access to information resources beyond the campus boundaries; and
- a service infrastructure to enable streamlining of institutional management and outreach activities.[14]

As discussed, if the fundamental assumption that most academic information resources will be digital is true, the economics of academic publishing will change. It is axiomatic that the unit costs of print publications rise as production volumes fall. Therefore, as publishers move in-

---

[14] William H. Graves, "A Strategy for I/T Investments," in D. Oblinger and S. Rush, eds., *The Future Compatible Campus* (Bolton, MA: Anker Publishing Co., 1998), 27–8.

creasingly toward a set of practices that assume the primary medium of distribution to be digital and network-based, the size of print runs will shrink and their unit costs will rise.[15] As the cost of print publications rise, campus leaders will need to guide the strategic collection development and management investments of their campuses. In the specific case of static budgets, campuses will have to choose increasingly between investments in the campus network infrastructure and investments in additions to the library physical plant. In such a potentially divisive decision-making context, campus leaders must acculturate the campus to the notion of network investments *as investments in the library*. Regardless of the particular strategic mix of resources chosen, investment in high speed and ubiquitous campus networks must be viewed not as a luxury but as a necessary cost of doing business in the future.

Most universities currently support modem pools to handle external connections to the campus network and resources, but find it increasingly difficult to finance the growing demand for connectivity. These technical and financial concerns will escalate, with the growing complexity of information resources. The evolving potential of data communications networks to provide differential quality of service and to price for such differentiated service will raise new, and possibly divisive, policy issues about allocating network resources among faculty members and academic disciplines. These new capabilities will also drive the need for new funds to support core instructional and research activities.

Foster a Culture of Collaboration

The execution of any of the foregoing strategies will involve unprecedented levels of collaboration within and between colleges and universities and with a variety of public and private organizations. Successful institutions will need to foster effective alliances for the acquisition, storage, and distribution of academic information resources. Campus leaders must create an environment and a set of reinforcing incentives that will encourage deep, unprecedented, and sustainable cooperation

---

[15] It is important to note that the demand for print-on-paper resources for instruction and research continues to rise despite the availability of electronic sources. Although paper will no longer be the primary archival and distribution medium, it has shown no signs of disappearing as a "use" technology. The capability of digital technology to produce paper products creates a potential strategy of "publication on demand" with no archival or dissemination functions.

among faculty members, librarians, technologists, and media specialists to transform their traditionally compartmentalized responsibilities. If the challenge of the networked information vision is the challenge of integration,[16] then new levels of intra- and interinstitutional collaboration must be fostered. In addition, campuses must become increasingly adept at those skills related to the oversight of a variety of outsourcing and shared-service arrangements as they move from unified academic information resource management models, to models in which major elements of the resource delivery system are owned and operated by others. The need to collaborate will be heightened by growing shortages of the key skills essential to achieving institutional excellence in these areas of campus endeavor.

Investigate and Invest in the "Search Engineering" Infrastructure

Key to the creation of distributed virtual environments is the deployment of technologies that enhance users' ability to find academic information in cyberspace. By late 1997, there were more than 640,000 sites and 100 million pages on the Web, and the number continues to double approximately every six months. In the immediate future, systems will be delivered that provide "visual representations of data, collaborative filters that gather recommendations from users, enterprise software with search capabilities, and advanced Web search engines."[17] In the longer term, technologies will be available that will answer questions not with lists of documents but with "multi-dimensional, immersive environments that provide a more intuitive view of large collections of data grouped or clustered by meaning."[18] Colleges and universities must actively monitor the market for search, filtering, personalization, and "agent" technologies, experiment with these technologies, and deploy the best of them in campus servers and workstations. These technologies will allow campuses to begin building the compelling virtual environments that will foster user loyalty. To be effective, these technologies must be bundled with on-line help services that correspond to a mix of current activities: (1) faculty office hours (for subject expertise); (2) reference library services (for search support); and (3) help desk services (for technical support).

---

[16] Donald N. Langenberg, op.cit.
[17] Jeff Ubois, "Casting an Information Net," in *Upside.com* (February 2, 1998): 2.
[18] Ibid., 5.

Focus on Directory Services, Authentication, and Authorization

Many campus librarians and information technologists are engaged in deep conversation about the authentication and authorization of the users of campus technical and information resources. These conversations are likely to seem arcane to most university presidents and provosts. While the technical aspects of managing authentication and authorization may indeed be arcane, the policy and economic issues that accompany these technical discussions deserve early attention at the highest campus levels. These issues ask important questions of who is a member of campus community, and what authorities and entitlements accrue to such individuals.

These essential differences between electronic and print-based information resources give rise to the earlier assumption that overall use of academic information resources, in the electronic context, will rise. Rising use will place new and different strains on the campus user support infrastructure. For example, the use of collections of physical information resources—books, periodicals, microforms, and other such resources—is self-limiting to the extent that academic resource centers maintain limited copies of any particular item. These limitations, plus the expense incurred by users of the collection by coming to campus, browsing catalogs and collections, waiting in lines, and so forth, limit further the use of collections. Network-based information resources are readily available from one's home, office, or other location, and are available simultaneously to any authorized user with a network connection. The removal of those barriers that limit usage will increase institutional service loads and costs. Policy makers will need to develop new strategies for allocating the costs of reference services and of printing network-based information resources.

In addition, the changing legal interpretation of an information resource's fair use, along with shifts toward information site licensing and pay-per-view pricing, will cause the unit (institutional) costs of information access to rise, even in cases where total institutional costs may fall.[19]

---

[19] The comparative economics of print and network-based information management are poorly understood. It is possible that certain strategies, such as those involving a shift of collection activity away from print materials and toward consortially-acquired networked materials, can lower total institutional costs in the long run. Such strategies replace rising labor and real estate costs with declining mass storage and network capacity costs.

These changing support requirements and economics of access suggest strongly the need for institutions to: (1) develop and implement sound infrastructures for identifying, authenticating, and authorizing users; and (2) revisit existing assumptions about the nature and size of the "university community." As Dr. Clifford Lynch put it, "It has become clear, rather suddenly, that our existing systems of authentication and authorization were not really designed to support the new [networked] environment, and that they can't do so."[20]

Many universities, for example, define the boundaries of their communities broadly to include the families of employees, retirees, and alumni. These inclusive boundaries are reasonable as they relate to academic information resources in the context of self-limiting physical materials. In the context of access, via institutional networks and modem pools, to university-licensed electronic resources, the policy, economic, technical, and support issues become significantly more complex.[21] Such complexity rises as: (1) members of the broader campus community come to expect access to campus printers, content and technical advisers, and other expensive resources; (2) the price of information resource site licenses must take account of the extended campus population, and (3) campuses must ponder the complexity and cost of managing the accounting and billing infrastructure that will be needed if costs are to be recovered.

In sum, campus policy makers must begin now to determine who, for the purpose of accessing electronic information resources, will be deemed a member of the campus community. Campus leaders will need to develop policies that differentiate the rights and authorities among community members and to revisit policies regarding the appropriate use of institutional resources. Campus technologists will have to develop complex campus directory services, determine what levels of support can be

---

[20] Clifford Lynch, "The Changing Role in a Networked Information Environment," in *Library Hi Tech*, 15:1–2 (1997): 30. Lynch describes the authentication and authorization challenge very clearly and argues, "that there is a need for large-scale service infrastructure, institutional and consortium initiatives, and broad agreement on the roles and responsibilities of the various players."

[21] In several extreme cases, colleges and universities find themselves serving in the role of Internet Service Provider (ISP) to the spouses and children of campus employees, emeriti, alumni, and others. In many of these cases, internet access is provided at no cost, or at rates that are below campus costs. This situation is not only problematic financially, but may be legally unsustainable, vis-à-vis commercial providers' concerns regarding predatory pricing by nonprofits.

offered to which members of the campus community, and implement authentication and authorization solutions that implement the campus policy. None of this will be easy. Finally, in addition to securing access to campus information resources, campus policy makers and technologists will need to revisit institutional policies and practices regarding the protection of the privacy of members of the community. The administration of a robust infrastructure for authenticating and authorizing members of the community, along with the powerful accounting environments to support electronic commerce in academic information resources, will require the maintenance of significant information about students, faculty, alumni, staff, and others. The administration of this information about campus community members and their network and information predilections will raise significant privacy concerns on campus.

Focus on Standards

Another major area of campus technical concern must be the management of campus standards. Robust commerce in technologically complex academic information resources will require the creation of and adherence to a variety of emerging technical standards and specifications. The Internet2 initiative, for example, is developing the standards and specifications that will enable differentiated quality of service across the Internet. Campus networks will have to be upgraded to support the protocols that will make these services possible. Other efforts, such as the National Learning Infrastructure Initiative's Instructional Management System (IMS) are bringing together commercial and academic interests to develop the standards and specifications that will make it possible to develop and share course materials, instructional resources, and academic processes via networks. Organizations like IBM are developing electronic course catalogs for the Western Governors University that will form critical and necessary components of a multi-institutional and global infrastructure that will be needed to share academic information resources across networks. Campuses should either actively participate in these endeavors to build regional and national infrastructures or should follow them closely. When opportunities arise, campuses should invest in their local infrastructures in ways that recognize and leverage national and consortium-based investments.

In addition to participating in initiatives designed to create standards for interinstitutional commerce in academic information resources, campus technologists must continue to manage campus workstation and network standards. As the complexity of networked information rises, with the inclusion of graphical, audio, video, and other components, the complexity of campus network technical resources to decode, compress, and decipher this information must also rise. In the near term, workstation capabilities and software environments will also need to rise in power and complexity. Therefore, there is no likely relief in sight for those campuses caught in the seemingly never-ending funding race against short hardware depreciation cycles. Similarly, until and unless Java-based networked computing solutions are deployed, the only hope for supporting this growing and technically insatiable community of information resources users is the adoption and support of campus technology standards.

Focus on Rights Management

The last, and perhaps most complex, area demanding the attention of skilled campus administrators is the management of intellectual property rights. The current academic information resources property rights model calls for: (1) the transfer of ownership from author to publisher; (2) the sharing of economic rents between author and publisher, and (3) the administration of rights, under law, by college and university academic resource centers. In most cases, authors of academic works give copyrights to publishers in exchange for the recognition that accrues from publisher's commitment to publish. Publishers, often with the support of faculty reviewers and editors, convert manuscripts into publishable resources, underwrite the expense of printing, marketing, and distribution, and sell finished publications back to college and universities. Colleges and universities, aided by the self-limiting nature of physical publications, make these materials available to members of the campus community under fair use limitations specified in statute and case law.

This model benefits the author who derives academic privilege, tenure, and promotion based, in part, on publishing activity, and it benefits the publisher who receives a time-limited monopoly on the sale or license of material written by others. Colleges and universities realize no economic benefit except goodwill and prestige. These institutions ultimately bear the total cost of this activity insofar as faculty time spent on research and writing is an institutional cost of business, along with direct expenditures for published materials held by libraries. Publishers, of course, have the opportunity for the greatest economic gain under this model.

As discussed, the economics of network-based delivery of academic information resources differ fundamentally from those economics related to print publishing, with the critical exception of copyright ownership. Print publication costs are highly influenced by scale, because of the costs of printing, storage, and distribution. Network publication costs are relatively insensitive to scale because of the very low costs of mass storage and marginal cost of network bandwidth. In the short term, these changed economics will tempt faculty and institutions to eschew the commercial publisher in favor of self-publication or university press publication. In the longer term, as electronic publications are enriched with audio and video, and are bundled with other services such as student chat rooms, databases, and on-line office hours, these publications will behave economically like capital goods. Colleges and universities (or consortia) with preeminent faculty, media studios, unique information resources, and the organizational glue to hold together those responsible for those resources may be uniquely positioned to become suppliers. To create a new rights management model, along these lines, institutions will need to create a new compact with their faculty. Under such a compact, institutions would invest in the production of faculty information resources, would hold the copyright jointly, and would share net revenues from the sale or license of these materials. Institutions or consortia in this fortunate position may be able to finance a portion of their technology infrastructures in this fashion.

Most institutions, of course, will not have the combination of talent, capital, and infrastructure to become major suppliers in the network-based marketplace for academic information resources. Institutions that will predominantly *use* networked information must become aware of, and organized for, changes in property rights that are being ushered in. In addition, the new technology infrastructure that will be developed to support the commerce in academic information resources will make it possible to account for activities such as browsing, lending, and printing. Such capabilities will make it possible for publishers to charge users who browse, share, or make private noncommercial use of copyrighted works. Recognizing the revenue implications of these new capabilities, commercial publishers, distributors, and entertainment firms are seeking to expand current legal definitions of fair use to include use currently deemed under law to be private.[22] Such changes would raise higher education academic information resource costs tremendously and could even threaten the relatively free flow of academic information.

Higher education has been largely disorganized, divided, and ineffectual in shaping public policy in this arena. As perhaps the largest supplier and certainly the largest consumer of academic intellectual property, higher education has a huge stake in the outcome of new public copyright policy and law. College and university leaders must join this debate, align disparate views among potentially conflicting elements of the campus community (faculty, librarians, and university press officials), and organize an effective presence among policymakers and lawmakers.

SUMMARY

The World Wide Web is growing at an extraordinary rate and is still in its infancy. The Web currently satisfies more the needs of authors to publish than the needs of readers for high-quality information. The Web does not mediate quality or deliver service in ways that libraries do. In the short term, it will be tempting to consider the Web as a substitute for libraries and publishers and to link authors of academic information resources directly with the end consumers of such resources. A longer-term view recognizes the important role of university consortia, learned societies, and commercial publishers in managing academic information resources. In particular, new economic realities will drive most campuses towards establishing consortia to make networked information resources economically accessible.

In a post-Web world, campuses must begin to create distributed virtual environments that mediate the quality of academic information resources and foster high levels of interaction among those who use them. Campuses must develop a variety of consortium relationships and create the organizational incentives and structures to foster collaboration among librarians, technologists, media specialists, faculty members, and others. Campuses must track, test, and implement new technologies for searching, browsing, and filtering network-based academic information resources. New technologies will make it possible to render information

---

[22] Pamela Samuelson, "Intellectual Property at your Expense," in *Wired* (January 1996): 135.

in new visual forms, creating meaningful groupings and clusters of information. Such technologies will go far toward making distributed virtual environments for teachers and learners a reality.

Networks will make it possible to deliver major elements of our missions independently of either time or place. The Information Age presents an opportunity for higher education to assume a position that is near the center of the societies we serve. Higher education's success in assuming this position of centrality will depend on effective leadership around a shared vision and on strategic investments in the key technologies and skills that will be needed to implement the vision.

11

Structure and Crisis: Markets and Market Segmentation in Scholarly Publishing

PAULA KAUFMAN

INTRODUCTION

"Crises reveal a deeper structure of things."

—Karl Marx

Mergers and consolidations. Declining profits. Commercialization. Oligopoly and monopoly. Copyright. New information technologies. Scholars interconnecting globally. Pressures on higher education financing. Increasing output. Rising prices.

These converging trends are creating turmoil and crises in the structure of scholarly publishing and, indeed, in the entire system of scholarly communication in critically important ways. To some observers, these changes are very positive; to most others, however, they seem to threaten the core purpose of scholarly communication itself. What is clear is that they give rise to fundamental questions about how scholarly information will be disseminated and communicated in the future.

Examining the state of the markets for scholarly publications will reveal the deeper structure of scholarly communication and thereby suggest ways in which the crises may be slowed or diverted. A brief analysis of the crises in two market segments, scholarly books and scholarly journals, may help to clarify the nature of the enterprise and to increase general understanding about how evolutionary and revolutionary approaches to facilitate the distribution of new knowledge might develop.

THE ROLE OF SCHOLARLY PUBLISHING

Because most authors of scholarly publications are affiliated with institutions of higher education, understanding the important roles higher education plays in contemporary society is important. Higher education teaches the next generation of professionals and leaders, educators and citizens. It provides opportunities for continuing life-long learning. It creates new knowledge through basic and applied research. And it disseminates and transfers that knowledge to society at large.

Although scholars communicate the results of their research in a number of ways, most do so through books and journals whose quality is verified by a publisher-run peer review process. This process validates publications both for colleagues around the globe and for local colleagues and administrators who control the fate of academic tenure and promotion decisions. Once published nearly exclusively in print, increasing numbers of books and journals have begun to be issued electronically. Regardless of format, however, the formal scholarly literature serves several important functions: dissemination, credentialing, and archiving. Their publications are more important to most scholars as vehicles for disseminating new knowledge and for gaining tenure, promotion, and prestige in their disciplines than for accruing any monetary gain. The formal scholarly literature also affords scholars ongoing access to the work of others and plays a critical role in the accumulation and resulting growth of new knowledge.

These functions drive the market supply and demand for scholarly publications. Because, in general, scholars do not share publishers' expectations of financial gain, tensions between scholars' need to disseminate their scholarship and publishers' need to generate revenues and/or profits contribute to the changing state of scholarly publishing.

Put in rather simplistic terms, the flow of scholarly communication begins with authors and ends with readers, many of whom use what they read to inform their own subsequent work. The chain of scholarly communication is rather more complex, however, and includes many other important components—for example, primary publishers, secondary publishers (print, CD-ROM, on-line content aggregators), - on-line information services, abstracting and indexing services, subscription agents, book wholesalers, retailers, document delivery services, copyright clearing organizations, libraries, and library purchasing consortia.

Each sector adds value to scholarly publications—and contributes in some way to the current crisis. But this chapter is concerned primarily with the markets for two types of scholarly publications: books and journals. It will examine them in terms of buyers and producers, explore

some of the changing dynamics in the marketplace, and suggest possible
changes that could emerge to abate the current crisis.

SCHOLARLY BOOKS

In general, scientists tend to communicate the results of their research primarily, but not exclusively, in refereed journals. Humanists rely more on
communicating through books, which may be on a single subject or which
may gather a group of similar or diverse essays into a single volume.

Although there are publishers who specialize in scholarly books, they
are not the only source for them. In addition to university presses, scholarly societies, and a handful of independent scholarly publishing houses,
some trade publishers also participate in the market. There appear, however, to be only two types of buyers of scholarly books: individuals and
academic libraries.

The market for general trade books is in many ways intertwined with
the market for scholarly books and trends in one market closely parallel
trends in the other. Book publishers are in the business of selling content;
yet, at the end of the 20th century and in the age of information, while
other content-focused businesses such as music, television, newspapers,
radio, and software flourish, trade and scholarly book publishers are
struggling.

Sales of all adult hardcover books—trade and scholarly—have been
under enormous pressure since the start of the decade. The *Huenefeld
Report* notes that sales of "modest-sized" publishers have fallen from
11.2% average growth rates in the 1980s to around 8% in 1996,[1] and
journalist Ken Auletta reports that the number of adult trade hardcover
books, and the money being spent on them, has declined in the last two
years.[2] University presses, too, report that they can no longer afford to
publish many academic books.[3] To make ends meet, many publish the
general interest books trade houses once published and issue scholarly
books only in less expensive paperback editions.[4]

---

[1] "Coming to Terms With Changing Realities of Book Trade Distribution," *The Huenefeld Report* (June 20, 1997): 12.
[2] Ken Auletta, "The Impossible Business," *New Yorker* (October 6, 1997): 50.
[3] Colin Day, "Digital Alternatives: Solving the Problem or Shifting the Costs?" Paper delivered at the Specialized Scholarly Monograph in Crisis Conference, Washington, DC,
September 11, 1997. Also, Marlie Wasserman, "How Much Does it Cost to Publish a
Monograph and Why?" Handout distributed with paper delivered at the Specialized
Scholarly Monograph in Crisis Conference, ibid.
[4] "UPs Wonder Will 'Publish or Perish' Perish?" *Publishers Weekly* (October 13, 1997):
14.

Indicative of the crisis in the publishing industry are the recent profit reports and sales, and attempted sales, of major publishing houses. In past decades, modest, or even non-existent profits, did not seem to affect the value of the commercial publishing companies themselves. Today, however, profits are the dominant driving factor of success. In 1996, Henry Holt was not profitable, and Simon and Schuster, Bantam, Doubleday Dell, and Penguin Putnam generated profits of no more than 10%. The Seagram Company, which owned the Putnam Berkley Group, exited the book business because, as its CEO reported, "there was no likelihood of comfortable double-digit growth . . . [I]t was perceived to be the lowest-growth cyclical business we were in."[5] Similar financial pressures abound among university presses, who are faced with decreasing sales and diminishing subsidies from their universities.

Although successful trade books can earn enormous sums for their authors, and smaller but nonetheless substantial sums for their publishers, most books do not see such success. It is the rare scholarly book that attracts large numbers of buyers or generates even a modest amount of profit. The costs of producing and distributing books include acquisition, editing, printing and binding, distribution, market, overhead, author's royalties, and discounts to middlemen and retailers. Auletta estimates that the typical book earns about $1.75 on a $25 cover price.[6] Marlie Wasserman, Director of Rutgers University Press, estimates that a typical print run of 600 copies for a scholarly book loses more than $8000.[7] And these figures are before "returns."

The decades-old practice of allowing middlemen and retailers to return all unsold copies to the publisher for credit places all the financial risks squarely with the publisher. Return rates have nearly doubled in the last decade and there is substantial evidence that the volume of returns is growing steadily, perhaps to a level that cannot be sustained by publishers.[8] Many publishers believe that the returns policy could be "the demise of the industry."[9]

The general trends and conditions that prevail in the adult trade book market are also important factors in the market for scholarly books. Today, as retail prices rise, the number of buyers is declining. Sales to individuals are diminishing rapidly[10], and most scholarly books are pur-

---

[5] Auletta, op. cit., 54.
[6] Ibid., 54
[7] Wasserman, op. cit.
[8] "Coming to Terms With Changing Realities of Book Trade Distribution," op. cit., 1.
[9] Auletta, op. cit., 59.
[10] "Book Sales Flat in '90s-Report," *Publishers Weekly* (October 2 1997): 14.

chased by increasingly fewer academic libraries, making print runs of even 600 copies too large. There appear to be several reasons for the shrinkage in both market segments.

First, some scholars report that there is so much information in their disciplines that they cannot possibly keep up with it, and they can no longer afford to purchase very much of it. They rely instead on libraries to provide the access they need. Alternative sources of "free" information, such as that available through various Web sites, seem to some scholars to negate the need to purchase scholarly books and, as Eli Noam argues, may be better suited to the new "short attention span" generation.[11]

Libraries have long comprised the major market segment for publishers of scholarly books. In decades past, most academic libraries purchased a steady percentage of all books published in fields in which their faculty were interested—or in which they might be interested in the future. Recently, two things have changed that policy. First, the output of scholarly publishing seems to be increasing, even as sales decline. The growth of specialized disciplines and the internationalization of scholarship contribute to the rise in production. Thus, even if they purchased the same numbers of monographs as they had previously, academic libraries would be purchasing a smaller percentage of the world's output. Second, and perhaps more significantly, the precipitous rise in prices of scholarly journals, especially but not solely in scientific and technical disciplines, has diverted funds that libraries might have used to purchase books. From 1986 to 1996, the number of monographs purchased by the members of the Association of Research Libraries declined 21% while the number of serials purchased by the same group declined by only 7%, despite the enormous rates of inflation in the prices of serials.[12]

The decreasing number of buyers and the increasing number of book returns threaten many publishers of scholarly books with financial downturn or closure. Prominent trade publishers continue to withdraw from the scholarly market. And yet, the pressures for credentialing scholars, the challenge to faculty to achieve tenure and promotion, and the need to communicate the results of scholarly research continue to in-

---

[11] Eli Noam, "The Future of Books," Paper delivered at Educom '97, Minneapolis, MN (October 29, 1997).
[12] Association of Research Libraries, *ARL Statistics: 1995–96* (Washington, D.C: ARL, 1997): 2.

crease. The result is a collision between the realities of the book market and the basic underpinnings of academia.

Maurice Bowra once remarked that while the dream of every British scholar is to be knighted, the dream of every American scholar is to be paperbacked.[13] Today, the dream of every American scholar is just to be published. Without significant changes, however, that dream will grown every more difficult to attain.

EMERGING MODELS

Is the scholarly book dead or dying, or will it be transformed into something else? The rather traditional strategies that many university and trade publishers continue to follow do not seem destined to succeed. However, some interesting models are evolving that might provide a foundation on which the scholarly book can survive—and even thrive.[14]

- Delivery of traditional printed books by nontraditional means—publishing printed books or parts of books on demand. Although this strategy has not brought great success to textbook publishers, its use by scholarly publishers could increase the individual buyer market. Customers will contact either the publisher or its designated distributors for a "just-in-time" printing. Customers will choose to have printed output delivered (bound or unbound) through traditional delivery mechanisms, including fax; or they will choose to have an electronic version sent to their own systems, where they can use the materials on-screen or produce printed output locally. New technologies enable efficient storage and near-print quality for outputting text and graphics.
- Delivery on fixed digital media. Customers—individuals or libraries—will purchase a CD-ROM or other analogous medium on which the text has been stored. Individuals can read and/or print out parts or the entire text on local equipment.
- Delivery in a mix of formats. Customers in both market segments will purchase the text in the traditional printed form and access the underlying data through a CD-ROM or on the Internet. Customers may also have access to publisher-sponsored Web sites that contain additional information about authors, continuing dialogs, and links to post-publication reviews.
- Delivery in non-fixed digital form (on the Internet, for example). In this model, likely to become more predominant, scholarly books can incorporate multimedia, hyperlinks to references and other resources, and the un-

---

[13] Wendy Doniger, "The Academic Snob Goes to Market," *Scholarly Publishing* 24:1 (October 1992): 3.
[14] Colin Day, op. cit.

derlying data. Individual buyers may prefer to purchase access to the material on a remote server, while libraries may prefer to purchase a copy they can mount on a local server. Access by license rather than purchase could become the norm as publishers develop new financial models.

- Distribution of scholarly books in tangible and intangible forms through emergent channels. Through powerful search engines, new on-line bookstores, for example, provide customers with quick access to hundreds of thousands of titles searchable by subject. By using this distribution channel, publishers could expose their scholarly titles to many potential customers who are not scholars but who may be interested in purchasing specialized titles once they know about them. The use of new distribution vehicles by individual or consortia of publishers could expand the individual-buyer segment of the market.

- Delivery of differently packaged forms of disciplinary-related materials that include monographic texts, chapters, article abstracts, Web sites, bibliographies, and the like. In this model, the publisher will identify specific disciplines (e.g., Columbia University Press's Columbia International Affairs Online) and will serve as both traditional publisher and integrator of materials that have been refereed by it or by other credible certifying sources.

- Delivery by individual authors rather than publishers. Noam argues that well-established authors do not need the marketing, distribution, or gatekeeping skills of traditional publishers and that post-publication review will emerge as a significant long-term qualitative measure, supplanting prepublication review as a credentialing service.[15] Authors, acting as publishers, can distribute their works quickly to targeted audiences and foster an ongoing dialog through a Website, but they may not be able to provide widespread and long-term access and archiving.

One or more of these models may emerge as the standard in the future. It is clear that as long as tenure and promotion continue to be important reasons why many authors publish, publishers will continue to play their gate-keeping roles—at least, that is, for as long as the market remains viable enough for publishers to survive.

SCHOLARLY JOURNALS

The roots of the scholarly communication system are generally acknowledged to have their origins in the 1640s, when a group of scholars who met regularly at Oxford found that they had difficulties communicating with each other. Private letters, then the primary means of communication, grew in number, but they were hard to share widely with others.

---

[15] Eli Noam, op. cit.

And so the scholarly journal, designed to exchange those private letters on a broader scale, was born when in 1665 the Oxford group, known as the Royal Society, published its first journal, *Philosophical Transactions of the Royal Society of London.*[16]

Scholarly journals—scholarly articles bundled together—are the mainstay of scholarship in most disciplines. The journals marketplace is so complex that the book market seems almost simple by comparison. Many observers, especially those in higher education, consider that today's market for serials is in a state of crisis seemingly without end.

Prior to World War II, most scholarly journals were published by scholarly societies. The rise of "big" federally funded science and the growing accessibility of higher education after World War II created an outpouring of research results and attracted a new breed of entrepreneurial company—for-profit commercial publishers of scholarly journals, many based outside the United States. The current publishing environment is an oligopoly-like global market, increasingly dominated by large commercial companies, especially in such disciplines as science, technology, medicine, law, and business. As in the trade book publishing industry, commercial publishers of scholarly journals are consolidating rapidly. The proposed merger of Reed Elsevier and Wolters Kluwer will unite two of the largest academic publishers, who together in 1996 had sales of $6.6 billion and published almost 2,200 titles.[17]

Faculty members write most scholarly articles—and then transfer their exclusive copyrights to publishers, who in turn sell the materials back (in large part) to the academic community. Much of the research carried out by faculty is supported by federal, state, and private funds, yet once they transfer their copyrights to publishers, they often must seek permission, and sometimes even pay a fee, to use their own materials for educational purposes or to develop derivative products. In addition to the copyrights they usually receive at no cost, publishers rely on faculty to serve on editorial boards and to review manuscripts for publication, often for no remuneration. Many observers think that the market for scholarly journals and their contents may be on the verge of collapse.[18]

---

[16] Robin P. Peek, "Scholarly Publishing, Facing New Frontiers,." in *Scholarly Publishing: The New Frontier,* eds. Robin P. Peek, and Gregory B. Newby (Cambridge, MA: The MIT Press, 1996).

[17] "Reed Elsevier and Wolters Kluwer Plan to Merge," *Publishers Weekly* (October 10, 1997): 10.

[18] Eli Noam, op. cit.

Carol Tenopir and Don King's recent study (1995) provides some data about the segmentation of the market for scientific and technical journals: commercial publishers accounted for about 40% of the output of titles, professional societies about 25%, and university presses and educational publishers about 16%, with the rest being published by such organizations as governments, government laboratories, non-profit organizations, and businesses.[19]

The market for scholarly journals is more segmented than the two identified for scholarly books. In addition to individuals and academic libraries, Tenopir and King identify government organizations, businesses, and special libraries as significant buying segments. Thus, efforts by publishers to market and sell their products, and efforts by purchasers to influence prices, are more complex and demanding than in the market for scholarly books.[20]

Many of the forces that characterize the market for scholarly books are present in the market for scholarly journals. As research activities increase, scholarship becomes more international, and, as the pressures for credentialing grow, so too does the output of scholarly articles. But, increased output alone does not account for the precipitous rise in the prices charged for scholarly journals. Tenopir and King calculate that the increased number of pages, coupled with inflation and the fluctuating value of the U.S. dollar, accounted for only 52% of the price increases in scientific and technical publications.[21] They attribute much of the remaining price increase to the pricing policies of commercial and, to a lesser extent, scholarly society publishers.

Because the market for scholarly journals is atypical of markets for consumer goods and services, publishers can raise prices even higher without suffering revenue losses. Contemporary scholarship reflects many relatively small groups of disciplines, subdisciplines, and specialties, each with its own communities and its own vehicles for disseminating scholarly articles. Each journal is perceived to have a unique level of quality, and thus each holds a unique spot in the hierarchy of publication in its discipline. Unlike bread or cars, individual journals are not substitutional for one another. Each presents itself as a unique good.

---

[19] Carol Tenopir and Donald W. King, "Trends in Scientific Journal Publishing in the United States," *Journal of Scholarly Publishing* 28:3 (April 1997): 136–7.
[20] Ibid., 154.
[21] Tom Abate, "Publishing Scientific Journals Online," *BioScience* 47:3 (1997): 177.

Further, academic libraries, which are the largest market segment for many scholarly journals, do not act as typical consumers. They are often unable or unwilling to cancel subscriptions to specific titles even when prices rise, for they purchase on behalf of their faculty and students, who together with librarians make decisions about the specific titles the library purchases and cancels. The differential pricing practices of publishers, who charge one price to individual subscribers and a higher one to libraries and other organizations, further complicates the marketplace.

Subscriptions held by individual subscribers are much more discretionary than those held by institutions. As prices rise, individual subscribers often cancel titles, particularly when they can access them in libraries or from colleagues. Subscribers to titles published by scholarly societies may have much less discretion, however, because the cost of their subscriptions generally is integrated with their dues to the society.

Scholars and their university libraries are not the only purchasers of scholarly journals. Researchers located in nonuniversity organizations, for example, also rely on scholarly communications for their work. Tenopir's and King's work showed that university scientists read only slightly more articles per year than scientists in other organizations, and that scientists who read more perform their work better and are more productive.[22] Nonuniversity organizations, mindful of the effectiveness of providing their researchers with a wide array of journals, would thus seem to be more price insensitive than university libraries or individual subscribers. As new technologies create new industries and new businesses, the profit sector's buying needs and price insensitivity provide a powerful force for publishers to sustain continuously increasing prices. Although Tenopir and King report that most scientific journals are purchased by libraries, the growing strength of the nonuniversity segment of the market will continue to introduce new complexities and unpredictable forces to the marketplace.

As digital information technologies have pervaded academia, government organizations, and businesses, scholarly journal publishers have begun to seek other ways to deliver their products. Electronic journals would appear to have a number of advantages over print. They can contain searching capabilities, full reference retrieval, graphic images and multimedia, embedded internal and external links, links to bibliographic

---

[22] Tenopir and King, op. cit., 143.

finding tools, links to underlying research and data, and instantaneous delivery to the desktop. Although many publishers have begun to produce their journals in electronic form, acceptance among buyers is not yet enthusiastic or universal. There is a marked ambivalence about electronic publishing in the academic community that John Cox, Managing Director of Carfax Publishing, Ltd. (UK), thinks goes beyond a reluctance to learn how to use new technology. Although the power of searching bibliographic databases to identify references is widely appreciated, many academics are openly skeptical when it comes to using primary research literature in digital formats. Although acceptance will grow over time, scholars today still want print.[23]

Uncertainty about electronic journals is not restricted to scholars. Librarians are skeptical about new pricing models, about the growing trend to license rather than sell access to titles, and about how long-term access to titles licensed but not owned will be provided. This skepticism makes publishers' investments in new formats risky. Nevertheless, some commercial and large scholarly society publishers are investing—sometimes substantially—in the transition to electronic publishing, with their early products either replicating print journals or creating entirely new publications. Clearly, over time more scholarly journals, or their unbundled contents, will be available in electronic formats.

EMERGING MODELS

The market for scholarly journals is in a state of upheaval and transition. Simultaneously, as libraries and individuals are increasingly less able to afford to maintain their subscriptions, digital versions of journals are emerging. The principal issue *librarians* face is how to meet faculty and student needs for information in multiple formats that may involve significant support costs at a time when budgets cannot even keep pace with the cost of information in the traditional print medium. The primary issue *publishers* face is how to maintain, or increase, the financial viability, or current returns, of their operations. The investment costs of the transition may reduce substantially the number of publishers. Some noncommercial publishers are turning to the commercial sector to take over

[23] John Cox, "The Changing Economic Model of Scholarly Publishing: Uncertainty, Complexity and Multi-Media Serials," Paper delivered at the Charleston Conference, November 1997.

parts of the publishing process for them, often at a considerable price to the customer. These factors will continue to contribute to major changes in the structure of the market, and one or more of these models may emerge.

- Delivery of groups of digital journals (old and new types) by licensing, rather than selling, subscriptions to libraries. Some publishers are attempting to license access to the entire set, or selected subsets, of their titles to individual libraries or groups of libraries, and some are attempting to build links among all journals in a single discipline or across related disciplines. (e.g., URANIA[24])

- Continued delivery of printed scholarly journals. Many university presses and scholarly societies will be unable to find sufficient investment capital for the transition to electronic publishing or to deliver their digital journals to society members who do not have access to digital technologies. The journals they publish likely will be targeted for "takeover" by the large commercial publishers, which will thereby further strengthen their market positions.

- Delivery of print and digital journals to groups of libraries that are forming formal purchasing consortia to take advantage of their collective buying power. Many consortia are comprised of libraries of all types, not just academic libraries. These consortia may aid in combating the rise of prices or expanding access to titles previously unavailable in a member institution.

- Delivery of digital journals by newly established aggregators who negotiate license agreements, mount the titles on their own servers, provide access through a common interface, provide powerful search engines, provide access through a number of bibliographic databases, and guarantee long-term access to the titles they vend. Aggregators will likely offer a number of spin-off products and services, such as searching across titles and delivery of individual articles. Organizations currently entering this market include Journal Storage Project (JSTOR), OCLC, and traditional serial vendors. Libraries and other organizations will comprise the market for these services.

- Delivery of individual articles, or groups of related articles, to individuals, libraries, and other organizations. Publishers, aggregators, and document delivery firms will all vie for a share of this market. Some libraries and organizations will subsidize the cost of the service to individuals, especially if they choose to offer the service in lieu of subscribing to some individual titles. Copyright ownership will become a significant key to financial success as each transaction can include revenue in exchange for permission to make a copy of the article for delivery to the end user.

---

[24] Peter Boyce, "Not Your Father's Journal: It Takes Links, Performance, and a Whole New Process," Paper delivered at the Charleston Conference, November 1997.

Development of these models is at an early stage, but they may offer prospects for new ways in which publishers and libraries can do business. However, there seems little likelihood that the current crisis can be subdued without significant changes in the structure of the market.

CAN STRUCTURAL CHANGES QUELL THE CRISIS?

There can be no doubting the changes, turmoil, chaos, and crisis in the markets for scholarly publications. The increasing output of scholarship and the need for its dissemination, the pressures for academic credentialing, the transfer of copyrights without compensation, the free labor provided for the review process, and the need for long-term access are creating more goods at higher prices than buyers can afford and are causing institutions to buy back materials created and given away by their faculty and researchers. The continuing emergence of new technologies and the transitory nature of the current state of development, the unique character of the market in which one good cannot be substituted for another, and the need for large capital investments and, as critical, for behavioral changes all mitigate against easy solutions.

There have been several proposals for collective action among scholars, librarians, and others in the chain of scholarly communication to change the current oligopoly-like marketplace increasingly dominated by commercial companies.[25] As yet there has been no consensus built around any one or more of these strategies.

- *Separation of the peer review and publishing processes.* In separating the credentialing component of scholarly publication from its eventual archival component, this proposal requires a new model for financing an academically managed credentialing process that could put peer-reviewed, sanctioned digital articles into circulation faster and cheaper than the current publication process. The role of scholarly societies in this model would be funded by manuscript submission fees paid in part by an author's employer. With the revenues from the fee, a society would conduct the peer-review process and render an evaluation of the article, which could then be affixed to any electronic version of the article. (Thus, the fees differ from the decades-old practice of "page charges" imposed by some publishers of science journals after an article has been accepted for publication.

---

[25] Association of Research Libraries, *Talking Points: Issues in Scholarly Publishing* (Washington, DC: ARL, 1997).

- *Transforming prepublication peer review into postpublication peer review.* This proposal would enable individual authors, scholarly societies, universities, and others to publish works quickly in traditional and nontraditional channels but would require new mechanisms for review following publication. Libraries would provide long-term access to works that survive review along with their now-public reviews. Chaos might quickly ensue in this new market structure, and new relationships between individual authors who distribute their own works and libraries would need to be developed.
- *Rethinking ownership of intellectual property.* In urging rethinking of the ownership of copyrights of scholarly works, especially scholarly articles, this proposal suggests that universities view them as they typically view patents and software, in which they traditionally retain some rights. Recommendations range from requiring individual faculty to retain ownership of copyright (i.e., not to transfer it to a publisher) to having the university own the rights to establishing an educational consortium to own and manage the rights.
- *Developing affordable alternative publishing outlets.* By seeking to create competition in the marketplace, this proposal encourages organizations that more closely share the values of the scholarly community to develop innovative publications that take advantage of new technologies. A proposal currently under development within the Association of Research Libraries, for a project called *Partners in Scholarly Communication*, seeks to find, work with, and fund publishing or technology partners interested in new publishing ventures; to endorse new publications and information products; and to help recruit authors, editors, and advisory board members. The emphasis will be on encouraging partners to enter the journals market in areas where prices are highest and there is greatest need for alternative models of research communication.

CONCLUSION

As this brief examination has shown, chaos and crisis pervade today's markets for scholarly publications. Studying the crisis reveals the deeper structure of the markets, but identifying reasonably practical solutions is much harder. The current change-filled environment and the introduction of new information technologies, coupled with the tensions between scholars who seek to disseminate knowledge and receive validation of their work and commercial publishers who are driven to earn high profits complicate the unfolding drama.

Without catalytic change the current crisis will continue and even deepen. Publishers will seek new ways to deliver their wares, and some will succeed and some will not. Not-for-profit publishers, struggling for positive financial results, will find it hard to raise sufficient investment capital to support the transition to new modes of publishing. Commercial publishers, striving for large profits, may find sufficient capital to invest in new formats and products but will have no motivation to change their current pricing practices. Libraries, the major segment of the markets for both scholarly books and journals, will continue to spend increasing amounts of money to buy decreasing amounts of materials.

But the catalytic changes that might quell the crisis will not occur without the intervention of the scholarly community itself. Only by working together can individual scholars, scholarly societies, and universities begin to take control of the scholarly communication process. The crisis will not subside until coalitions and partnerships of scholarly societies and universities create new competitive publishing ventures, commit new capital to their nonprofit publishing arms, devise new strategies for retaining valuable copyrights, and develop and implement new pre- and postpublication review processes. The leadership must come from all sectors of the scholarly community: higher education associations, scholarly societies, organizations of academic librarians and academic information technologies, and individual faculty members. The crisis will deepen unless those who write, use, and buy scholarly publications collectively change the structure of the market. The solutions will be multifaceted but the resolve to act must be singular.

12

Steps Toward A System of Digital Preservation: Some Technological, Political, and Economic Considerations

DONALD J. WATERS

The use of technologies, including the use of those that underlie emerging digital libraries, is subject to what historian Edward Tenner calls a "rearranging effect." Malcolm Gladwell called attention to the phenomenon in a recent commentary in *The New Yorker*, where he observed that "anyone standing on a city subway platform on a hot summer day" experiences a rearranging effect. Subway platforms seem as if they ought to be cool places, since they are underground and are shielded from the sun. Actually, they're anything but. Come summer, they can be as much as ten degrees hotter than the street above, in part because the air-conditioners inside subway cars pump out so much hot air that they turn the rest of the subway system into an oven. In other words, we need air-conditioners on subway cars because air-conditioners on subway cars have made stations so hot that subway cars need to be air-conditioned. It's a bit like the definition the Viennese writer Karl Kraus famously gave of psychoanalysis: "the disease of which it purports to be the cure."

Not all technological advances result in this kind of problem, of course, but it happens often enough that, when someone comes along making spectacular claims in behalf of a new technology, it's worth asking whether that technology really solves the problem or simply rearranges the hot air from the car to the platform.[1]

And so it is with digital library technologies. Popular rhetoric attributes considerable transforming effects to them. Yet, digital information and the technologies on which they depend are extremely fragile.

---

[1] Malcolm Gladwell, "Chip Thrills," *New Yorker* (January 20, 1997): 7–8. See also Edward Tenner, *Why Things Bite Back: Technology and the Revenge of Unintended Consequences* (New York: Vintage Books, 1997), 9.

Their fragility makes it highly uncertain that digital libraries can endure over time and it causes one to wonder about the durability of their supposed benefits. Rapid cycles of change and obsolescence infect the hardware and software products now in common use to create new knowledge. As the underlying technology changes and becomes obsolete, digitally encoded records of knowledge must systematically and regularly migrate to newer technology or they will become indecipherable and vanish before our eyes.

The examples of lost or endangered records of knowledge stored electronically are numerous and growing. Who can now read files that were created on a Kaypro machine using early versions of WordStar, or on other machines using the earliest versions of still popular word-processing programs such as WordPerfect or Word? A highly publicized example of the difficulties of preserving digitally encoded records of knowledge is the "Year 2000 Problem," in which aged software cannot accurately record transactions and other critical information containing dates in the new century. And the *New York Times* recently featured an article describing the difficulties of preserving for future researchers the agricultural records, labor statistics, penal registration lists, personal data of party functionaries, and other materials stored electronically in the Central State Archives of the former Communist East Germany. According to the report, "The technology for reading them and the keys to the software that created them were often missing."[2]

Two years ago, the Task Force on Archiving of Digital Information focused on this problem of keeping the digital records of knowledge aligned with the underlying technology needed to read them. It argued that "the problem of preserving digital information for the future is not only—or even primarily—a problem of fine-tuning a narrow set of technical variables." Rather, the problem of regularly migrating digital information to new, up-to-date technology is one of "organizing ourselves over time and as a society to maneuver effectively in a digital landscape. It is a problem of building—almost from scratch—the various systematic supports, or deep infrastructure, that will enable us to tame our anxieties and move our cultural records naturally and confidently into the future."[3]

---

[2] Gerd Meissner, "Unlocking the Secrets of the Digital Archive Left by East Germany," *The New York Times*, (March 2, 1998). *http//www.nytimes.com/archives*

[3] Task Force on Archiving of Digital Information, *Preserving Digital Information. Report of the Task Force on Archiving of Digital Information* (Washington, D.C.: Commission

The challenge of creating the deep infrastructure needed to sustain digital records of knowledge over time consists, at least in part, of marshaling a complex set of political, economic, and technological forces toward the development of a system of organizations that have come to be known generally as digital libraries. This paper analyzes a subset of the forces at work in the development of digital libraries and suggests how the developments are transforming the processes, particularly the scholarly processes, of communicating about knowledge. It argues that these developments amount to concrete steps in the creation of a system of digital preservation. The analysis depends on a series of assumptions.

ASSUMPTIONS ABOUT CREATING DEEP INFRASTRUCTURE

The first assumption is that the pressures to create the systematic supports for preserving digital information do not arise solely, or even primarily, from technological imperatives. Rather, new digital technologies give us tools with which to respond to profound political and social impulses in an emerging knowledge economy. Peter Drucker and others have identified and analyzed many of these impulses.[4] Our success in responding to them depends on how astute we are in identifying and understanding the key organizing principles of the knowledge economy and, then, in designing appropriate means of applying the technologies as part of its overall development.

The second assumption is that libraries play an essential preservation role in the pursuit of knowledge and that this is one of the key organizing principles of the knowledge economy. Libraries can, of course, take a variety of organizational forms, including those that individuals manage for their own personal use, as well as much more elaborate entities embodied in such forms as public, corporate, academic, and research libraries. The time frame over which libraries preserve works of knowl-

---

on Preservation and Access and Mountain View, CA: The Research Libraries Group, May 1 1996), 6. Also available at *http://www-rlg.stanford.edu/ArchTF*

[4] Peter Drucker, *Post-Capitalist Society* (New York: Harper Business, 1993). See also, for example, Frank Webster, *Theories of the Information Society* (London: Routledge, 1995). For the library community, see Clifford A. Lynch, "The Technological Framework for Library Planning in the Next Decade," in Beverly P. Lynch, ed. *Information Technology and the Remaking of the University Library. New Directions for Higher Education* 90 (San Francisco: Jossey-Bass Publishers, Summer 1995), 93–106.

edge can also vary from the relatively short span of an individual's personal library to the centuries covered by a large national or university research library. Regardless of their particular form or the time frame of their preservation objective, what libraries preserve is the integrity of the works they contain so that these works are reliably and economically available to the individuals or communities whose pursuits of knowledge they support. Depending on their scale, libraries preserve the use and usability of works of knowledge through the more or less elaborate management of a set of operating features, such as the selection of particular works for the collection, as well as their acquisition, cataloging, storage, retrieval, and circulation.[5]

As a new variant of the form, digital libraries manage collections of digital works. Like libraries of other kinds, digital libraries must organize themselves to preserve the integrity of the works they manage for use over time by the individuals or communities that they support in the overall knowledge economy. However, the fragile nature and other distinctive features of digital information give special shape to the essential preservation function of digital libraries and to the core features of their operations.

The third assumption is that preservation means different things to different people. A significant challenge of the digital environment is for communities of common interest to ensure that the information crucial to their pursuits of knowledge endures. One can make great sense of the apparent chaos of the World Wide Web by focusing on the various, and sometimes interlocked, communities of interest that have found a home there.[6] So too, one can chart the building of the "deep infrastructure" needed to preserve the use and usability of digital information in the emerging knowledge economy by distinguishing and tracking the development of the various communities of interest in the pursuit of knowledge. These communities differ, of course, and continue to change, in the nature and subjects of their common interests, in their uses of digital information, and in the corresponding development of their digital li-

---

[5] The Report of the Task Force on Archiving of Digital Information (op. cit., 9–27) analyzes in detail the functional and organizational requirements for preserving the integrity of digital information.

[6] See, for example, John Hagel and Arthur Armstrong, *Net Gain: Expanding Markets Through Virtual Communities* (Cambridge, Mass.: Harvard Business School Press, 1997) and Robert Hof "Internet Communities," *Business Week* (May 5, 1997): 64–80.

braries. This paper focuses on the uses of digital libraries in the communities embraced by research universities.

Finally, let us also remember the distinctive characteristics of digital information. One can readily copy digital information without changing the original, and one can transmit it widely over networks. These and other features have a variety of implications, but among other things they mean that the use and preservation of digital information are subject to economies of scale and to organization in digital libraries that differ from those in libraries of paper-based materials. Many of the functional attributes—the need for circulation, cataloging, and reference, for example—are the same. However, the division of labor to realize digital economies of scale can, and almost certainly will, result in digital libraries that effectively manage their collections by allocating functional responsibilities for their operation in ways that are quite different from how we are presently accustomed to seeing them. Indeed, if we look closely at research universities, we can see that the political, economic, and other conditions that shape the use and preservation of digital information in the communities bound to them are giving rise, before our eyes, to new and distinctive kinds of library organizations.

DEVELOPING A SYSTEM FOR DIGITAL PRESERVATION

To illustrate how the "deep infrastructure" for the enduring use of digital libraries is developing in and affecting the research university community—and our research libraries—let us focus on three specific issues: the distributed organization of repositories of digital information, which must be the locus of any digital preservation activity; the dependence on contract, rather than copyright law, as the basis for using and preserving the information in these repositories; and the evolution of integrated systems of discovery and retrieval, which must support the information that we aim to preserve.

Distributed Repositories

The problems in the scholarly communication process, which appear as a spiral of escalating prices and journal cancellations are, at least in part, problems of ensuring the durability of the electronic record of knowledge.[7] In increasing numbers, scholarly communities, such as those in high-energy physics, astrophysics, engineering, computing, and genomic, studies are recognizing the diseconomies of the present system and have accepted responsibility for setting up and maintaining electronic channels of communication for their disciplines. Conventional publishers, such as Elsevier, Springer-Verlag, and Academic Press, are also opening electronic channels for disseminating scholarly works.

In the shift from conventional printed publication to the use of the electronic medium, the scholarly community is today experiencing significant transition costs. Publishers and scholarly societies suddenly need to invest in the systems engineering of processes that have been relatively stable for years, and they have to provide annual budgets for research and development where previously they had little or none. Libraries worry about the 5 to 10 percent of their collection budgets that they currently have at risk in electronic information.

However, the transition to electronic media for scholarly communication is not only incomplete but also highly uneven across disciplines. Some scholarly communication, such as that about genomic studies, is dependent on massive electronic databases that are growing at exponential rates. Meanwhile, stakeholders—publishers, scholarly societies, and libraries—in other disciplines maintain both print and electronic streams of publication as they experiment with electronic resources and decide when, or whether, to shift permanently to the electronic medium.[8]

In the unevenness of the transition, the differences in skill and products among the publishers, scholarly societies, and libraries provide an intense learning environment, which under substantial competitive pressure generates a highly productive "leap-frog" effect. Each new investment builds on known solutions, even as it advances the field by offering competitive solutions to problems still remaining. The cumulative result,

---

[7] For a version of this argument, see Donald J. Waters, *Realizing Benefits from Inter-Institutional Agreements: The Implications of the Draft Report of the Task Force on Archiving of Digital Information*, (Washington, D.C.: The Commission on Preservation and Access, 1996). Also available at *http://arl.cni.org/arl/proceedings/127/waters.html*

[8] Ann Okerson is an especially acute observer of the development of electronic publishing. See two of her recent papers: "Can We Afford Digital Information? Libraries? An Early Assessment of Economic Prospects for Digital Publications," in *The Prospect of Digital Library*, KIT International Roundtable for Library and Information Science, November 9–10, 1995 (The Japan Foundation: Library Center, Kanazawa Institute of Technology, 1995) and "Recent Trends in Scholarly Electronic Publishing," (presented at the Seminar on Multimedia Scholarly Publishing, Helsinki, May 29, 1997). *http://www.library.yale.edu/~okerson/recent-trends.html*

compounded by continuous improvements in the underlying technologies, is a rapid, sometimes disorienting, advance in the quality and reliability of the electronic systems.

Despite the rapidity of the changes underway, the dust is not likely to settle for some time on the transition from print-based to electronic scholarly communication. Still, the transition is far enough along in many disciplines to discern that there is demonstrably little economic benefit in having every library manage the costly logistics of disk storage, software compatibilities, and the forward migration of scholarly works that publishers distribute in electronic form.[9] Instead, economies of scale in the storage and accessibility of digital works raise a significant challenge for collection management in digital libraries. Although digital libraries may hold portions of electronic scholarly collections under their direct control, they will increasingly collect, and need to preserve the use and usability of, works that are stored remotely in repositories under the control of various widely distributed agents.

There is a growing body of research now underway that investigates the technical requirements for constructing a distributed network of digital repositories and explores how these requirements change with different genres of material and under varying conditions of use.[10] In addition, organizational models are emerging that give digital libraries a variety of options for ensuring the long-term preservation of the scholarly record. For example, some libraries might position themselves to serve as cache or mirror sites for the electronic repositories of publishers, thereby opening the possibility of replication and redundancy as a preservation tool. Others might contract with publishers and scholarly societies to serve as external agents for managing repositories of data. Stanford University's High Wire Press is a pioneering example of bringing library and other university resources to bear in devising ways to manage the

---

[9] See Task Force, op. cit., pp. 29–35. Also see Andrew Odlyzko, "The Economics of Electronic Journals" (presented at the Scholarly Communication and Technology Conference of the Andrew W. Mellon Foundation, Emory University, April 24-25, 1997), *http://www.arl.org/scomm/scat/odlyzko.html*; and Malcolm Getz, "Electronic Publishing in Academia: An Economic Perspective" (presented at the Scholarly Communication and Technology Conference of the Andrew W. Mellon Foundation, Emory University, April 24-25, 1997). *http://www.arl.org/scomm/scat/getz.html*

[10] For a seminal paper outlining the scope of such research see Robert Kahn and Robert Wilensky, "A Framework for Distributed Digital Object Services," May 13 1995, *http://www.cnri.reston.va.us/k-w.html*. See also, for example, Ron Daniel, Jr., and Carl Lagoze. "Extending the Warwick Framework: From Metadata Containers to Active Digital Objects." *D-Lib Magazine* (November 1997). *http://www.dlib.org/dlib/november97/daniel/11daniel.html*

scholarly record in digital form.[11] Still others might follow the lead of JSTOR, the journal storage enterprise created with venture capital from The Andrew W. Mellon Foundation, and position themselves to serve as fail-safe repositories for back-issue works that publishers themselves no longer wish to manage.[12]

Much more work is needed, of course, to determine how the structure and organization of repositories affect the durability of digital information. However, even as technical research proceeds and as organizational models for repositories emerge, libraries in the community of research universities are rising to the challenge of preserving digital information on at least two other major fronts. They are developing licenses for digital works, and they are helping to redesign systems of discovery and retrieval.

Dependence on Contract

A common means today for libraries to acquire the rights to use scholarly works in digital form is through execution of a detailed contract, or license. For owners and providers, the general protections that copyright law presently affords in the sale of intellectual property seem inadequate in the digital realm. There, copying is technically so easy that it seems to put at great risk of loss the rights that owners have in their property. Thus, in the application of contract law, they seek directly from users the greater protections they feel they need.

Libraries, on the other hand, have regarded with suspicion the resort to licensing. They have viewed it as an attempt to subvert or sidestep the general protections, such as fair use, that copyright law affords to users of intellectual property in the interest of promoting "the progress of science and the useful arts." Indeed, in the worst case, licensing may actually constrain the rights of users in substantial ways. For example, if libraries terminate a license and the provider withdraws previously licensed information, the prior investment becomes worthless and the user experiences a loss of the record of knowledge.[13]

[11] See *http://highwire.stanford.edu/*
[12] See *http://www.jstor.org/*
[13] Ann Okerson, "Buy or Lease? Two Models for Scholarly Information at the End (or the Beginning) of an Era." *Daedalus* 125:4 (1996): 68–9. Also available at *http://www.library.yale.edu/~okerson/daedalus.html*. See also, Ann Okerson, "The Transition to Electronic Content Licensing: The Institutional Context in 1997" (presented at the

Although licenses for the use of digital works appear to put libraries and their users at a disadvantage, the growing experience of both providers and libraries in creating them suggests not only that contracts are appropriate to present circumstances in the digital arena, but that they can actually benefit both parties. Contracts provide the means for divergent interests to meet in times of uncertainty, high risk, and great promise. By engaging in the negotiation of content licenses, publishers and libraries do more than forge agreements; they craft the durable and trustworthy political relationships so necessary to sustaining the electronic information products they both need. In their contract-making, publishers and libraries are, as Ann Okerson has put it so well, "making [their] own peace, thoughtfully and responsibly, one step at a time."[14]

When publishers and libraries are as unsure of one another as they are today in the digital environment, one way that licenses enable them to "make peace" is to define formally and legally who the parties to the agreement are. Licenses also enable the parties to specify their mutual responsibilities and provide for ways to settle disputes, should they arise. A growing trend in the creation of content licenses is for libraries joined by regional affiliation or other common features to define themselves as a consortium or buying club in relation to a publisher for the purpose of acquiring a license to use a digital work or set of works. Such an arrangement benefits publishers because it reduces the overhead of marketing products separately to each institution. For the libraries, the benefits include discounts on the purchase price, or inclusion in the purchase of more works than any institution acting separately could have afforded. Perhaps more importantly, licenses that define groups of libraries as buying clubs are beneficial because they serve to align library interests where previously there was disunity. Such alignment is especially critical in an environment where repositories of digital information are widely distributed and under external control. To assert any influence over the information products, libraries must be able to act in concert with themselves and the publishers. Buying clubs provide libraries an identity, defined by contract, for such concerted action.

Scholarly Communication and Technology Conference of the Andrew W. Mellon Foundation, Emory University, April 24–25, 1997). *http://www.library.yale.edu/~okerson/ mellon.html*

[14] Ann Okerson, "Licensing Perspectives: The Library View" (presented at the ARL/CNI Licensing Symposium, San Francisco, December 8, 1996). *http://www.library. yale.edu/~okerson/cni-license.html*

Publishers seek to limit their risk under contract by defining and limiting the community of users who can use the electronic information they provide to libraries. The categories of authorized users generally tend to exclude alumni and corporate partners in the research university community, the very categories to which these institutions are aiming to extend their services. Libraries, however, focus in the development of content licenses on what authorized categories of users can do. Can they make copies? On what terms can they make copies for colleagues or readers who do not have a license to this particular resource? How can the resource be used in the rapidly evolving world of classroom access? How can use be preserved over time? Libraries are finding that, within the defined categories of users, the answers to these questions lead both parties back to the provisions of fair use and other rights generally afforded under copyright.[15]

Finally, when the need and promise are as great as they are in the emerging knowledge economy, content licenses afford a way for libraries and publishers together to create and develop new markets and ways of conducting business. They provide a space to experiment and explore. They afford a pragmatic way to achieve change and to build the necessary infrastructure for improving the quality, lowering the cost, and expanding the reach of education in research universities, and for ensuring that the information that is the subject of these transactions endures over time. If we are to meet these objectives—especially the preservation objective—we need to give particular attention to how new electronic information products are integrated into the larger mix of resources that digital libraries provide their users. How do electronic systems of discovery and retrieval, as the current jargon would have it, "interoperate?"

Systems of Discovery and Retrieval

The information that digital libraries in research universities are licensing for use from various distributed repositories is composed of works that have diverse document and data structures and that depend on various search engines and vocabularies for access. The heterogeneity of the information in structure and form significantly challenges the ability of users to identify, retrieve, and evaluate the quality of information. De-

---

[15] Ibid.

signing and constructing systems that lower the barriers for discovery and retrieval of these heterogeneous materials are essential for the enduring use of digital libraries, and, as more and more materials become available to members of the research university communities, they become increasingly urgent tasks.

To reliably stimulate the attention of users over time, information from a distributed set of repositories must be integrated into the information space of a digital library. Such a space typically consists of four areas: a catalog of the works selected for the library or set of libraries; a series of index structures that describe works in greater detail than the catalog, or in ways that the catalog does not permit; the works themselves; and tools with which to use or analyze the works.

The library catalog describes and organizes at either an item or collection level much of the material selected for a library and judged to be most pertinent to the community of users it serves. MARC is the standard interchange format in which catalog records are represented electronically. Concern about the complexity of the MARC record and its inability to represent complex hierarchical and certain other kinds of relationships among source works has led in recent years to the development of the so-called "core" record and the exploration of alternatives such as the Dublin Core and the use of SGML (Standard Generalized Markup Language) for tagging fields. MARC has proved remarkably durable, however. The development of the 856 field in the MARC record, which links to related objects in digital form, the Z39.50 protocol, and World Wide Web interfaces to the protocol have made it possible for MARC-based library catalogs to integrate seamlessly into a networked environment.

Although they are crucial, library catalogs simply are not sufficient for digital libraries to provide intellectual access to the world of knowledge. Traditional abstract and index files have long been available electronically to provide detailed information about the contents of journals, and providers are moving quickly to place them in the networked environment. Significant work recently on the Encoded Archival Description (EAD) has produced a standard method for detailed on-line descriptions of archival collections. Similarly, work is progressing under the auspices of the Inter-university Consortium for Political and Social Research (ICPSR) for a standard means of encoding the data dictionaries, or codebooks, for data files. Efforts to organize the methods for describing and classifying visual resources, such as photographs and works of art are less advanced but moving rapidly. Finally, inverted indices for full-text documents and the means of searching them also figure prominently in the digital landscape.

As catalogs and index structures for various types of works—books, serials, archives, data files and visual resources—all appear on-line in a distributed networked environment, so too are the sources, or digitized surrogates of them, also appearing there in greater quantities. In some cases, the library may have licensed the sources; in other cases, it may own and hold them locally. In addition, tools for on-line textual, data, and image analysis and manipulation also exist on-line and have become increasingly sophisticated in function.

Given the short span of time since the invention of the World Wide Web, it is almost miraculous that so many of these components—catalogs, index structures, sources, and tools—now live on the Web and that together they comprise a fully navigable information space for discovery, retrieval, and use. One can, for example, search a catalog, find a record and link from it through the Web directly to the source book. One can also search, find a catalog record for an archival collection, link to the EAD for collection, traverse the finding aid, and then link again to a surrogate of a photograph contained in the collection. Alternatively, one could skip the catalog search and start directly by searching an EAD or a collection of them. Perhaps more complex is the example of a student searching the catalog, finding a data file of survey results, linking to the relevant on-line codebook, and extracting a subset of data for analysis using a favorite statistics program.

Experiencing for the first time an integrated on-line information space for discovery, retrieval, and use in these ways can leave one breathless with excitement. However, except in some specific cases, it is mostly the excitement of anticipating a future full of promise rather than of having it realized. As publishers deploy their repositories into this on-line space, they are learning about weaknesses in design and how to correct them. For example, some publishers provide journal titles that are directly addressable from a catalog or other index structure. Many, however, do not, and this deficiency, in effect, cripples the navigation mechanism for the reader who cannot move from a catalog record or journal index directly to the title. Some publishers, in fact, designed their system to force the reader, upon entry, to initiate another search to find the title, regardless of the information the reader brings to the repository from other electronic searches elsewhere.

Repositories are also learning that they need more than the descriptive information contained in catalogs and other indices to manage on-line collections most efficiently for long-term use. They also need to manage in standard ways other forms of metadata—information about objects in their collections. For example, they need to store, organize, present, and preserve structural metadata, which include information about page sequencing or other divisions that enable a reader to navigate a work effectively in a digital environment. They also need to manage administrative metadata, which include information about the manner of creation, the provenance, and the ownership of a work that enables a digital library to manage effectively the rights in the intellectual property of a work.

Design flaws in the addressability of digital objects and inadequacies in the metadata structures clearly prevent collections of digital works from being well integrated into a prevailing information space, and the appropriate solutions are not always obvious. The development of supporting mechanisms, such as standard protocols for structural and administrative information about digital works and the means for searching across a multitude of index structures, would facilitate integration. These and other related mechanisms are presently the subject of sustained research on agent architectures at the University of Michigan and at Stanford University under the auspices of the National Science Foundation's Digital Library Initiative.[16] Another area of intensive research and development is exploring how to support dynamic links among citations in electronic works through standard document identifiers, such as the Digital Object Identifier (DOI), the Serial Item and Contribution Identifier (SICI), and other means.[17] In the end, however, the success of this research and of its eventual implementation cannot be measured solely by how well or poorly they support integrated systems of discovery and retrieval. Rather, the measure is against a higher standard: Do they lower the barriers to effective use of digital libraries by those in the communities they serve? And do they thereby fulfill the essential library

---

[16] For the University of Michigan Digital Library Project, see http://www.si.umich.edu/UMDL/ For the Stanford University Digital Library Project, see *http://walrus.stanford.edu/diglib/*

[17] Clifford A. Lynch, "Identifiers and Their Role in Networked Information Applications." *ARL: A Bimonthly Newsletter of Research Library Issues and Actions* 194 (October 1997), Washington, D.C.: Association of Research Libraries. See also *http://www.arl.org/newsltr/194/194toc.html*

goal of preserving for future members of those communities the use and usability of the record of knowledge?

CONCLUSION

The development of digital libraries described here suggests that significant political, economic, and technical forces are already at work to generate the systematic supports, or deep infrastructure, for preserving the cultural and scientific record of knowledge in the digital environment. However, the history of the unintended consequences of technical innovation invites skepticism. Rather than help to invigorate and support research, learning, and other forms of scholarly communication, does the emergence of digital libraries promise merely to rearrange the hot air from car to platform, shifting the balance of information services from enduring to immediate access? If such a rearranging effect is indeed at work, then systems of scholarly communication will have to pay dearly to compensate for the loss of the information they generate, on which the quality of future scholarship depends. At a time when higher education is already under fire for, among other things, its soaring costs, we must avoid so perilous an outcome.

13

Technical Limits of Digital Libraries

MICHAEL E. LESK

President Clinton called in his 1998 State of the Union address for "an America where every child can stretch a hand across a keyboard and reach every book ever written, every painting ever painted, every symphony ever composed." Can we do this? Most of the barriers are legal and economic, not technical. Look on the Web for the works of any famous writer; whether they are present will depends more on copyright status than upon their length or their fame. Hemingway, no; Hawthorne, yes. Orwell, no; Ovid, yes. We can certainly digitize books, paintings, and sounds; the Web already contains gigabytes of each. But we may not be able to afford to do large scale digitization, or to pay for the right to do it, or to pay for cataloging, archiving, and access.

Much of the effort required for the President's vision will be an engineering effort as we move from demonstration systems to services that deliver a large library of useful content in an affordable and maintainable way. Other parts of the effort required will deal with user interface issues. The rapid move of computer information systems from software intended for use only by library professionals who have taken a one-semester course in on-line search systems to software intended for use by teenagers logging on for the first time has left us with some rough edges that need improvement.

In addition to these interface issues, and the major focus on economics and on legal issues, there are still other technical limits impeding on-line information systems, particularly involving multimedia. This chapter discusses some of the technical barriers to expanded digital libraries, under three headings: (1) input limits, (2) content analysis issues, and (3) interface limits. To achieve the President's vision, we need to get the material into digital form; we need to organize it so that it can be retrieved; and we need to be able to present it back to users.

LIMITS ON INPUT TO DIGITAL LIBRARIES

If President Clinton's hypothetical child is to find something through a keyboard, first it must be converted to digital form. Although essentially everything written today is written on a word processor and is potentially already in digital form, vast numbers of existing books may need conversion. There may be perhaps 100 million printed books in the world's libraries. Converting them is feasible, but not necessarily practical.

Among the technical improvements we need are cheaper scanning, higher-quality optical character recognition (OCR), automatic cataloging, and better image handling.

Scanning

Although scanners have become extremely cheap, most are still designed for well-made modern paper. Scanning old and fragile material, or oversized material, can still be comparatively expensive. And although slow scanners have become cheap, it is not possible to scan much faster.[1] To scan the world's libraries would cost several billion dollars, and that money is not available today.

There are some technological advances, such as a new scanner which scans an open book from above and corrects for the curvature of paper as a result of tight bindings. Unfortunately, the library market is not a really lucrative one. A really fast amorphous silicon scanner, for example, was demonstrated in prototype as a book scanner with a configuration that did not require books to be opened flat, but the production version of it is targeted at the medical community (see *http://www.dpix.com*).

What more could be done? A few years ago the MIT Media Lab suggested that books could be scanned without opening them (imagine taking MRI scans of books). If this were feasible, it would help scan extremely fragile materials, such as manuscripts and papyri. Papyrus scrolls

---

[1] A discussion on the practicalities of scanning can be found in *Conversion of Traditional Source Materials in Digital Form,* by Anne Kenney, (see *http://www.ahip.getty.edu/ agenda//hypermail/0004.html*), and *The Digitization of Primary Textual Materials* by Peter Robinson (Oxford University Computing Services, 1993).

are difficult to unroll and, for preservation reasons, it would be advantageous to handle them as they are. Old manuscripts have many of the same problems. Scanning the only original copy of *Beowulf* was an extremely expensive activity, with great care taken for preservation concerns.[2]

Even for ordinary books, scanning could be much cheaper and simpler. We have passed one important benchmark: it is cheaper to scan a book than to build a space for it on a shelf in a new building in the center of a university campus. That cost is as high as $30 per book (for the new stack at Berkeley, which is underground and earthquake-resistant). But warehouse space off-campus can be as cheap as $2 per book, and, for many old books, that alternative is appropriate. The largest cost in scanning is labor cost; if no one had to turn the pages, costs could be much lower. Eliminating the need to cut pages from the binding would also overcome some of the distaste felt for digitization by traditional library users and avoid problems when books do have artifactual value. Returning to legalities, unfortunately, one notices that President Clinton said, "every book ever written" rather than "every book ever published." This implies that even unpublished works are to be converted and placed on the Web. Under United States copyright law, material written even a century ago but never published remains potentially copyrightable until printed. Suffice it to say here that, unless you were very lucky with the author's will, the cost of typing a hundred-year old manuscript, even if several hundred dollars, is insignificant in comparison with the difficulty of clearing copyright.

Conversion

Just having a set of scanned pages of every book is only the start of an on-line library. If this material is to be found when needed, it is desirable to convert it to searchable ASCII. The commercial OCR industry has made considerable strides in text recognition, but has still not reached a level where the typical page is recognized without any errors. Libraries need both higher accuracy and also programs which can recognize the variety of fonts found in older documents. Compared to the machines of

---

[2] See Kevin Kiernan, "The Electronic Beowulf," *Computers in Libraries* (February 1995): 14–15; on the Web as *http://www.uky.edu/~kiernan*

the 1980s, OCR software today is generally less trainable and starts with more knowledge of modern fonts; it often fails on 19th century printing. A text which has been processed by OCR but with a large number of errors will cost as much to correct as it would cost to rekey entirely; if we wish to get costs down, we need significant improvement in the accuracy rate of OCR, not just lower cost programs running on faster computers.

Automatic format identification, as well as just OCR of the text, would be highly valuable to libraries. The effort spent cataloging and formatting digitized material can exceed what is required just to get the text. OCR software is improving in its ability to untangle columnar text or tables, and to identify headings, but librarians would like systems that take in a book and determine an appropriate MARC record as well as producing structured rather than typographic markup. Ideally, for example, scanning a page of bibliographic references would produce identified journal names and volume numbers, not just notes about italic and boldface type. OCLC investigated the ability to do descriptive cataloging from title page images some time ago, with general success.[3]

Similarly, despite the great progress in speech recognition and the increasing number of commercial software packages which perform speech transcription, there are still great limits to the ability of programs to replace keying. *PC Magazine* recently reviewed two consumer speech dictation programs and found that after correction the output rate was below 30 words per minute. Even a poor typist is able to do that well.[4] Speech recognition does not perform well with noisy background environments, multiple speakers, or complex conversational dialogues with several people speaking at once. In most library applications, we do not have the freedom to pick constrained dialogues (e.g., about the weather) where speech recognition can be most effective.

The ability to convert items other than language is still missing. We can not take drawings, for example, and easily turn them into vectors. Maps, data plots, chemical structure diagrams, mathematical equations, architectural drawings, musical scores, and other items are difficult or

---

[3] See John Handly and Stuart Weibel, "ADAPT: Automated Document Analysis Processing and Tagging," in *Proceedings of the International Conference on Electronic Publishing, Document Manipulation andTypography*, ed. R. Furata (NewYork: Cambridge University Press, 1990), 183–192.

[4] See Alfred Poor, "Watch What You Say," *PC Magazine* 17:5 (March 10, 1998): 129–148.

impossible to convert automatically. Not only does saving this material as bitmap images use lots of storage and delay transmission to a user display, but it impedes searching or manipulating the content. Image technology is often very specialized; the software for handling Computer Aided Design (CAD) records and the software for handling machine-readable chemical diagrams have little in common. The development of more standard vector representations, as well as better raster to vector conversion routines, would be a great simplification for libraries.

Multimedia Conversion

The cost and efficiency of converting more complex materials to digital form vary widely. Digitizing music, for example, is relatively well understood, and, of course, sound on CDs is already in digital form. Image handling, whether photographs, art works, museum objects, or the like, is now fairly common, and there are examples of effective and efficient conversion, such as the Judaica posters project at Harvard.[5]

Digitizing movies is not now routine, but the advent of digital television is likely to produce floods of digital video, along with much expertise and devices suitable for the conversion. Some movie studies are now doing all their production work in digital form; many television stations also routinely use digital recording. Devices to capture TV signals into a PC are now sold as consumer gadgets, although they produce a low-quality image. The Carnegie-Mellon University (CMU) Informedia project, described later in this article, is exploring many technological options for storing and searching video.

Storage demands and bandwidth needs for video are both high, but year-by-year costs of disks continue to come down, and network transmission speeds increase rapidly. The advent of digital video data (DVD), with the introduction in early 1998 of writeable DVD disks, moves us close to the day when a few thousand dollars of equipment will let individual libraries create their own digital video material. Our main problem, regretfully, is a lack of standards for high-resolution digital video storage. The entertainment industry should settle this fairly quickly.

Multimedia conversion is often bottlenecked at cataloging. CD audio

---

[5] See Charles Berlin, "Digital Imaging at the Harvard Library: the Judaica Division's Israeli Poster Image Database," *Harvard Library Bulletin* 5: 4 (Winter 1994–1995).

is already digital, but until recently had no form of machine-readable label and still has nothing approaching a library catalog record. Identifying the composer and performer of a piece of music is much harder than getting the descriptive cataloging off a book title page. Image collections were rarely item-level cataloged; the cost of generating catalog records for each print in a photography library usually exceeds the cost of scanning the images. Thus, libraries may find themselves with material that is not adequately described for retrieval and may need to substitute search technology for cataloging effort.

The practical problem facing a research library is that converting material without cataloging it may be pointless, since content which can not be found might as well be lost; and yet there may be no money to pay for cataloging. To break this logjam, we need technical advances that will let us do some kind of semiautomatic cataloging.

To summarize, we generally know how to convert materials into a pile of bits, but we may not be able to afford it; we may not be able to get legal permission to do it; and we may not be able to make a searchable version. Only the last of these problems is really a technical issue. We need research on cheaper conversion, better methods for automatic cataloging, and improvements in multimedia organization.

CONTENT ANALYSIS ISSUES

It is easier to search a small collection than a large one. If every library becomes a gateway to the entire history of the world's creative effort, better ways of searching it and organizing it will be necessary. Some new technology will be needed to handle the variety of digital information that now arrives at libraries. Although we have adequate free-text search systems for keywords, systems that go beyond this method of text searches as well as systems that are capable of dealing with other kinds of media are needed and important.

Text Analysis

Despite years of research in natural language processing, we still do not have routinely available systems for sentence parsing or discourse analysis. As a consequence, digital library tools are usually for document retrieval, rather than for answering questions. Nor is it usual to find a digital search system that actually carries on a dialog with the user and is capable of improving the query results through several iterations of the search; instead the usual search system handles each query as an isolated unit. The shrewd user can do the equivalent of relevance feedback, but the novice may simply be frustrated. In fact, we still know so little about retrieval systems that, in general, we can not even look at a query and tell whether it will be easy or hard to answer.

Among the tools we do have are some very promising methods based on statistical text analysis. For example, it is possible to identify the part of speech of words in a sentence by using a database of statistical patterns, a method discussed in *The Computational Analysis of English: A Corpus-Based Approach*, by R. Garside et. al.[6] Ken Church, using three-word patterns, achieved higher accuracy in determining which words are nouns, verbs, or serve other grammatical roles.[7] Similar work has been done at the University of Pennsylvania, which has also extended such technology to parse sentences, and by researchers like Fred Jelinek at IBM and Johns Hopkins, and Geoffrey Sampson at Leeds and Sussex Universities.[8] Parsing can help identify phrases, as opposed to merely words that appear near one another. One would not wish to find that a sentence such as "authors whose other work is solid state that Kennedy was shot by more than one gunman" as relevant to a query about "solid state physics" because it happens to contain the two words *solid state* in the stipulated order, though not as part of a phrase.

More promising are some techniques for sense disambiguation based on context analysis. Research at Digital Equipment Corporation (DEC) by Sue Atkins and others has built on earlier efforts to show how one can decide which meaning of an ambiguous word is meant, even if no part of speech shift is involved. Yet, we do not have a general solution to this problem. In fact, little structure is involved in most search systems. Aside from searches for multi-word phrases, Tom Landauer has pointed out that most search systems would give exactly the same results if all the

---

[6] R. Garside, G.Leech, and G. Sampson, *The Computational Analysis of English: A Corpus-Based Approach* (London: Longmans, 1987).

[7] See Ken Church, "A Stochastic Parts Program and Noun Phrase Parser for Unrestricted Text," Association for Computational Linguistics, *Proceedings of the Second Conference on Applied Natural Language Processing* (Austin, Texas: ACL, 1988).

[8] This research is described, among other places, in Fred Jelinek, "Self-organized Language Modeling for Speech Recognition," *Readings in Speech Recognition*, Alex Waibel and Kai-Fu Lee, eds. (San Francisco: Morgan Kaufmann, 1990), 450–506, and E. Black, R. Garside, and G. Leech, *Statistically-driven Computer Grammars of English; the IBM/Lancaster Approach* (Amsterdam: Rodopi, 1993).

documents in their system had the words rearranged at random. A message given by Karen Sparck-Jones and Martin Kay in their book *Linguistics and Information Science* twenty-five years ago is still valid: linguistics ought to be of some value in retrieval, but so far no one has figured out how to make it useful.[9] Instead, effort focuses simply on speeding up word-by-word searching. That is an admirable and difficult effort and for a description of the process, see *Managing Gigabytes,* by Ian Witten et. al.;[10] but we need to go beyond pure word searching someday. Although simple text search systems looking for words are legion, algorithms to identify genre, reading level, and other properties of text are much less common. Thus, it is still rare to be able to do a search for a tutorial on a subject, or for a children's book with a given theme. Rating Web pages as tutorial, reference, monograph, historical text, or the like, would simplify some searches. Some work at Stanford has looked at the evaluation of Web pages, but not at their categorization; Columbia has looked at categorization of newswire articles.

Summarization

Another key gap is the inability to summarize long text documents. Research is needed on both how to make general summaries, and how to extract a summary relevant to a particular question. Much of the work on automatic abstracting has tried to do automatic extraction of an abstract, that is, the identification of sentences within a document that will represent the whole text. Unfortunately, there may not be suitable sentences in the text to do this. Pronoun references, for example, may make sentences pulled from context hard to understand. Except in genres (such as conventional journalism) where text is written to be abbreviated by truncation, automatic extracting is hard to do. An example of this work is that of Chris Paice in the United Kingdom.[11]

---

[9] Karen Sparck-Jones and Martin Kay, *Linguistics and Information Science* (New York: Academic Press, 1973).

[10] See Ian Witten, Alistair Moffat, and Timothy Bell, *Managing Gigabytes* (NewYork: Van Nostrand Reinhold, 1994).

[11] C.D. Paice and P.A. Jones, "A 'Select and Generate' Approach to Automatic Abstracting," *Proceedings of the 14th Information Retrieval Colloquium,* Lancaster, 1992, in the series *Workshops in Computing,* eds. T. McEnery and C. Paice (New York: Springer-Verlag, 1993):114–154. Earlier work is in C.D.Paice, "Constructing Literature Abstracts by Computer: Techniques and Prospects" in *Information Processing and Management* 26:1, (1990): 171–186.

Some research has been done on modeling texts, so that better summaries can be obtained. Typically, a template is made up for the kind of material to be summarized, and then the slots are filled in by text analysis of the original. Although this will prepare a grammatically correct summary, it requires that a semantic model of the subject matter be available, and that's relatively hard to make for most real documents. Most success has been on fairly stereotyped newswire stories. The best-known effort in this area is that of Roger Schank's group in the 1970s and 1980s.[12] Schank's research identified standard patterns for stories about bus crashes and natural disasters; they then attempted to find the key facts and fit them into these patterns.

Some more recent work is that of Kathy McKeown in "Generating Coherent Summaries of On-Line Documents: Combining Statistical and Symbolic Techniques." McKeown's work involves a greater variety of documents, and the material produced is fluent enough and useful enough that, for example, it has been used to produce justifications of capital investment scenarios in industry.[13]

Navigation

In general, we lack good techniques for dealing with large documents. Some such documents come with tables of contents or other ways of organizing their content. If they don't, we need tools to help users find their way through them, beyond scrollbars and searches for individual words. And we also need collection-based methods of navigating the new kinds of libraries. Most Web pages don't come with Dewey or LC class numbers, and we lack a well-accepted alternative for how to present a digital library.

Some very interesting work in this area has been done by Bruce Schatz at the University of Illinois and collaborators in their "Interspace" effort. They have used correlations between words in documents to produce concept maps of the material in their digital library. Using two-dimensional layouts, they can present a more vivid portrayal of an area of

---

[12] See W.C. Lehnert, "Plot Units and Narrative Summarization," *Cognitive Science* 4, (1981): 293–331.

[13] Kathleen R. McKeown and Judith L. Klavans, "Generating Coherent Summaries of On-Line Documents: Combining Statistical and Symbolic Techniques," see *http://www.cse.ogi.edu/CSLU/isgw97/reports/mckeown2.html*

knowledge than is possible with a normal hierarchy, which is essentially a linear layout. The Interspace investigators can divide a set of articles into subject areas, each labeled with a noun phrase found automatically from the articles. More recently, Schatz and his associates have moved on to perspective three-dimensional displays, making even more use of the ability to organize material visually.[14]

Of course, each collection analyzed by this technique will have a different set of subareas and labels. Whether it is worth trying to make an overall knowledge classification to function as traditional library classification schemes do for books is not yet clear. Yahoo does this for the Web, but we need more research on the ways in which knowledge can be organized and on the value of the different kinds of organization. Is it better to produce such organizations on demand, a new one for each query? Or is it better to have some maintained system that persists? We don't know yet.

Multimedia Searching

One extremely difficult project is searching video collections. They are very bulky, and time-consuming to index or to search. The *Informedia* project at Carnegie-Mellon University (CMU) is one of the leading efforts in this area. They have considered several of the main problems and attacked them broadly. Their efforts include the use of the text in the audio track and the ability to pick apart the images and search for pieces of them.

In handling the narration, CMU tries to deal with both closed-captioning text and speech recognition. The closed-captioning text is perhaps more accurate, but it still contains many spelling errors, and it is not well synchronized with the actual sound. Thus, they try to take advantage of both sources, using each to improve the other. Once a properly synchronized narration is transcribed as accurately as possible, they can then do text searching and use the narration to help divide up the video into segments.

Meanwhile, they also study the images. Rapid changes in the pictures can be used to divide the video into scenes, which then permits a story-

---

[14] Bruce Schatz, "Information Analysis in the Net: The Interspace of the Twenty-First Century," *American Society for Information Science Annual Meeting*, Chicago, October 11 1995, or *http://csl.ncsa.uiuc.edu/IS.html*

board-type summary to be presented. Images are also analyzed in more detail for several special features. For example, televised news often contains words on the screen. CMU attempts to find these words, isolate them from the background, and then feed them to an OCR program. They can then be used as additional search data; sometimes, for example, locations are identified only in such captions, not in the narration.

Other image processing software attempts to find all human faces in the pictures. These can then be compared with a dictionary of faces to try to find particular people; and the dictionary can be made by finding places where a TV scene which shows a person also has a narration component that gives the person's name. All of this work is described in various publications.[15]

Although such projects are making great strides in image analysis and searching, there is still considerably more to do. We need to be able to search many kinds of images and for many kinds of image features. At the moment, image searching is too often about finding color blobs, and not about the kinds of detail users often wish to know. Robert Wilensky of the University of California at Berkeley warned against demonstrations in which the image search system can only find pictures of sunsets. Further research is needed in this area.

Language Translation

Recently, mechanical translation systems have appeared on the Web for assistance in reading Web pages in foreign languages. As an example, here is the opening of Jules Verne's *Around the World in 80 Days*:

DANS LEQUEL PHILEAS FOGG ET PASSEPARTOUT
S'ACCEPTENT RÉCIPROQUEMENT L'UN COMME
MAÎTRE, L'AUTRE COMME DOMESTIQUE

En l'année 1872, la maison portant le numéro 7 de Saville-row, Burlington Gardens—maison dans laquelle Sheridan mourut en 1814—,était habitée par Phileas Fogg, esq., l'un des membres les plus singuliers et les plus remarqués du Reform-Club de Londres, bien qu'il semblât prendre à tâche de ne rien faire qui pût attirer l'attention.

---

[15] M. Christel, T. Kanade, M. Mauldin, R. Reddy, M. Sirbu, S. Stevens, and H. Wactlar, " Informedia Digital Video Library" *Communications of the ACM* 38:4, (1995): 57–8.

A l'un des plus grands orateurs qui honorent l'Angleterre, succédait donc ce Phileas Fogg, personnage énigmatique, dont on ne savait rien, sinon que c'était un fort galant homme et l'un des plus beaux gentlemen de la haute société anglaise.

Here is the English version from the Systran software:

IN WHICH PHILEAS FOGG AND PASSEPARTOUT
ACCEPT ONE AS MASTER RECIPROCALLY,
THE OTHER AS SERVANT

In the year 1872, the house carrying number 7 of Saville-row, Burlington Gardens—house in which Sheridan died in 1814—, was inhabited by Phileas Fogg, esq., one of the most noticed members most singular and Reform-Club of London, although it seemed to take with task anything to make which could draw the attention.

With one of the largest speakers who honour England, thus succeeded this Phileas Fogg, character enigmatic, of which one knew nothing, if not which it was a fort gentleman and one of the most beautiful gentlemen of the English high society.

Not a literary translation, or even complete, but serviceable for some purposes. How much better can we do? Cross language indexing has also been getting considerable attention and seems to be a much easier problem.[16] In 1997 AAAI ran an entire symposium on cross-language retrieval and indexing.

Certainly, multilingual issues will only become more prominent as the percentage of the Web which is in English steadily declines. All predictions suggest that the Web will become world-wide, with all languages represented. Again, the President called for every child to be able to get every book; for this to be meaningful we must have machine translation, since, no matter what we can do with language teaching, every child will not read every language.

---

[16] Tom Landauer and Michael Littman, "Fully Automatic Cross-language Document Retrieval Using Latent Semantic Indexing," *Proceedings of the Sixth Annual Conference of the UW Centre for the New Oxford English Dictionary and Text Research* (Waterloo, Ontario, 1990): 31–38 also *http://www.cs.duke.edu/mlittman/*

INTERFACE LIMITS

Even digitized and organized content must still be delivered to the users. This will require significant advances in our interface software, particularly if those users include children, as they do now and as the President insisted. We need better screens, better use of our screens, better ways of browsing and searching, and better support for navigation and learning. The most important issues here may be social. What kinds of cooperation among users can let them help each other? What kinds of communities will develop among digital library users?

Technical Concerns

Laptop screens were limited to 640 × 480 pixels until early 1996. Many maps are on sheets of paper 3 feet wide; scanned at 300 dpi, they would need a resolution of about 10,000 pixels across to represent full detail. Today the maximum laptop resolution is 1024×768 and the largest screens in conventional desktop machines can do 1800×1440. A factor of 5 in resolution and size is still needed to make screen displays comparable to paper. Some compensation can be gained by zooming and panning software, but often such changes are frustratingly slow compared with holding a sheet of paper nearer or farther from one's eyes.

Beyond plain graphical displays, video is still limited in accuracy and motion capabilities. Perhaps we notice this less, having become used to the low resolution of the conventional United States videotape format. An ordinary typed page, displayed on a TV screen, is illegible. Other difficulties with screen displays include the difficulty of reading them in bright light and the inability of some cheaper systems to do satisfying color displays for subtle shadings.

Speech is even less developed as a communications medium with computers, despite major strides recently in commercialization of speech research. Speech synthesis from computers has not met with much user acceptance (remember Microsoft Bob). Whether this is a function of inadequate speech quality, or of our ignorance of how best to use speech in a user interface, is not yet known.

Other modalities are even less developed. Despite efforts over the years at force-feedback devices to be touched, held, or pushed, and the occasional demonstration of a smell-producing device, sound and vision are still the basic senses for communication. This is not too serious, since relatively little in conventional libraries uses any other modality.

Perhaps more important than the technical limitations of on-line devices is our continued lack of use of even the capabilities they do have. In early 1998 many libraries and on-line services still use terminal-oriented systems. Relatively few information retrieval systems employ graphical interfaces, although work by Hearst and Fox show some of what can be done.[17] Hearst represents each document by a bar with light and dark spots, indicating which search terms appeared in the document and where they showed up. Fox lets the user pick various aspects of the search (date, keywords, author) and then assign them to colors, shapes, or coordinates in one or another dimension. Another project at the National Institute of Standards and Technology represents a search result as a globe drawn in perspective, with latitude showing the number of matching terms and longitude indicating which terms matched. All of these systems start to exploit new computer screen technology; none is yet in common use.

Mobility

Many people wish to use digital libraries from their homes, cars, boats, and other places. There is an enormous amount of research and development being done on mobile computing. Some of this work will interact with digital libraries; for example, no intellectual property protection technique that depends on land-line connections to identify users can be successful in a world of mobile laptops and radio modems. Technically, issues of caching digital library data will be more important for mobile users whose trains go into tunnels and who may otherwise need to operate in a disconnected mode from time to time.

Caching, in this context, refers to the idea of local storage of information that will be fetched again. Such strategies can become very complex, as systems attempt to minimize response time by prepositioning

---

[17] Marti Hearst, "TileBars: Visualization of Term Distribution Information in Full Text Information Access," *Proceedings of the ACM SIGCHI Conference on Human Factors in Computing Systems (CHI)*, (Denver, CO, May, 1995): 59–66, on the Web as *http://www.sims.berkeley.edu/~hearst/papers/tilebars-chi95/chi95.html*; see also E.A. Fox, L.S. Heath, and D. Hix, *Project Envision Final Report*, Department of Computer Science, Virginia Polytechnic Institute and State University (Blacksburg, VA) at *http://ei.cs.vt.edu/papers/ENVreport/final.html*

material on the user's machine. This is particularly important for mobile users, since they not only have the problem of drop-outs (when the machine becomes inaccessible) but they also often have lower basic transmission rates than those with permanent wired connections. Is it effective to try to guess what the user will want next, and try to fetch it before it is asked for? What success rate at this kind of prediction will yield a net benefit, as opposed to wasting so much transmission that it merely congests the network instead of actually helping the user?

Other problems for mobile users will involve how they identify themselves and what agreements apply to them. Many libraries sign license agreements limiting use of digital material they have purchased to their particular geographic sites. Does this include someone wandering around the campus with a mobile machine? It would seem that it should, but it is not at all clear that mobile networks will actually identify the location of a user accurately enough to decide whether the user is on or off campus. Perhaps someday every mobile computer will have a Global Positioning System (GPS) receiver, making this point moot; but then there may be questions of personal privacy on the order of: "It's ten o'clock, do you know where your laptop is?"

Universal Access

President Clinton called for digital libraries to be open to every child; this includes those with limitations on their vision, hearing, or finger dexterity. There are, of course, many more adults who also have such limitations, and who need to use digital libraries. Research is proceeding, but still slowly, at making it possible to access the Web through alternate media. Speech synthesis and speech recognition, for example, can help those with restricted vision or restricted hearing. Some more specific topics, such as Braille devices, are also important in this context.

Many of the techniques that would be needed for universal access would also be useful in other contexts. Automobile drivers, for example, should not be taking their eyes off the road to look at computer displays or their hands from the controls to type on keyboards. The same devices and techniques that would help the blind or those with severe limitations on finger motion would also permit development of computers that could be used by car drivers. Should speech devices be common but unusable in noisy subway trains, keyboard and display combinations that would help in such a situation might also be useful for the deaf.

Perhaps most relevant to the digital library context specifically are questions relating to the different experiences people have and their knowledge of the systems they use. Often, interfaces are designed specifically for expert users or specifically for novice users. Sometimes they are designed only to appeal to someone walking around a trade-show floor and looking at a machine for thirty seconds. Universal access implies being able to support a wide variety of people with different needs. Some wish a quick, rapid interface; some wish a more detailed, step-by-step approach to getting information. We do not now have any idea what the spread of public needs is or how to design systems that are forgiving of a very wide range of public attempts to deal with them.

Organization

The problems of organizing and displaying information are more serious than the more technical questions of screen resolution or disk space. A reference librarian traditionally phrases answers to users in terms of what the user has asked and the context of the question. We would not expect that a reference librarian asked for references relating to Randolph Churchill would give the same answer to a fifteen-year-old secondary school student as to a professor in a university. Yet typing that query at a search engine returns an answer independent of the questioner. In her paper, "Why are Online Catalogs Hard to Use?" Christine Borgman suggests that it is our inability to understand and model the searching process that has made it difficult for users to adapt to on-line searching systems.[18]

In particular, we have not learned much new about organizing subjects—not only lately, but over the centuries. Tom McArthur, in his wonderful book, *Worlds of Reference* (Cambridge: Cambridge University Press, 1986), traces our debt to Aristotle throughout all Western information organization. We still have college courses and Dewey class numbers with titles like "Economics" and "Politics" and "Rhetoric" because Aristotle used those names. Can we find any better ways to organize material? Computer clustering of subjects is now practical. Would

---

[18] Christine L. Borgman, "Why Are Online Catalogs Hard to Use? Lessons Learned from Information-Retrieval Studies," *Journal of the American Society for Information Science* 37 (1986): 387–400.

reclustering a document collection for each user be useful, if we could do it? Or would a constantly changing organization confuse people more than help them?

Somehow, we need to learn what people do in a search and what would therefore help them. Although some excellent studies have been done by researchers such as Christine Borgman, Nick Belkin, and Miche Beaulieu, we still need additional research to understand what is going on during a search, and how to help out.[19] Most people, furthermore, are only beginning to learn what on-line searching is about. Imagine, for example, that you are trying to find books written in a language you do not understand, and all you have to help you is a half-complete bilingual dictionary. Worse yet, you don't understand that this is what you have, so you have extreme difficulty understanding what queries will work and what will not. This is perhaps our understanding of users with search systems today; we need to learn more.

Rating and Ranking

Users are often dismayed by the very large number of responses to queries found by search engines. If the President's goal of encouraging children to use the Web is to be pursued, we need some way of organizing the returned lists of information so as to help them understand what the long lists mean. It would be particularly useful if there were a way of indicating the relative value of the material retrieved. At present, Web pages tend to be indiscriminately listed. Requests for information on computers may return for-sale ads mixed with serious technical papers.

Various kinds of technology, as mentioned before, can improve retrieval performance. Text analysis may disambiguate word meanings, so that people searching for oranges can avoid being drowned by instances of the color word "orange" (or the Orange Line on the Washington subway, or Agent Orange, or William of Orange, among other possibilities). Perhaps someday we will have fielded data more commonly available, so that people can distinguish between books written by Henry James as op-

---

[19] See M. Hancock, "Subject searching behaviour at the library catalogue and at the shelves: Implications for online interactive catalogues," *Journal of Documentation* 43 (1987): 303–321.

posed to books written about Henry James. If we can do genre identification, we can try to sort out the undergraduate essays, the children's books, the advanced monographs, and the various other kinds of literature which exist. In paper form, these can sometimes be told apart merely by format; the bright colors in the children's book section of a bookstore are recognizable from a distance when no title can be read. All of these methods, however, even if successful, will still leave us with a great many apparently similar items. Is there a way of picking out the best ones; which should be studied first?

Now, it is true the President didn't say that children should only be able to access good books. Although it may appeal to some sense of fairness among authors to have a random choice of items at the end of a search, the readers could use additional help in choosing what they should read when there is too much to read. It costs much less to put an essay on the Web than to print it with traditional book technology. That may be good for the authors, but, at times, it is bad for the readers. Can we manage to actually find higher-quality items to present to people when they are looking at the Web? One possibility is, of course, to reinvent refereeing, and, in fact, the Yahoo site is known for including only approved and selected material, rather than all pages that can be found. Publisher sites, such as those run by professional societies or commercial publishers, also limit their content to something which has been approved by somebody who knows about editorial judgment. But this involves more manual effort. Is there an automatic way of picking quality documents?

Presenting "better" Web pages is a difficult problem. After all, we don't even grade student essays in college with mechanical programs. Rather than rely on text analysis, there are systems attempting to use the way people manage the Web as a way of ranking items from a search. Perhaps the most developed is a Stanford system which looks at the links between pages and values pages highly if they are linked to by many other highly valued pages. This process resembles citation indexing. The operation involves adjusting the entire structure of pages and links, since the values assigned to pages determine the values they place on other pages. The Stanford software finds a stable solution; and it can then put value ratings on the pages and use those to decide which pages should be presented higher in search lists. This system has the great advantage that users need not be asked for any judgments at all; the mere linking that authors do as they create their pages is used to decide which are most valuable.[20]

If users can be asked for more information, even better ranking might be possible. Two experiments are those run by Alexa Internet (*http://www.alexa.com*) and by Paul Kantor at Rutgers.[21] Both Alexa and Rutgers ask users to judge and rate pages they are using; the Rutgers project asks for somewhat more information at each query than does Alexa. We do not yet know the effect this has on the willingness of the users to cooperate. Part of any rating problem is knowing the specific context of any particular user's information quest; a page may be very valuable to someone in one situation but not in another. Both Alexa and Rutgers are trying to gather situation-specific data, so that they can give situation-specific advice. Whether these systems will work well in practice is not yet known.

Browsing

Much of the focus of current Web search engines, of course, is on retrieving documents in response to queries. The support of browsing is less focused and less studied, relying mostly on the hypertext links provided by authors. Additional technology to support a browsing mode would be welcome. For example, most search engines do not know which documents you have seen before and which are new to you. Thus, you can not phrase a search asking for material which is new to you (as opposed to material that has simply been written after your last session). Nor can you say "I know I saw this before" as a way of helping with a search.

Traditionally, many users of libraries have not known much about what they wanted when they came into a library. Their information seeking has been a combination of searching and serendipity, reacting to what they saw on the shelves and what was in their mind. Computer systems have emphasized searching very heavily. We do not have a good

---

[20] Lawrence Page, Sergey Brin, Rajeev Motwani, and Terry Winograd, "The PageRank Citation Ranking: Bringing Order to the Web," to appear in SIGIR '98 (also see *http://google.stanford.edu/google_papers.html*)

[21] P. Kantor, B. Melamed, and E. Boros, "A Novel Approach to Information Finding in Networked Environments," *http://scils.rutgers.edu/baa9709*

model of imperfectly expressed information needs or effective ways of helping people with vague requests find what they want.

Browsing may be particularly important with image collections. Image searching is still a difficult task, and, although it is one of the most studied subjects right now, success is still hard.[22] Yet people can skim through pictures extremely quickly; experimental systems have presented as many as 8 or 10 pictures *a second* and people are still able to recognize images they know. How can we take advantage of the ability of people to browse images quickly to compensate for our difficulties doing formal searches? The standard answer is "thumbnails" (thumbnails are small size versions of pictures), but other ideas are needed.

As the Web grows, more sophisticated browsing and searching techniques will be necessary. Already, Excite reports that the average length of queries is getting longer, as people learn that very short queries are inadequate to deal with the current Web size. Image, video, and sound searches are all going to be important problems that we face—in addition to the need for easier technology to search text collections. We need to cope with very large collections, combined with users who have only part of an idea of what they want. We need to look for ways in which fast browsing techniques can make up for our inability to do really accurate searching.

Communities

The users of digital libraries may be able to help each other even more than do the users of conventional libraries. Scholars today regularly exchange comments about information resources and where material can be found. Yet a user standing in a library may find it hard to locate someone working nearby who might be doing closely related research and who might be interested in sharing search ideas. On the Web, though, it may be more possible to quickly find others with similar interests. People frequently post pages of links as guides to other places where information on one topic may be found. What kind of communities will develop around digital libraries?

There has been recent, thriving research on the subject of "collabora-

---

[22] David Forsyth, Jitendra Malik, and Robert Wilensky, "Searching for Digital Pictures," *Scientific American* 276:6 (June 1997): 72–7.

tories." Perhaps the best known is the Upper Atmosphere Research Collaboratory (UARC) run by the University of Michigan. Professors Dan Atkins and Gary Olson lead a team that has built and supports the UARC system. UARC lets researchers around the world access the data obtained by instruments located in Greenland. Obviously, remote instrument control saves the time of individual researchers who don't have to make a particularly long trip to a place which may have some radar instruments but lacks libraries, computers, and colleagues (as well as warm weather and most creature comforts). But it also lets them interact with each other, even though the researchers are scattered around the world.[23]

Other collaboratories work on environmental or engineering subjects. A further extension of the idea of collaboratories is the CoVis (collaborative visualization) system, built at Northwestern University, which emphasizes the ability of precollege students to use the system to interact with researchers. This lets students find out, early on, what researchers do and gives them the excitement of talking to the actual researchers. It avoids the more traditional system in which a student who is thinking of becoming a research chemist must first take several years of courses which bear little relation, in their style, to what a research chemist actually does. Instead, the collaboratory lets the young students gain contact with researchers and with equipment that their schools could not usually provide. And the researchers are not excessively imposed on; Professor Benjamin Shneiderman, of the University of Maryland, for example, is enthusiastic not only about the benefits to the students but also the benefits to himself of these interactions.

The research issue here is only partly how to make it easy for people to exchange information and share their knowledge. We have electronic mail, discussion lists, groupware, and the like. Further progress in videoconferencing may help, as can matchmaking software and adaptations of the virtual environments common in multiperson computer role-playing games. Although this technology is important and the advantages of community use of material particularly exciting, perhaps even more important than the technology is how to arrange our research system so that the participants in a collaboratory benefit the most from their par-

[23] See Nancy Ross-Flanigan, "The Virtues (and Vices) of Virtual Colleagues," *Technology Review* (March/April 1998) or *http://web.mit.edu/techreview/www/articles/ma98/ross-flanigan.html*

ticipation. Enthusiasm will carry us far, but if we really wish our faculty and our students to exchange information, more than enthusiasm may be needed. Tenure committees and economists must see that it is beneficial not just to accumulate information and results oneself, but to share them with others throughout the process.

SUMMARY

Although the primary obstacles to creating large digital libraries are economic and legal, there would be technical problems using such libraries if we had them. The most serious problems revolve around using multimedia (although traditional libraries never provided particularly good support for multimedia searches), and around the organization of on-line material. We do not even know whether we are likely to get dramatically better technology for these problems or simply learn better how to assist each other in community-based systems.

If we are to achieve President Clinton's goal of access to "every book ever written, every painting ever painted, every symphony ever composed," we need primarily relief from the administrative burdens of the copyright law and an economic understanding of the value of digital libraries and who will pay for them. But we will also need technical ways of indexing and searching the paintings and symphonies, and, if we also wish to fulfill his goal of making this material available to every child, we need breakthroughs in our educational systems and our computer interfaces.

14

Why the Web Is not a Library

JOSÉ-MARIE GRIFFITHS

INTRODUCTION

Information resources on the Internet, and especially resources on the World Wide Web, have grown at a truly astounding rate in recent years. At no known time in the history of civilization has there been such a quantity of information available to such a large population. And for those with access to a computer and a modem, that information is available without regard to the traditional barriers of time or geographical location—it is available 24 hours a day, 7 days a week, from the comfort of home.

As I write these words, the population of Internet users worldwide is greater than 90 million.[1] At least 56 million American adults, or 27% of the U.S. population age 16 and older, have been on-line sometime in the last 5 days.[2] Sixteen million more Americans plan to connect to the Internet by June 1998,[3] bringing the total to 72 million.

For those involved in the creation, sharing, and archiving of knowledge, millions of people publishing, discussing, and archiving information should be wonderful news. So why is it that many of us are feeling our enthusiasm checked by caution? Why is there an assumed headlong dash into digitizing everything in sight while beating a chaotic retreat from the functions our libraries and librarians have fulfilled for centuries? What does the Web have to do with libraries anyway? What dif-

---

[1] NUA, Dec 9, 1997; *http://www.nua.ie/surveys/*
[2] IntelliQuest, Nov 18, 1997; *http://www.intelliquest.com*
[3] IntelliQuest, Nov 18, 1997; *http://www.intelliquest.com*

ference does it make to higher education and libraries that the Web is there and being used by so many millions of people?

There is a need for higher education leadership to stop and reflect seriously on the implications of this information revolution and for the library community, especially, to reaffirm the principles and skills it can bring to this new medium. Whether we like it or not, millions of people are using the Web as if it were a library, as a place to go for information retrieval, validation, and discussion.

The Web is not a library. But it has the potential to change the most basic foundations of knowledge creation, sharing, and application—worldwide.

WHAT THE WEB IS AND IS DOING—AND WHY WE HAVE TO TAKE IT SERIOUSLY

It Is Rapidly Becoming a Ubiquitous Information Source

As the numbers above make clear, the Internet, and most especially the Web, is becoming an almost ubiquitous information source for millions of people. Further, the most rapidly growing population segment using the Web is school-age children. These future adults are already forming skills and habits of acquiring and working with information, and for many of them the Web is a much more engaging medium and teacher than their textbooks or local librarian. Why?

It Has an Almost Bewitching Attraction

The Web has an almost bewitching attraction. Personal computers now come out of the box with an internal modem and already-configured Web browser software installed. The process of making a network connection is now often as easy as plugging in a phone cord. With a double-click of an obvious icon, users suddenly have an incredible amount of information at their fingertips.

They can get at that information without needing the assistance, involvement, or supervision of any other person, such as a teacher or librarian. They do not need to know the Dewey Decimal System to find what they want. They do not have to leave the comfort of their own mousepad, hunt for a parking space, or worry that it is 2:00 on a Sunday morning and that the library does not open again until 10:00 a.m. on Monday.

It Makes Rare Resources Available Anywhere

Academic researchers often need resources in special collections available in only one location in the world. The time and expense of travel can make those resources completely inaccessible to these individuals, and so they must work from what they can access. People looking for information for themselves or their families often have highly esoteric interests, based on very specific backgrounds or needs. Increasingly, some of what they need is on the Web.

So what is wrong with this picture? We have millions of people who want access to billions of pieces of information, and the Web seems to be making this access possible. What is the problem?

The problem is that the Web is not a library in some very important ways.

WAYS THE WEB IS NOT A LIBRARY

The Information Is Not All There

First and foremost, the information is not all there. The vast amount of information one is able to retrieve from a search on the Web gives the impression that one has plumbed the depths of information available on a topic. This is not true, not today and certainly not for the next many years.

David Barber, in an article in *Library Technology Reports*, makes the point that " . . . the proportion of available digital content is tiny compared to the amount of printed materials available. Nor is conversion from print to digital form likely to substantially reduce the size of the collection of print materials. Many resources are so large that complete digital conversion is not a possibility. At the Cleveland Public Library, there is a collection of over a million photographs. Assuming that the necessary financial resources could be found, and assuming that digital conversion of each photograph might take five minutes of handling and scanning, this task would take one person over two thousand 40-hour work weeks, or 40 years."[4]

This illusion of depth and comprehensiveness is, as any good re-

---

[4] David Barber, "Building a Digital Library: Concepts and Issues," *Library Technology Reports* 32: 5 (Sept.–Oct. 1996): 573–738.

searcher knows, incredibly dangerous. Given the reasonable assumption that most people are searching for information with some purpose in mind, retrieving a highly skewed or incomplete set of information on a certain topic while assuming that one has the full story is not something anyone could ever consider wise. History gives us too many examples of the danger of the invisible.

The Web Is Lacking Standards and Validation

Secondly, much of what is available on the Web does not conform to reasonably accepted standards of validation, which libraries and librarians have traditionally been able to establish when building their collections. A great deal of what is on the Web has been "published" there without peer review by individuals who are without identified or reliable institutional affiliation. For instance, the medical community is increasingly expressing concern about the amount of medical information being posted on the Web that, just because it is "published and in print," appears to be authoritative and part of accepted medical practice. While any medical professional reading it may immediately spot the inaccuracies or contradictions, a layperson may have no background or context to do so.

Medical institutions especially have established themselves in certain camps, or they employ particular philosophies of medicine. Given affiliation information, medical professionals can understand the underlying context of the information presented and know before they start reading it whether or not they accept the basic premises on which an article is written. Without that identified affiliation, or an understanding of what that affiliation might mean, a layperson has difficulty knowing what is merely one person's new idea or opinion and what has a history and has won consensus among many knowledgeable people in that discipline.

It Has Minimal Cataloging

Thirdly, the Web is not a library in that at present there is almost no cataloging (content, form, or version description). There is very minimal collection structure or organization. What a researcher finds depends on the adequacy of the search engines, the researcher's skill in using them, and the number of sources retrieved. Most, if not all, search engines retrieve through an analysis of the frequency of word presence, not through information content or meaning. If one is dealing only with quantitative information, a statistical approach rather than a semantic one may be adequate. But, in our increasingly complex world, there are fewer and fewer problems that can be solved with a statistical approach alone.

It Does Not Yield Effective Retrieval of Information

Unfortunately, what we see in today's easy-to-use Web interfaces and navigational tools is a "dumbing down" of the retrieval process. Already we hear cries of information overload and information anxiety. The tools available today are too simplistic for effective retrieval for many purposes, especially in an environment that can support an explosion in the amount of information made available. The Web is an excellent tool to find some information about a topic, to find very current and rapidly changing information, and to communicate with others who have similar interests. But it provides less and less support to the serious searcher for information. The statistical (word frequency) approach implemented in most Web navigation tools, even with topic or type modifiers, is simply not sufficient to discriminate among collections, let alone among individual items or further disaggregations of content. Research on semantic approaches to retrieval has a long history but has tended, for the most part, to be ignored by those developing Web-based tools. Further interaction between the Web tool developers and the information retrieval research community is essential for progress to be achieved.

America Online, Netscape, and Yahoo, among others, are beginning to provide a structured organization with a clickable hierarchy of sites by topic. However, the ranking is only by site and, again, is based on word frequency or source type. However, even these minimal efforts reinforce the fact that for information to be helpful to people, it must be organized. What is interesting is that the cataloging that is being done on the Web is generally happening outside the academic and library worlds. The Web at present is much like the entire Library of Congress with all the materials shelved randomly or, perhaps an even more accurate image, all the materials in large, unorganized piles on the floor.

It is also the case that search sites are becoming destination sites: a poll conducted by NPD On-line Research on search and navigational guides has revealed that while people are using search sites to search the Internet, they are also using them for the growing number of services available on the search sites themselves, such as links to new sites, news contents sites, and entertainment/game sites. When asked what kind of sites they visited most, 50 percent of users said "Education," 45 percent said "Magazines/Newspapers," and 42 percent said "Technology."[5]

WHAT THE IMPACT OF THE WEB WILL MEAN FOR THE FUTURE OF LIBRARIES AND LIBRARIANS

Many who have glimpsed the potential of the Internet and the Web to deliver vast quantities of information to user communities ranging from the scholar to the average person have questioned the need for the library. Interestingly, predictions of the library's demise coincide with an increase in the use of libraries. This seeming paradox can be explained partially by the lack of understanding of what a library is and what added value is provided by the qualified librarian. Can and will libraries survive the onslaught of digital publishing and the predicted ubiquity of access to electronic material? The library will indeed survive because it has played, and will continue to play, a critical role in facilitating access to a wide range of recorded information/knowledge resources. However, how the essential elements that constitute a library and the core competencies of the librarian will manifest themselves in an increasingly digital world of recorded knowledge is less easily foreseen.

The Role of the Library

From the days of the library at Alexandria, libraries have contained purposefully identified collections of recorded knowledge (referred to as "content" in the Web era). As these collections grew in size, and as librarians helped provide more individuals access to more collection items, it became necessary to develop tools to facilitate access. These tools evolved in the form of classification systems, catalogs, bibliographies, indexes, abstracts, and other finding guides, and, along with the secondary information resources they generated, they described the contents of library collections according to carefully designed models of the structure

---

[5] NPD Group Inc., Nov 19, 1997; *http://www.nua.ie/surveys/*

and relationships among disciplines and subdisciplines. Libraries must be committed to the long-term preservation of these collections and secondary resources.

Libraries provide a range of services facilitating access to collections of recorded knowledge (both local and remote collections). These services include intellectual access (via the descriptive tools) and physical access (either directly or via interlibrary lending agreements). The services can be used directly by the user or by the librarian on behalf of the user. Instructional services have also evolved to give users an understanding of, and the skills necessary to use, the collections and the tools to access them.

How the Role of the Library Will Change

In the rapidly growing, Web-enabled, digital publishing environment, there is a continued need for all the above-mentioned roles of the library. However, they will expand in scope and change in manifestation. The library of the future will continue to provide:

- **Purposefully identified collections of items,** although these will no longer need to be physically collocated and housed in a library building. However, the library as a physical location for non-digital materials and as a point of access for those who are unable to afford the necessary access tools will continue to exist. The physical manifestations of the library as a community facility may eventually be replaced by technology-enabled collaboration and the evolution of "knowledge communities."
- **Metadata** or content descriptions of both individual items in collections and of collections themselves, collaboration and the evolution of "knowledge communities." including descriptions of how to access them and of access rights. In the Web environment there has been an increasing call for "metadata" descriptions. The term metadata has traditionally been used to refer to descriptions attached to numeric databases to facilitate interpretation of data values. The term is increasingly used to refer to the entire class of content descriptors in the digital environment. Needed linkages between digitally published materials and non-digitally recorded materials most likely will be provided through combined metadata descriptions made available through the Web. Librarians will expand their role in the management of the variety of access rights associated with individual items and collections. The area of rights management is becoming much more complicated.

- **Preservation of collections and their associated metadata,** including preservation of the tools necessary for access. The removal of items from what might be considered "active collections" and their identification in archival collections, and their preservation for long-term access, are essential but often overlooked functions.
- **A range of access and instructional** services including search and retrieval (navigation), question-answering, navigational training, and so on. Librarians will need to expand both the scope and availability of analysis and interpretation of information content on behalf of users.

The Changing Roles of Librarians

These evolving and expanding roles of the library are reflected in a parallel shift in roles for librarians. These roles are increasingly identified in discussions of the Web environment; unfortunately, they have not always been recognized outside the field of librarianship as roles long-held by librarians. It is important to acknowledge that librarians have always had two overriding imperatives: knowledge of the users they serve (ranging from the general public in public libraries to highly specialized groups in research and special libraries), and knowledge of recorded knowledge domains. These two primary foci of the librarian's role will not change; in fact, they will be reinforced, although they may well become more specialized in the Web environment simply to cope with volume.

Librarians Will Increasingly Be "Dedicated Subject Specialists" in the User or Collection Areas for Which They Are Responsible

The formal information needs of individuals and groups will increasingly be best served by librarians who build collections and access tools and navigate those collections and who have in-depth knowledge of the user community interests and needs and the knowledge resources relevant to those needs. A recent presentation emphasizes this need: "Most users need the libraries' resources primarily at certain critical junctures in their research. . . . The maintenance of pointers to resource sites is critical . . . . sporadic users cannot hope to keep up with the changing nature of the Web, but dedicated subject specialists (who analyze their subject areas continuously by searching, evaluating, organizing and presenting the material with their specific user group in mind) can and should."[6]

Other roles of the librarian will be reshaped in various ways. Examples of these role shifts include:

Librarians *Will Evolve From Collection Builders to Knowledge Prospectors*

In an environment in which almost anyone can "publish," the librarian will have to sift through vast quantities of Web-published material to identify those "nuggets" that contribute to particular knowledge domains. The creation of validated collections of digital materials and their relationship to validated nondigital materials will offer a significant added value to the serious information seeker, while allowing other linkages to be developed and used. In expeditions through knowledge space it is likely that the librarians' paths which ensure that major finds and sightings are along the route will be the well-trodden pathways relied upon to hit the key attractions. Enterprising explorers will still be able to veer from the main path and tread their own paths through the space, identifying new attractions en route. Librarians will need to review the "tours" regularly to determine which ones to offer.

Librarians *Will Evolve from Classifiers, Catalogers, and Indexers to Metadata Developers and Publishers*

This role is an expansion of the librarian's traditional role of cataloging and classification. It will become increasingly important to provide tools that contain intellectual content, structural and procedural information that will facilitate the identification and selection of relevant information items and objects, and a much greater level of disaggregation and discrimination than previously available. For example, it may be necessary to be able to identify a data table or chart in a published report and link it to a database and a mathematical model that was used to manipulate

---

[6] Rob Aken and Mary Molinaro. "What I Really Want From the World Wide Web Is . . .". In *Realizing the Potential of Information Resources: Information, Technology and Services—Proceedings of the 1995 CAUSE Annual Conference* (CAUSE, 1996) 8-2-1 to 8-2-5.

the data. Librarians are uniquely qualified to perform this enhanced role: "Librarians know the idiosyncratic needs of their users. . . . A structured selection process is critical to encouraging the continued use of Web resources, especially since the growing size of the Web makes finding relevant material difficult. Mounting unique local materials and adding pointers to specific related materials contributes a resource that saves students and researchers invaluable searching time, especially given the limitations of current WWW search engines." [7]

Librarians Will Evolve from Information Retrieval Specialists to Knowledge Navigators and "Expedition Guides"

The information retrieval role of the librarian has expanded with the multiplicity of recording formats and retrieval tools that have developed to facilitate the identification of information content. To fulfill the role of knowledge navigator in the currently expanding environment, the librarian must be knowledgeable about the fullest range of finding tools and have honed skills in their effective use. This role has always been a value-adding role and allows the inexperienced searcher to identify more useful, relevant materials in less time.[8, 9]

In the expanding knowledge universe, the librarian and information user can be thought of as pioneers exploring new knowledge frontiers. "In this new future, one in which we really do not know where we will end up, the librarian often takes on the role of expedition guide. Librarians can be the physical guides, the procedural guides and the intellectual guides to knowledge resources in various formats. However, as the guide, one cannot always lead. Sometimes it may be necessary to follow while someone else steps up for awhile and cuts down the forest in front of us, clearing a new path. The success of the expedition requires the librarian to be both leader and follower, consistently providing guidance from either role."[10]

[7] Rob Aken and Mary Molinaro, ibid.

[8] José-Marie Griffiths, *Special Libraries: Increasing the Information Edge*, With Donald W. King. (Washington, DC: Special Libraries Association, June 1993).

[9] José-Marie Griffiths, "Libraries: The Undiscovered National Resource," With Donald W. King, in *The Value and Impact of Information*, eds. Mary Feeney and Maureen Grieves (London, England: Bowker Saur, 1994).

[10] José-Marie Griffiths, "The New Information Professional," Presented at the Annual Meeting of the American Society for Information Science, November 2, 1997. To be published in the *ASIS Bulletin*, Spring, 1998.

Librarians Will Evolve from Reference Librarians to Information Analysts/ Knowledge Interpreters

In an environment where the information content available is expanding so rapidly, users need help to extract the information they require and to interpret it in the context of the immediate need. This need has been identified in several studies[11] but meeting this need has been a role that librarians have shied away from. Regardless of which individuals play this role, the need for information extraction and analysis is increasing. Furthermore, the role requires the analyst/interpreter to be very close to the user(s) in understanding the context for the analysis/interpretation, although not necessarily in physical proximity. An entire professional group of information brokers has emerged to begin to fulfill this role, as has the practice of distributing librarians into product development and research groups in corporate and research organizations.

Librarians Will Need to Become Effective Collaborators as Well as Teachers

While librarians have been leaders among professional groups in their development of and ongoing support for cooperative services (interlibrary lending, shared cataloguing, and reciprocal access programs, for example) they must develop closer collaborations with their users. "Librarians will have to collaborate with others—and not only with people they know or people who use their services over and over again. Increasingly they will have to deal with unfamiliar people, remote users, about whom they have no prior knowledge. Moreover, librarians are going to have to learn how to collaborate with these new people in very short periods of time; in fact, in transitory periods of time."[12] Librarians will also need to continue to develop their traditional role as teachers, especially in assisting others to acquire the skills needed to find and evaluate appropriate sources.

---

[11] José-Marie Griffiths, "Competency Requirements for Library and Information Science Professionals," Keynote address. In: *Proceedings of the 20th Annual Clinic on Library Applications of Data Processing*, (Urbana, Illinois: University of Illinois, April 24–26, 1983).

[12] José-Marie Griffiths, "The New Information Professional," Presented at the Annual Meeting of the American Society for Information Science, November 2, 1997. To be published in the *ASIS Bulletin*, Spring, 1998.

WHAT THE IMPACT OF THE WEB WILL MEAN FOR THE FUTURE OF TEACHING, LEARNING AND RESEARCH IN THE 21ST CENTURY

So what do all these changes mean for the future of teaching, learning, and research in the 21st century?

Everyone Needs Skills in Information Searching and Retrieval

First of all, it is clear that everyone needs skills in information retrieval. In the same way that a basic education now is assumed to include English composition skills (all American colleges and universities require a certain proficiency level in this area), the Web requires that everyone have skills in information retrieval. These skills need to include understandings previously left to librarians of how to verify and establish the credibility of information sources.

Those in the business world are already well aware of their lack in this area. As higher education moves more into assisting adult and nontraditional students with life-long learning, colleges and universities need to make sure the curriculum includes classes that help students gain information retrieval and management skills. A survey from Reuters, which polled 1,000 business managers worldwide, reported that, while managers were constantly accumulating information, over 50% of them openly admitted they do not have the capacity to assimilate it; rather, they are overwhelmed by it. Ninety-seven percent said they believed their companies should provide information management training.[13]

This Redefinition of Roles Is not just an Issue for Higher Education or Libraries

Secondly, this is not just an issue for higher education or libraries. The Web is pushing us to redefine the roles of all public institutions relative to the creation and sharing of information. As has been noted in a report written by the Benton Foundation, "At issue is the very notion of a public culture—that nexus of schools, hospitals, libraries, parks, museums, public television and radio stations, community computer networks, lo-

---

[13] Reuters, Dec 16, 1997; *http://www.yahoo.com*

cal public access, education, and government channels of cable television, and the growing universe of nonprofit information providers on the Internet . . ."[14]

A Scenario Model for Viewing the Future

To a great extent, these various roles will be defined, especially for higher education and their libraries, by the direction society takes in the next 10 to 20 years. Lawrence Wilkinson, an organizational development consultant who assists companies making the transition into the information age, has developed a method of scenario building that highlights the large-scale forces facing society as a whole. As he states, "Given the impossibility of knowing how the future will play out, a good decision or strategy is one that plays out well across several possible futures." [15] In other words, we need first to develop some models of potential futures. Then we can begin to suggest some functions and roles that we need to assume or facilitate in the years to come.

Wilkinson asked the staff of *Wired* magazine to name the driving forces they think will define society and will influence "the future of the future." They came up with two dimensions of importance. They proposed that the first pull is between the individual and community:

Individual  Community

"Will the energy of democratization and the ascendance of the ultimate individualized "I" continue to prevail?"

"Or will our social organization and self-definition be rooted in a group — a nation, a tribe, a collection of users of a particular brand, a more communitarian 'We'?"

It is clear that neither the "I" nor the "We" will ever disappear, but it is a question as to which will become the prevailing influence in our society—or the portion of society we support or with which we identify.

---

[14] The Benton Foundation, *Buildings, Books and Bytes: Libraries and Communities in the Digital Age*; (the Benton Foundation, funded by the W.K. Kellogg Foundation, Washington, D.C., November 1996)
[15] Wilkinson, L, "How to Build Scenarios." Scenarios: The Future of the Future, *Wired* (special edition 1995):77–81.

The second set of forces they identified look to the uncertain character of social structure:

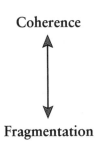

Coherence

*"Will social and political structures (either new
or traditional) provide a society-wide coherence
and order? Will there be a state to impose
order, level the playing field, and unify a
commonwealth?"*

Fragmentation

*"Or will society shatter into shards, the jagged
edges of which do not mesh into a coherent
whole? Will permanent fragmentation,
increasing plurality, and unfettered free-
marketism bring us to 'bottom-up' functioning
anarchy?"*

In other words, will society be the center that holds and provides stability, or will it fragment?"

Wilson[16] took these dimensions and explored their application to the
possible role of the librarian in each of the four scenarios. He introduced
another dimension that aligns with individualism versus community:

Information as      **Information as a**
a Market Good   **Common Good**

Wilson suggests that, if a focus on the individual defines the future, information will turn into a market good, and the future of our present
model of public libraries and universities does not look rosy. However,
if coherence and community are the dominant characteristics, our present model of public-funded, community-based information resources
will continue to be viable.

If we chart *Wired*'s two dimensions (albeit in a slightly different way
than Wilkinson chose to) and combine them with Wilson's addition of
the role of information, the following matrices and implications result:

---

[16] Tom Wilson, "The Role of the Librarian in the 21st Century," The Library Association
Northern Branch Conference (Longhirst, Northumberland, November 17, 1995).

The Emphasis of Society

First, in terms of societal changes, each of the 4 quadrants would map something like the following:

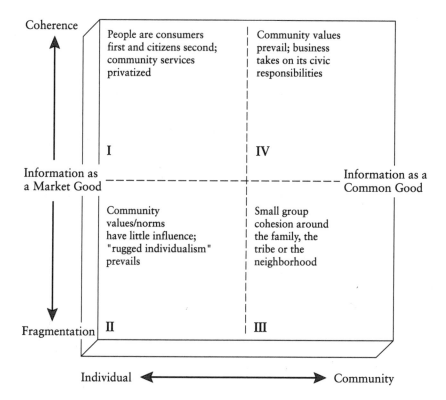

The Characteristic of Work

Work, when mapped on these two dimensions, would likely have the following characteristics:

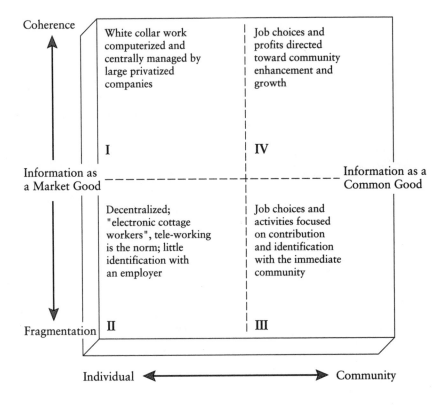

The Roles for Higher Education, Libraries, and Librarians

Against this background of societal and work emphases, we may see the essential roles of higher education, libraries, and librarians as follows:

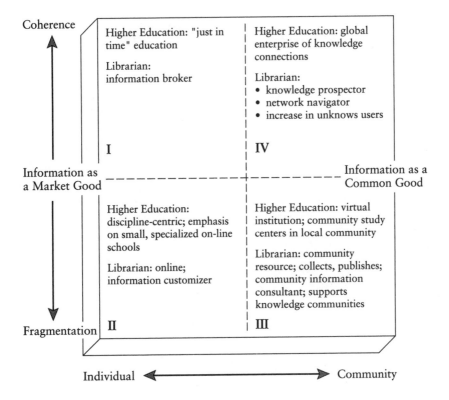

Coherence

Higher Education: "just in time" education

Librarian:
information broker

I

Higher Education: global enterprise of knowledge connections

Librarian:
• knowledge prospector
• network navigator
• increase in unknows users

IV

Information as a Market Good

Information as a Common Good

Higher Education: discipline-centric; emphasis on small, specialized on-line schools

Librarian: online; information customizer

II

Higher Education: virtual institution; community study centers in local community

Librarian: community resource; collects, publishes; community information consultant; supports knowledge communities

III

Fragmentation

Individual ⟵⟶ Community

Regardless of what direction society takes, all those concerned with information creation, sharing, and application will have to contend with the Web (or whatever follows it) . In addition, many layers of our society and many areas of our world are already strongly aligned with one of the four quadrants. Thus, educators, and especially librarians, must be looking to become fluent in the skills necessary for their relevant roles.

VI. CONCLUSIONS

It is imperative that we understand the Web and the ways it is not a library. But the Web, and whatever universally available electronic information system follows it, must be reckoned with, because an ever-larger population of our world is assuming that it replaces the library. We must address all the concerns the Web raises, find ways to compensate for its lacks, and reinforce the role of the library. We must understand what the changes in information availability and retrieval methods mean for the future of libraries and librarians and what they will mean for the future of teaching, learning, and research in the 21st century. In the years ahead, these issues will impact the foundations of knowledge creation, sharing and application. We must understand the roles and responsibilities the academic and library communities need to assume, and do so proactively—immediately and in the future.

Section 4

Leadership, Staffing and Management

15

Vision 2010: Digital Technology and the Future of Higher Education

DEANNA B. MARCUM

The June 23, 1997 issue of *Business Week* was devoted to the annual update on Information Technology. There were the usual projections for technology's becoming more and more integrated into the fabric of daily life. As the editors described it, "Computers, if they retain that moniker, will tend our children, meld with our flesh and blood, heal the sick, and restore eyesight to the blind." In other words, computer technology will be a part—and often a central part—of all that we do.

This comes as no surprise. We cannot go to the supermarket, a doctor's office, or even the fuel-emissions testing station without realizing how computers connect us and those with whom we do business to vast storehouses of digital data. In a few instances, the transactions seem easy. This is especially true in those areas where there is an economic incentive to make computer interactions user-friendly. But in other instances, as we attempt to utilize digital technology for instructional purposes and for virtual libraries, we are frustrated with the clumsiness of the computer interaction, and nearly all of the top computer labs in the country are spending most of their effort on creating "organic" systems in which computers function more like humans. At the same time, software is being developed to be more intuitive.

But computer developments are entrepreneurial and opportunistic. Douglas Englebart of the Bootstrap Institute in Fremont, California, one of the futurists who contributed to the *Business Week* review of technology, noted the disjunction between the pace of technological change and the purposes the innovation might serve: "The digital revolution is far more significant than the invention of writing or printing. It offers the potential for humans to learn new ways of thinking and organizing social structures. Right now, we're evolving without much vision. But if we could boost our collective IQ [with computers and networks], maybe we could see where we are going."[1]

We read the projections from the computer science community, in tandem with more skeptical essays about the effects of technology on our society. When it is not necessary to be specific about the effects on a particular institution, the projections seem safe enough. It is much more difficult to predict where digital technology is going, or more specifically, where it is taking the library, archival, and museum communities.

But one of the mandates of the Council on Library and Information Resources (CLIR) is to consider how information organizations will have to cope with the changes introduced by digital technology. We must help libraries position themselves to take full advantage of its benefits. And we must analyze what the changes mean for the way we prepare ourselves for our professions and for how we do our work.

VISION 2010

As we aimed to carry out this mandate in 1995 and 1996, the Commission on Preservation and Access, then a separate organization, created a project called Vision 2010. The rationale for the project was a conviction that digital technology is transforming our institutions of higher education. Daniel Atkins, Dean of the School of Information, University of Michigan, chaired the project's seminars, which were convened over an eighteen-month period. Three groups of seminar participants were asked to design the basic learning, teaching, and research environment, the undergirding scholarly communication networks, and the overarching organizational and economic infrastructure that will be required in twenty years. They were also charged with identifying the technological developments to support the creation of this vision, along with various implementation strategies and mileposts of success. The focus of the seminars was on what needs to be created, not on how universities are going to change. The Commission engaged some of the best minds to examine the many forces that will shape the system of higher education a couple of decades from now.

Four discussion groups—made up of technology experts, educational

---

[1] Douglas Englebart, "Technology Update," *Business Week* (June 23, 1997), 94.

administrators, educational theorists, information specialists, scholars, and librarians—met over the period of the two-year Vision 2010 Project. The process moved from the identification of issues, to a consideration of new forces and conditions and the promise and perils of the future, to an examination of the capacity and readiness of higher education to adapt to and, indeed, to help construct the future. The participants considered issues of governance, management, and culture and their cumulative effect on decision-making in higher education. The charge was to conceptualize the nature of information and its management in the broadest sense of that word in the year 2010—its flow, its stewardship, and its use in scholarship, teaching, and learning.

Seminar participants discussed creative leadership, flexibility, adaptability, resilience, and protectiveness in the academy. Provost Jonathan Cole of Columbia University described the fundamental problem of choice at the research university as one that has "more to do with the basic ambiguity over governance than the ability to articulate alternatives." The challenge, participants agreed, will be to give legitimacy in this environment to the kind of decision-making that these times call for. The pace of university life that is made possible by digital technology requires a clearer process of decision making.

The Commission recognized that large research universities, in particular, view change cautiously. Their cultural and organizational fabric contains built-in impediments that enable them to resist, if only with partial success, outside pressures for change. Research institutions, and their libraries, are tied simultaneously to the past and to the future. Even though many of the most promising technologies were born in the labs on research university campuses, the institutions have lacked the full measure of technical capacity needed to adapt them to their own uses. Yet change is evident everywhere on these campuses.

The Internet has grown dramatically in just a few short years. It provides powerful search and collaborative tools that allow new access to information and to distant colleagues. Networked university supercomputers, together with the Internet and the World Wide Web, have enhanced research throughout academe. But even as institutions of higher education are busy raising and allocating funds to wire their campuses to take fuller advantage of networking, and as library access is being transformed, the fundamental nature of education and teaching has not been significantly affected by existing technologies, let alone by the promise of the coming digital revolution.

Vision 2010 was an effort to focus attention on the profound transformation likely to take place in higher education and scholarly communications as a consequence of digital and related technologies. Planners chose the year 2010 as a symbol of the threshold of a new era. But significant changes already have occurred, and the date is close enough in time for concerted planning to be underway. Present planning efforts in the academic and publishing communities are focused primarily on how existing organizations need to evolve gradually in response to the new technologies and to concentrate on coping with current problems that are only partially created by current technologies. This approach is simply inadequate for dealing with revolutionary changes. Vision 2010 aimed to project thinking and imagination far enough ahead to enable universities to teach themselves on the basis of current dilemmas. It was created to be a more revolutionary planning process to deal with revolutionary change. The experience of shaping, carrying out, and reflecting upon the outcomes of the Vision 2010 project has led to several conclusions and recommendations.

THE FINDINGS OF VISION 2010

After examining four scenarios of the future of higher education and its management of information resources, Vision 2010 participants issued four general findings:

First, there is a broad consensus that the technological transformation predicted for decades by futurists is now taking place and will have tremendous significance for higher education for generations to come.

Second, the analysis and planning required to prepare for and take full advantage of new benefits and opportunities during this period of transformation call for a different process—longer-term, more imaginative, and expansive—than what higher education has been accustomed to. Academe has been a principal supplier of research and expertise to the private sector, which considers the academy an essential source of its vital growth and renewal. And yet, educational institutions have allocated insufficient resources to reinventing themselves or predicting their futures.

Third, higher education now must respond effectively and in a timely manner to financial exigencies and to calls from within to reexamine a host of fundamental educational issues. In the traditional lecture and print-on-paper communications environment that has evolved on the campuses over many years, there have been few outward and visible changes in the classroom, lecture hall, library, or laboratories, despite significant changes in the students and curriculum. The lectures, textbooks, and library reserve lists have remained the key elements of classroom support. Physical place, time, and the calendar have served as boundaries of the institution and its activities. In the mixed digital and paper world, both elements are enhanced by instantaneous global communication and access, and all forms of intellectual resources—including those contained in the world's libraries, current publishing, and recordings, as well as dialogues with professors and colleagues—are no longer restricted by place, time, or distance. It is clear that our conceptions of the student, the instructor, and the location of teaching, learning, and research will undergo radical change in a technologically transformed global environment. It is no longer practical or desirable to see current planning activities and future planning efforts as totally separate and sequential tasks. For both current and future planning, we must engage in a process of reexamining the mission, character, and appropriate future role of an institution. For both current and future planning, we must consider how operational decision-making of the requisite magnitude can be accomplished efficiently. Every institution should approach the two planning efforts in a coordinated, indeed integrated, manner.

Fourth, while educational and scholarly associations, foundations, and other supporting groups should examine collectively all these issues and questions, it is also essential that each institution engage in its own effort. Reading studies and conference reports and pondering the implications of others' visions of the future may be helpful for suggesting new directions or greater breadth, but neither can take the place of the individual exploration of itself each institution must undertake. A demanding, creative process of strategic and operational planning is essential if an institution is to develop a shared vision. Technological developments, themselves characterized by continuing change, will transform society and the institutions within it. Universities must change their internal processes for understanding issues and making decisions, lest they become overwhelmed by the technological transformations that will inevitably take place.

DRIVING FORCES FOR CHANGE

These findings came after intense discussion by seminar participants and through wide reading and the examination of a variety of universities' planning documents. As they considered the changes universities can expect because of developments in digital and related technologies, the Vision 2010 group saw changes occurring in three stages:

In the first stage, digital technology has a direct influence on the way traditional services or functions are provided. For example:

- Pedagogy and the learning environment have changed dramatically to include more interaction with the learner.
- Libraries are providing access to information far beyond that found in the physical holdings of the institution.
- Laboratories and research computational facilities are carrying out collaborative research, experimentation, and data gathering and distribution.
- Communication networking allows cost-effective global connections to colleagues, students, and information resources.
- Distance learning provides new opportunities in teaching and learning with digital applications.

As the digital technologies advance to the second stage, the changes will not be limited to accomplishing traditional tasks more effectively. Advances will bring new approaches to tasks that heretofore were impossible to accomplish, or even to imagine. The way we share resources and collaborate, and even the way we learn, will change. We do not yet know the exact form the virtual campus or university will take, or how it will combine traditional space and socialization with distant digital capabilities. But we do know that the virtual library is close at hand and more readily discernible.

The third stage of technology transfer is by far the most significant and difficult to predict, in both its scope and its timing. This stage involves the transformation of much of our society and economy, including higher education by revolutionary, and eventually pervasive, technologies.

This transformation is likely to be of far greater magnitude—and realized over a much shorter time span—than earlier technological revolutions. In his widely quoted article, "The Age of Social Transformation,"[2] Peter Drucker has dealt with the profound societal changes, particularly in the world of work, that we are already experiencing as a result of these technologies.

For higher education, Drucker cites the looming challenges:

---

[2] Peter Drucker, "The Age of Social Transformation" *Atlantic 274* (November 1994): 53-80.

- *Demographics.* The continued explosive growth in the world's population, primarily in the developing and third-world countries, will result in a global population of well over two billion teenagers by the year 2010.
- *Rapidly expanding knowledge base.* Since World War II, we have experienced an unprecedented exponential growth in our knowledge base, spurred by the increase in government-funded research in space and technology. More recently, the growth has occurred within the health sciences and biomedicine. While the rate of government-sponsored research is likely to diminish, at least in the near term, the high rate of growth in our knowledge base will continue in the digital era throughout a competitive global economy.
- *The Economy.* There will be pressures on student and family income resources, tax support of institutions and research, and student grant and loan legislation. As the very structure of our tax system is examined, changes could result with both positive and negative effects. The societal changes in past decades brought about by our technologically driven economy are likely to continue having a negative effect on higher education in the 1990s, but then to turn positive in the following decades if higher education can make the appropriate adjustments.
- *New Learning Theory.* Recently, there has been a growing emphasis on learning, as distinct from teaching, and on new and rediscovered research regarding how and when we learn, both as individuals and in groups. A number of institutions, primarily colleges, are already taking significant steps in moving from a teaching to a learning and networked environment.

HIGHER EDUCATION'S REACTIONS TO THE DRIVING FORCES FOR CHANGE

Vision 2010 participants found it simple enough to identify the forces of change but more difficult to identify the effects of these changes on institutions of higher learning. Among the current issues they identified were:

1. Cost Containment, Rising Budget Deficits, and Other Economic Issues

   In the foreseeable future, few institutions can continue to anticipate rising revenues from increased enrollments, federal funding for research, or the incremental state appropriations that they have become accustomed to. To continue to be successful, most institutions will have to live with low-growth or no-growth budgets and practice effective cost-containment. The costs associated with new opportunities, programs, or courses will have to be met by equivalent new sources of revenue for the purpose or through the elimination of other costs.

2. Facilities Infrastructure

   The significant growth in infrastructure over a number of decades has left higher education with physical plants worth more then $3.5 billion, according to some estimates. These aging facilities have a replacement value of perhaps a hundred times that figure and accumulated deferred maintenance, by one estimate, of between $60 and $100 billion. The situation is aggravated when technological and other factors have rendered some facilities obsolete and when critics, primarily of greatly expanded budgets for deferred maintenance at public institutions, draw attention to facilities. As digital technologies begin to have their impact on the way in which education and scholarly communication take place, institutions will be faced with having to shift resources gradually from a physical to a virtual mode and with exploring increased sharing of physical facilities with other institutions.

3. Traditional Budgeting and Accounting Practices

As institutions face the growing dilemma of capital costs, demands on their expense budgets in the digital age will increase as well. There will be more license and access fees to cope with, rapidly changing software to upgrade or replace, and exploding communication costs that reflect the heavy use by both faculty and students of the networks. The accelerating advances in technology will result in an increasing rate of obsolescence, to which educational institutions, unlike business firms, are generally unaccustomed in their accounting and financial planning.

4. Tuition

Even though they have slowed a bit, tuition increases have generally continued to exceed increases in both the cost of living and family incomes. On the other hand, except for the most heavily endowed institutions, or those with access to additional funds for this purpose, universities cannot continue to increase, or even maintain, their current levels of financial aid or other means of tuition discounting.

There are serious policy debates about the appropriate federal and state assistance that should be provided in the public interest. The arguments are magnified when an increasing portion of potential college-age students are low-income or international students.

5. Productivity

There will be a growing demand for increased productivity and for more cost-effective allocation of faculty and staff time. Closely allied to this demand will be one for increased attention to assessment in learning strategies and outcomes. New learning approaches through technology will need to be explored, including greater realization of effective learning by students within collaboratory environments and greater faculty mentoring. There will undoubtedly be increased exploration of possible cost-effective applications of technology, which may substitute equipment costs for personnel costs by making teaching and learning less interdependent.

6. The Added Costs of Operating in Both the Analog and Digital Environments

While there will be many sites of added costs in this transition period, the library is the most obvious example of the hybrid (analog/digital) institution. The dilemma of accommodating the combined costs of print materials and new digital surrogates will continue for the foreseeable future. An increasing amount of the print or analog collections will require costly preservation, perhaps through new cooperative preservation arrangements, and institutions will have to develop new mechanisms for equitable access.

7. Balance between Teaching and Research

The familiar dilemma of striking a balance between teaching and research, particularly in research universities with large undergraduate enrollments, is the focus of attention, both inside of and outside of academe. The issue is extremely complex practically, philosophically, economically, and ethically. The library will experience new and demanding expectations as institutions move to accommodate the appropriate claims of teaching and research.

8. Relationships with Community and Society

Digital technology offers many new opportunities for creating a wider range of relationships with the community and society. But the relationships remain elusive. The university is being urged, in the words of Provost Billy Frye of Emory University, to be "more sensitive to its public responsibility and relationships and less self indulgent," but little is understood about the organizational and economic changes that are necessary to bring institutions to this new level of realization. Universities must articulate what they have to bring to these relationships, as well as their motivations for entering into them. They must also be specific about which segments of the institution are prepared to take part in collaborative efforts.

CONCLUSION

Vision 2010, as a project, drew to a close in July 1996. And, in strict terms of assessing projects, it was less than a success. The scenario-building process used by the management consultant/futurist for the project proved a stumbling block, especially for university administrators. While developing alternative futures for higher education, the participants developed many questions and offered many ideas, but the scenario-building process itself seemed too artificial to apply to their own situations. Perhaps the technique itself was flawed, or perhaps the lack of familiarity with the technique kept many of the participants from taking it seriously.

Nonetheless, the themes that emerged from the discussions have continued to frame the agenda for the Council on Library and Information Resources, and Vision 2010 participants convinced us that we must pay sustained attention to them. The challenge is to analyze the probable new environment and to influence the directions libraries and archives will take as they collaborate with information technologists on future information delivery systems. The themes and their implications include:

1. New Literacy

Universities must accommodate the different learning styles of individuals. University presidents, in particular, were convinced that visual literacy will be an important addition to learning, teaching, and research in the 21st century. Faculty also report that undergraduate students, in particular, are inclined to work with electronic resources exclusively. Does this combination of factors mean that the massive collections in research libraries will be used less and less frequently? What kinds of information resources will be needed by future generations of students and scholars? CLIR may be able to shed light on the problem by commissioning a study of how the digital environment affects teaching and learning.

2. Institutional Competition

Higher education's monopoly on credentialing is threatened as commercial enterprises and professional societies use digital technology to offer alternative avenues to certification. Distance education programs can be offered by any institution willing to make the investment in technology, and established hierarchies of institutional prestige are thereby questioned. We must go beyond individual opinions to a careful, thoughtful consideration of the appropriate role of higher education in society. A committee within the Association of American Universities is exploring a modification to the tenure process by decoupling editorial review and publication. Libraries can make a contribution to this effort by establishing a secure, reliable method of digital preservation. CLIR is in the process of setting forth the requirements for digital archives, but the cooperation of many partners, both not-for-profit and commercial, will be necessary to assure long-term preservation of "certified" scholarly works.

3. Stability

Some of the Vision 2010 participants considered the digital signal as a prime liberator breaking down barriers of time, place, and institutional affiliation and spawning virtual communities; others saw in it the power to create new outlets for faculty individuality and creativity within the institutional structure. Most agreed that only flexible and adaptive institutions would survive.

For CLIR, the important task is to provide information about managing information resources in a way that allows for flexibility and adaptation on the part of the university. A group of university administrators, economists, and library directors has begun to develop an Investments in Information project that will produce a model for universities to use in determining where the investments are being made in information resources on a campus, with some guidelines for analyzing the effects of those investments.

4. Finances

Without exception, the Vision 2010 participants identified finances as the primary force in determining the future of universities. Their discussions ranged over declining public esteem and support for higher education, demands for accountability, and the substantial investment costs of digital technology. More research and analysis of these issues are needed. In this area, CLIR can help by providing information, but the responsibility for increasing accountability and undertaking strategic planning will be largely on the shoulders of individual institutions.

Despite all of the projections that digital technology will level the playing field for universities, the participants in the Vision 2010 Project were not convinced. Technology can be put to many effective and productive uses, they concluded, but planning by individual institutions for the transformation will be the critical ingredient that determines the shape and form and promotes the general health of higher education and the libraries that serve it. Colleges and universities may properly think of themselves as citizens of the larger polity of higher education, but if each does not first set its own institutional house in order, it can be of little use to its fellows or contribute to the communal enterprise in which all are engaged and all have a stake.

16

The Information Resources Professional

BRIAN L. HAWKINS AND PATRICIA BATTIN

An important dimension of the challenge facing our campuses is the inadequate supply of information resource leaders. Higher education desperately needs leaders who can integrate the formerly compartmentalized responsibilities of libraries and information technology divisions and assume an expanded role in the management and allocation of these important resources in support of the institutional mission. Implicit in any technological transformation is the need for ongoing education, training, and skill development for both information providers and information users. The rapidity of change and the increasing complexity of digital technology and its information products further complicate the situation, since such programs must be designed for an unknown future and a short life-span. Digital technology continues to pose fundamental challenges to the academic and financial organization and management of higher education. The reliance on traditionally defined institutional responsibilities and—in the case of the library—on a structured postgraduate professional degree to supply continuing leadership to meet those responsibilities, as if they were unchanging, is no longer valid.

As more and more information has become available in electronic format, formerly distinct organizational responsibilities have overlapped and blurred, creating costly duplication for institutions and frustration for users. During the past decade, digital information and communications technologies have created an urgent need for new relationships among librarians and their information technology counterparts. At the same time, the increasing scholarly use of information technology continues to influence pedagogical and research methodologies in a manner that requires the skilled collaboration of librarians and information technology specialists. Decisions that affect the provision of information services to students and scholars must now involve librarians, technology specialists, faculty members, and key administrators responsible for the allocation of academic and financial resources.

The shortage of talented individuals to fill these newly defined leadership positions on campuses is acute. In response to persistent financial stringencies and the perception that library schools were slow to adapt to change, some universities closed their library schools, while others began to fundamentally restructure their traditionally conservative approaches to librarianship. In contrast to the historic and relatively static educational program for librarians, there has never been a clear career path for the role of chief technology officer, a position that has drawn talent from the ranks of technologists, faculty members, and professional administrators. The traditional patterns of preparation are not adequate to the new age of information and technology, though the demand is at its highest point.

Although the changes occurring in some library schools are welcome, it will take ten to fifteen years until the graduates of these innovative programs have the experience to assume major leadership roles in our colleges and universities. Consequently, people already in the pipeline need to make a major commitment to their own personal and professional development to prepare them for the challenges posed by our campuses, and institutions must reorganize traditionally compartmentalized functions to enable the new leaders to effectively manage the demands of a volatile mixture of knowledge resources in a variety of formats and media.

With higher education in the midst of the greatest restructuring it has ever experienced, it is not surprising that the two major information service units—the library and the information technology organization—are being closely scrutinized. Over the last ten to fifteen years, both have gone through wrenching changes. Neither of these units can continue business as usual. The unbelievable inflationary increases in the costs of journals have decimated the acquisitions budgets of our libraries, just as the explosion of knowledge, the limitations of space, and the influx of new technology and its associated support structures have put enormous strains on the larger campus budget. There are no solutions to these problems *within the traditional organizational structure*. We must reconceive the overall information and service strategies of our campuses in a manner that incorporates continuous change as a way of life and is unconstrained by the historical legacies of institutional organization. To draw from the work of Peter Drucker, a *transformation* of our institutions is called for. It is critical to recognize that, while transformation may begin with reconceptualizing the functions of libraries and information technology divisions, such change must go hand-in-hand with institutional reorganization and a concerted effort to develop professional leadership in this new realm.

The information resource (IR) professional who is qualified to lead our campuses through these difficult times, both today and in the future, must have an appreciation of the historical, cultural, and technical roles of all information resource functions. In recent years, we have acknowledged an ever-increasing interdependency between the library and computing, as well as among other information service providers who support media services, telecommunications, the print shop, and the classroom needs of the institution.

HISTORICAL PERSPECTIVE

Despite widespread reluctance to relinquish traditional concepts of library and information technology divisions, the responsibilities of these areas have been substantially changing over the past several decades. The old roles are much too narrow. The contemporary IR professional needs to develop a much broader and more inclusive responsibility for the various information resource functions, and unprecedented individual commitment to develop new skills is essential. But the legacies of turf and professional credentials have seriously impeded progress. A brief review of the metamorphosis of librarians and technology specialists into today's information resource professional reveals a startling similarity in process. Librarians enjoyed a centuries-long period of relative stasis before the advent of 20th-century information technology turned incremental change into transforming change. The metamorphosis occurred through four phases which can be characterized as periods during which information providers functioned as follows: technical do-ers, service providers, resource managers, and overseers of integrated resources.

Technical Do-ers: "Here's what I have"

Until the advent of electronic technology, librarians offered printed materials. Technology specialists initially supplied terminal access to mainframe computers. The professional librarian/specialist was responsible for maintaining the infrastructure, managing the operation, and supervising a centrally allocated budget. The characteristics of the printed book defined the nature of instruction, scholarly research, professional qualifications, library operations, and relatively primitive concepts of service, including the chaining of books and restricted service hours for security purposes. In the same manner, the characteristics of mainframe computers and hard-wired terminals shaped the skills and mental outlook of technology specialists.

Service Providers: "What do you want?"

Although the movement into the second phase occurred much earlier in time for librarians, the process of change is remarkably similar in both circumstances. As the demands of readers became more sophisticated, a customer service orientation developed with a focus on sustaining a consistent set of services and developing a broader system orientation beyond those controlled by the service providers, for example, "my library." Librarians recognized the need for universal schemes extending beyond a local collection for the organization of knowledge and began to require bibliographic and disciplinary specializations as part of the professional training. As the demands of computer users matured and equipment capabilities expanded, computer specialists developed a "systems" orientation beyond "my mainframe computer." In both areas, those with increasing administrative responsibility realized that growing complexity made it impossible to be an expert on all issues. The individual manager must know the key issues, have a generalized working knowledge of all relevant areas, and depend upon a community of experts for advice.

Resource Managers: "What are we doing?"

A significant change began to occur in the decade of the 1990s, as more choices and options became available. The information professional in both areas became much more aware of the need to manage people, technology, services, and information itself, all of which are encompassed under the broad umbrella of information resources. As financial demands grew and budgets became ever tighter, strong fiscal and budgetary skills became necessary. With knowledge now widely available in a variety of formats and media, formerly clear demarcations of responsibility blurred, and the need for internal and external collaboration markedly increased. The characteristics of digital technology demanded an ability to deal with capital planning and staff development, as well as the identification and forecasting of academic needs and priorities. Especially in the last decade or so, an enormous new resource infrastructure has emerged on campus, requiring prudent and sophisticated management skills from the leaders of both the IT organization and the library. But perhaps most importantly, this phase witnessed a dawning recognition that the role of the professional is not solely about books or technology but rather about the use of these resources in support of learning, instruction, and research.

Overseers of Integrated Resources: "What should be we doing?"

The current demands for leadership of information resources require all of the skills and roles from the previous phases, but also require that one be a generalist, a boundary spanner, and a partner in the broad institutional schema. The new leader must be literate in multiple languages, including fund accounting, teaching loads, research funding, legal contracts and liabilities, social policies, disciplinary specialties, government policies, scholarly and commercial publishing, fund-raising, and other academic and business lexicons. The focus is on the transformation of the university and the elimination of barriers to the optimal use of technology in support of instruction and scholarship. Rather than be limited to a technically specialized compartment in the institution, the information professional must have the ability to participate actively in setting institutional goals, to budget to the mission, and to appreciate and manage diverse cultures and constantly changing user needs. The following suggestions are illustrative of the kinds of changes necessary to develop current leadership and a talent-pool for the future.

DEVELOP A NEW MINDSET

IR professionals must change the mindset they use in approaching the problems faced in their areas of responsibility, and they have to do things differently. The IR professional needs to be able to define and demonstrate how information resources are integrated into the institutional mission. Just being able to administer or manage the library or the IT organization and its associated resources is no longer sufficient. Instead of accepting the institutional goals and listening to the loudest faculty committee, the new IR professional must be an active participant in the discussion and help other institutional leaders understand the complexities of information resources, service delivery, the technology, and the information demands of the community. The new IR professional must also learn the issues and concerns of these other constituencies. These changes are really no different from those called for throughout our society, as organizations reshape and reengineer themselves. The IR leader of the future needs to become more of a generalist, a more eclectic member of the university community, and a person who can span the boundaries of the various subunits on campus. The role of this new professional must transcend the traditional "stovepipe" structures and fiefdoms.

IR managers need to shape the discussion about how to budget to the institutional mission. What is the mission? How does the role of information, or the role of technology, fit into what the institution is trying to accomplish? This redefinition of roles requires a level of participation within the institution that emanates from a very different mindset. It means that the mission may require the cessation of traditional services that are no longer relevant. It means adoption of value structures driven from outside the IR units, rather than from within. The change means giving up exclusive control of these resources, and it means more actively sharing control with other segments of the community. The critical mindset is that the information resources needs of the campus must be fully integrated into the institution's strategic directions and mission—after broad campus discussion.

The role of the IR professional is not about books, and it is not about technology! It is about support of the comprehensive academic enterprise. It is only when this new mindset is fully adopted that IR professionals will be welcomed to the table where the "real" decision-making of the institution occurs. Only then will IR professionals be perceived as partners in the academic process rather than administrators of some specialized support unit.

APPRECIATE THE DIFFERENCES

Although it makes sense to have greater coordination and coherence between the library and IT functions, one must understand that these two professions have grown from very different backgrounds and cultures. Furthermore, the underlying values and approaches which often characterize these two groups are often in conflict, and, instead of being a source of mutual growth and learning, these differences more often than not have created barriers and challenges to effective cooperation.

Information resource professionals must move out of the current pattern of a restricted cultural view, all too often characterized by mutual contempt. The new professional in this field has to understand that the current cultures of both librarians and IT professionals have valid points of view, and these different perspectives need to be brought together. Professionals in one area need to learn the "business" of professionals in the other area. Whether through concentrated study, internships, cross appointments, or joint committee work, efforts need to be made to value the differences, the strengths, and the perspectives that the other professional group has to bring to the table. These new professionals have to understand what the other group contributes, to value that contribution, and not to fall prey to stereotypes. Perhaps the most critical and obvious starting point is when professionals in each field begin to accept the validity and integrity of the concerns of the other related professions.

Currently, a variety of biases and prejudices exist in libraries and IT organizations about the other group. Professionals in the information service fields have a real obligation to the future of higher education to address these issues and recognize not only that they need each other but that they need the involvement of scholars and students as well. New technology is bringing increased interdependency in higher education. While there is a recognition that librarians and technologists have to work more closely together, there is also a deep, visceral division that must be overcome as these professionals begin to see each other in very different ways, recognizing what each brings to the partnership. Although this recognition is threatening to many, because it implies the need for changing organizational structures and erasing territorial boundaries, a new level of cooperation is essential to enable our institutions to cope with the transformational pressures facing them today.

REDEFINE AND ELIMINATE HISTORICAL BOUNDARIES

One of the critical challenges to transformational change is the issue of "turf." If this problem is to be overcome, new decision-making processes that cross boundaries need to be sought out and developed. Instead of defining a project or initiative as one's own territory, the more appropriate questions should be: "What is it that the students and faculty need? What is it that the institution needs?" These more basic questions keep the focus on the mission and are likely to be an important way to unify loyalties that have been traditionally divided because of compartmentalized organizational units. This change in orientation is needed throughout the institution.

There is great value in bringing the different skill sets of different IR constituencies to bear on a common problem of the academy, but, increasingly, the contributions of one's scholarly colleagues must be incorporated as well. Faculty must work with IR professionals in ways that have neither been invited nor sought in the past. The incorporation of an increased faculty perspective brings an in-depth knowledge of the discipline; an understanding of how scholars frame questions, seek information, and organize their research methods; and an understanding of how different cognitive styles relate to teaching and learning. These perspectives are needed in the discussions to define the information resources—their content and formats and media—that are to be provided on a campus.

These decisions can no longer be intelligently made solely by professional librarians and/or technologists. The control over the decision-making process must be broadly shared, and this transformation will require organizations to develop new decision-making mechanisms to modify previously ordained structures, just as it will compel information resource professionals to enlarge their circle of colleagues.

MANAGE EXPECTATIONS

One of the most difficult challenges facing IR professionals is the establishment of a baseline of services in support of the institutional mission. In both IT divisions and libraries, staff are often called upon to provide everything that is requested by anybody who wants it. This demand-driven model can no longer be accommodated, much less sustained. Limits need to be defined in terms of the bundle of services included in tuition payments and faculty appointments. Resources cannot be effectively managed unless the limits are understood and unless a baseline of expectations has been clearly defined. These limits need to be both understood and accepted by the community, because while information may be growing exponentially, institutional resources to support this information are not. The administration and the faculty are probably more loathe than librarians and technologists to accept this reality, but failure to have this campus discussion will seriously curtail any planned and orderly provision of services within a coherent structure, and reactive and inconsistent responses will be the order of the day.

In addition to the business and technical skills required, the information resource manager needs to develop skills in "salesmanship" to "sell" new strategies to student, faculty, and administrative constituencies. These significant changes represent a new primary job responsibility of becoming a manager of expectations.

THINK DISCONTINUOUSLY

The primary attention of an information resource professional in the future will necessarily be on the process of discontinuous change. What are the changes destroying our ability to cope using our traditional practices? What are the activities that cross over traditional boundaries and, hence, are not getting appropriate attention? What are the major issues lurking over the horizon? A longer-term, more anticipatory approach will be critically needed. Instead of merely reacting to events, issues must be anticipated to the degree possible, and then presented to the campus community in order to frame the campus discussion and shape the new information and service environments available for students and faculty.

It is easy to postulate that people should "think discontinuously." It is much harder to actually do it. When one is an active part of an organization and caught up in the pressure of daily activities, it is difficult to see the currents of change. In a turbulent environment, a leader finds the time to contemplate what he or she is doing and why. The leader doesn't extrapolate from the past, but instead tries to visualize different scenarios for the future, studies the environment, and applies data to support one of these scenarios. The leader who can think discontinuously anticipates the future and challenges the historical assumptions inhibiting the possible realization of desired outcomes. The quality of such predictions will be a function of how well such figures are grounded in a thorough understanding of the current milieu; how broadly they scan the external environment; how committed they are to constant self-improvement, life-long learning and personal growth; and how willing they are to explore abandoning historically cherished values and skills that have enabled them to adjust to the world around them.

DEVELOP THE NEXT GENERATION OF LEADERSHIP

Information resource professionals in the 21st century must focus on professional development to an unprecedented degree. They must, as well, recognize that the demand for changing skill sets may not reflect traditional assumptions. It is the responsibility of each professional to analyze what skills are needed, not what skills are currently held. Enlightened self-interest is imperative, because one's job might well disappear because of the level of change likely to be experienced. It is threatening to realize that one's current skill-set may be of little use and, indeed, a liability. Pressures to acquire new skills exist at all levels throughout the organization. Specialized skills have been the source of security for many IR professionals, who say to themselves: "I know how to perform a given function," or "I know a given area better than anybody else." Yet the demand for that area may be eliminated, or, at the very least, changed at a rapid rate. Finally, it should be pointed out that there is a curious paradox associated with IR leadership: the path to success has always been characterized by the development of specialized skills, but the path to leadership requires the skills of a generalist.

A critically important responsibility for both the institution and the individual manager is the continuing development of information resource professionals. The manager of IR resources has the responsibility to ask certain questions in order to adequately staff the changing functions in the college or university. What are the processes needed to change, develop, or refine one's skill-sets? How much of the budget in the IR units should be committed to professional development to improve the abilities of institutional personnel to cope with these changes?

An additional responsibility accompanying the effort to transform and develop another generation of leaders is mentoring, a key obligation of leadership today. More importantly, it is mentoring in a different frame of reference that is so desperately needed to create a future cadre of transformational leaders. Senior-level IR professionals need to look forward and to anticipate what skills and abilities will be demanded in the future, including the ability to think discontinuously in order to give the younger generation an opportunity to identify and learn new skills and conceptual abilities for the 21st century.

CONCLUSION

The changing role of the information resource professional requires more than just increasing one's sensitivity to others, more than an improved set of management skills; it requires a broader orientation—a change in mindset. These concerns are not about turf but about viewpoint, and that viewpoint must constantly refocus on a commitment to the mission of higher education and the role that information, information services, and information technology can contribute to that crucial mission. Enlightened leadership on these issues is the responsibility of information professionals. However, if IR professionals do not assume this role, presidents and provosts will—by default. The needs of the campus will be better served if those individuals most knowledgeable about information issues initiate, lead, and facilitate these critical discussions. The provision of information resources—through a print, electronic, or technical infrastructure—combined with the power of digital technology must enhance, not define, our educational mission. The professional obligation of information resource professionals is nothing less than to participate in the definition of the 21st-century institution of higher education.

17

Leadership in a Transformational Age

PATRICIA BATTIN

Let me exhort everyone to do their utmost
to think outside and beyond our present
circle of ideas. For every idea gained is
a hundred years of slavery remitted.

—Richard Jefferies
The Story of My Heart (1883)

Writing on leadership and managerial style from the perspective of past experience in an age of technological transformation and upheaval is an exercise in self-deception. To engage in that time-honored practice and to dispense advice and wisdom accumulated from decades of managing library and information services in a relatively stable and predictable environment that no longer exists is useless to those who must grapple with today's challenges. Even the success stories of the recent past in managing the onset of technological change are of little use to those who must lead the transformation of the historically compartmentalized information systems into a seamless and coordinated multimedia array of 21st-century information resources. The most beneficial exercise may be to speculate instead on the changing nature of leadership required for a discontinuous future.

Perhaps one of the most devastating impacts of digital information technology on the higher education community, arguably the last bastion of institutional conservatism, is the imperative to change the nature of the very organizational and financial structures that have created and supported the existing strength and vitality of American higher education. The most difficult challenge faced in an era of transformational change is the recognition that our past strengths will become our liabilities if we do not act in time. It has become painfully evident that the promise of a rapid, money-saving electronic transformation of research, teaching, and learning has been made prematurely and oversimplified by technology gurus and visionaries whose interests are focused on the potential of information technology rather than on the specialized information requirements of working scholars in a variety of disciplines. The entrenched and resistant organizational and managerial bureaucracies of higher education and the particular leadership talents necessary to effect such a significant transformation have been largely ignored. Traditional budgetary procedures have supported initial investments without recognizing the unrelenting need for continuing hardware and software replacements and upgrades; technical access continues to be widely enhanced at the expense of intellectual access and archival reliability; the capacity to handle the rapidly increasing volume of demand as users adapt to new options and services has quickly become inadequate; the costs and technical complexity of digitizing existing print resources have been seriously underestimated; and requirements for the continuing educational opportunities for both information users and providers have been vastly misunderstood. The comfortable assumption that each new technology or management style will substitute for another in a one-size-fits-all formula entirely misreads the complex interactions of technology with the human mind.

Leading a transformational process and managing the fluid and chaotic transition period requires skills vastly different from those needed for ensuring "administrative law and order" in a stable, predictable environment. Rules no longer apply, boundaries disappear daily, ambiguity prevails, and the old cliche "the foreseeable future" is of no use at all. Where our spheres of responsibilities used to have well-defined borders, the only boundary is the new frontier. Effective leadership will require an extraordinary ability to maintain a delicate and continually changing balance in the management of technical, financial, and human resources to serve the academic mission of our universities and colleges. Print-on-paper technology enabled us to build the huge bureaucracies we call "research libraries," "information technology divisions," and "universities." The characteristics of print-on-paper shaped our research methodologies and concepts of scholarly services, permitted selective autonomy or collaboration on our own terms, and enabled our bureaucracies to become less responsive to the needs of our clientele as we turned our interests inward to managing the operation as an end in itself.

A major characteristic of networked digital technology is its simultaneous capacity for decentralization and for the central coordination essential to ensuring broad and unencumbered access. Effective leadership in the 21st century must manage that creative tension. We shall have to make judicious decisions that blend the strengths of the past, the demands of the present, and the uncertainty of the future, and we shall have to balance them continually from both local and interinstitutional perspectives within an organizational structure designed to support the past. The mission of librarianship has always been to preserve the past, serve the present, and create the future. Until the advent of digital information technologies, creating the future essentially implied an extension of the status quo within the traditional organizational structure. In a digital environment, however, new patterns for funding collaborative enterprises, network compatibility and hardware/software interoperability, institution-wide access for site-independent information resources, integrated administrative data systems, shared development of hardware/software with the corporate sector and other institutions, collaborative preservation and archiving responsibilities all pose managerial challenges that can no longer be isolated or compartmentalized within comfortable definitions of turf and authority.

Books and paper will not disappear. Digital capacities continue to be add-ons rather than simple replacements. But what must change are our human systems for organizing, managing, and financing continuing access to knowledge, be it through books, electronic databases, or lectures in the classroom. We cannot graft digital technology onto our existing system of social organization—the very fabric of our society—which has been designed around the characteristics of print-on-paper technology. We must learn to manage hybrid systems in which the newcomer—information technology—will determine the nature and design of our systems for managing scholarly information. We will have to learn how to distinguish and manage the strengths and weaknesses of a broad spectrum of technologies. Higher education will undoubtedly live in a hybrid environment for some time to come. The challenge will be to utilize the power of technology to enhance the intellectual mission of institutions rather than allow the mission to be defined by the technology.

Endless and incessant visions of the digital future surround us, but few voice the threatening proposition that to achieve the vision we must first destroy the familiar barriers to true collaboration and sharing of responsibility by taking steps that will revolutionize our traditional assumptions and managerial comfort level. The greatest psychic distance in the world may well be the gap between envisioning the future and realizing the vision. The obligation of leadership is to translate the talk into effective action.

The most successful leadership styles will be those that respond to the new reality with a blend of bold leadership, informed risk-taking, widespread consultation, and consensus building. Too often, events have overtaken effective action and resulted in costly missed opportunities because of drawn-out consensus processes that worked in a low-technology environment but now serve to excuse inaction. The zeal to establish templates and formulas for management style has encouraged both consensus and authoritarian decision-making—as management techniques—to become mindless ends in themselves, when they should be tools to be used in achieving the necessary balance. Leaders of the transition—those who will make it happen at every level of the organization—will need acute powers of analysis, abundant common sense, vibrant creativity, reasoned judgment, and a passionate commitment to the mission and goals of the extended higher education community.

A major obligation of leadership in a time of wrenching transition is the active development of the successor generation. There is no time to wait for the academy to debate the educational needs for an uncertain future. A major casualty of the chaotic transition period of the past two decades has been the practice of mentoring in the information professions. Mentoring in the library profession was a specialty of the "old boys' network" and served admirably to provide a continuing leadership cadre in an era of shared assumptions, prejudices, and stability. With the opening of opportunities to the formerly excluded, new vitality and talent entered the system. Unfortunately, the tradition of mentorship, rather than the manner in which it was practiced, was viewed with suspicion and largely abandoned. A primary leadership responsibility is the assurance of a talented successor generation capable of handling future challenges. In years past, that meant bringing up the young in one's own image. Today, it means identifying talented new individuals from unprecedented sources and attracting them into an ever-changing and expanding profession, helping those with traditional credentials and experience to develop the qualities necessary for success in an environment of ambiguity, and providing productive learning experiences that build on existing strengths and minimize weaknesses. It means the nurturing of a new generation of leaders who view their responsibilities in a totally different frame of reference. We are not producing future leaders by keeping the younger generation locked within the outmoded organizational schemes of the past.

The two professional obligations that are most critical today to the financial and intellectual survival of academic institutions are diversity and leadership. Diversity is imperative, because it is both morally right and, as the traditional talent pool continues to shrink, demographically smart. Equally imperative is the assurance of leadership succession to guide our institutions through a period in which there is no longer a stable, bureaucratic structure to compensate for the lack of leadership. The two best methods to achieve these goals are affirmative action (to seek out talent wherever it may be) and formal mentoring programs.

Affirmative action programs have broken open the formerly exclusive circle of opportunity, but well-developed mentoring programs are essential to fulfill the goal of ensuring a continuing flow of talent and creativity from a broad population. But neither affirmative action without mentoring nor mentoring without the assurance of equal opportunity will create the leadership cadre so desperately needed in a transitional society.

Affirmative action programs are under serious attack today, largely because they are widely viewed as preference and quota programs rather than as activities designed to level the playing field by seeking out qualifications and competence beyond traditional stereotypes and perceptions that tend to reinforce the status quo. Affirmative action does not mean the disenfranchisement of any segment of society, but the extension of the franchise to all. There has been much concern among those who have not experienced the widespread denial of opportunity in earlier times and who consider affirmative action programs to confer an unwanted stigma. In an imperfect world, a stigmatized opportunity is better than no opportunity at all! Each generation gains from the contributions made by its predecessors. Some day, social programs may not be needed to broaden our horizons, but that time has not yet arrived.

Mentoring programs in higher education seem to have lost their popularity. The struggle for individual and institutional survival apparently leaves no energy for developing future leaders. Perhaps the perception that mentorship was practiced in an exclusive manner caused general abandonment of the basic concept.

It is relatively easy for the individual manager to recognize the need for new skill sets and continuing education to develop a broader understanding of management techniques. In many instances, it is a question of finding the funds to provide opportunities for one's staff to attend seminars, workshops, and institutes. But mentorship is something quite different, much more demanding and without an immediate payoff—and possibly without a future benefit to a specific institution or to the individual mentor.

Mentorship represents an individual commitment to seeking out, identifying, and developing in a variety of ways the leaders of the future—people who have the creativity, the intellect, the conceptual skills, and the personal qualities necessary to provide true transformational leadership in the challenging contemporary environment of higher education.

- It means surrounding oneself with the most intelligent colleagues, despite the covert—and often overt—threat to one's own sense of security.
- It means urging others to develop their true potential, even when that potential surpasses one's own.
- It means delegating—but not abdicating—and being available to work through problems together, to advise, to support, and to accept ultimate responsibility. It is to be a coach rather than a commander.
- It means the conscious tailoring to individuals of opportunities that require them to stretch, and it means helping them through the opportunities and past any fear of failure.
- It means recognizing strengths and weaknesses: building on the strengths and strengthening the weaknesses through appropriate actions and opportunities.
- And particularly in today's world, where we know the future will be discontinuous, it means not "doing as I have done" but recognizing that the uncertain future will require different leadership abilities and having the courage to urge the younger generation to develop those styles with no assurance of their legitimacy or potential for success.

The "digital library" is an instructive example of several phenomena—the clash between the new and the old, the need to explore beyond one's own set of ideas, assumptions, and talent pool, and the challenge to reconcile different points of view in the interests of the institutional mission. To the computer scientists at the National Science Foundation (NSF), who created a multimillion-dollar program to encourage research into the concept of "the digital library," the term signifies the technological infrastructure. To librarians who hope to apply for the grants offered by the NSF, the term implies the storage and management of digital information. To college and university administrators seeking to restrain library costs, it means cheap and easy ways to provide access to knowledge resources traditionally held in libraries. And to scholars in the humanities, it means the demise of the book as the primary information medium. The "digital library" is all of this—and more. The use of the term itself is dangerously misleading because it imprisons us in an image of the past and illustrates, through its familiar connotations of turf and containment, either an inability or an unwillingness to accept the inevitability of unprecedented collaboration, shared expertise and responsibility, and new integrated working relationships.

The military establishment is often criticized for basing its strategies in a new conflict on the lessons learned from the previous war, rather than assessing the new situation from the perspective of a constantly changing reality. Those responsible for the management of information resources are also vulnerable to the charge of "fighting the last war." Despite our daily exposure to the enormous transformational power of digital information technologies and to the growing dysfunction of our environment as we try to stuff those technologies into our traditional management structures, we continue to define the battlefront as one between libraries and information technology centers. That stage passed some years ago. In today's environment, the simple merger of libraries and information technology center is a fruitless attempt to continue the traditional pattern of university organization rather than to begin the challenging and unsettling process of conceptualizing a whole new dynamic for managing information resources. It may well be that the next several decades will require fluid and changing organizational structures that combine both primary responsibilities for some functions with more broadly shared decision-making mechanisms for others, in search of a productive balance. Managing information technology will undoubtedly reflect the characteristics of the technology itself—lack of stasis, unpredictable change, reconciling contradictory capabilities, serving multiple audiences, and creating new interdependencies. One of the most difficult attributes for 21st-century leaders will be the ability to balance an understanding of the values, strengths, and vitality of our system of higher education as it has evolved to date with the capacity to conceptualize and bring into being a new system that integrates the strengths of the past with the promise of the future.

18

Developing Performance Measures for Library Collections and Services

SUSAN ROSENBLATT

INTRODUCTION

"The true university of these days is a collection of books."[1] Thomas Carlyle's evocation of the role of the library as university still resonates. The library's iconic status within the university: as its heart, the center of intellectual activity, a repository of the record of human knowledge and achievement, a laboratory for the creation of new knowledge persists. Yet at the same time, there is not only growing doubt about whether this symbolic vision of the library can be sustained, but also active questioning of its legitimacy as a vision for the library in today's world. The explosion in the creation of new knowledge, rapidly increasing rates of publication, escalating costs of scholarly and scientific journals, and visions of the potential of technology-based information to render traditional libraries less necessary, engender fundamental questions about the proper role of the university library: what constitutes relevant measures of its effectiveness and how should appropriate levels of funding be determined. Traditional measures of library quality rest largely on the size of collections, yet statistical evidence in many libraries indicates that only a small proportion of most research collections is actually used. If print collections are little used, expanding information output makes it impossible for libraries to aspire to comprehensive collections, and networked information allows scholars increasingly to do research without coming into the physical library, then how might the university define li-

---

[1] Thomas Carlyle, *Lectures on Heroes, Hero-Worship, and the Heroic in History* (Oxford: Clarendon Press, 1920), 147.

brary excellence? As a practical matter, what kinds of quantitative and qualitative evidence might be gathered to measure the quality of the research library and how well it is performing?

TRADITIONAL MEASURES OF RESEARCH LIBRARY QUALITY

Traditionally, research library quality has been measured by inputs, including such factors as size of collection, acquisition rates for new information (volumes added and serial subscriptions maintained), annual expenditures for library materials, size of staff, and operations budget. The primary resource for determining research library rankings is the annual report from the Association of Research Libraries (ARL).[2] The published report documents statistical measures in eighteen areas, including, in addition to the factors mentioned above, workload measures for interlibrary lending. Supplementary workload measurements not published in the annual report include circulation, library instruction, and reference transactions. ARL's algorithm for ranking university research libraries is heavily weighted towards collection size (an historical feature) and current expenditures. Thus, as explained by ARL, the ranking primarily reflects resource deployment rather than performance. Although expressly not intended as an indicator of quality, the ARL index is nevertheless is widely cited, featured prominently in the *Chronicle of Higher Education,* and commonly held to be an indirect measure, if not of library quality *per se,* at least of institutional commitment. Implicitly, the ARL statistics reflect the belief that the size of a university's library collection and the library's budget bear an important relationship to the quality of the university itself—its teaching and research programs.

Another measure of collections strength, the RLG Conspectus, was widely regarded during the 1980s and early 1990s as a reputable mechanism to assess the quality of library collections. Simply put, the Conspectus tended to rank collections on their degree of comprehensiveness rather than on their utility, and, although quantitative measures such as citation analysis were used to substantiate the ratings assigned by individual libraries, these rankings were largely subjective. Use of the Con-

---

[2] ARL Statistics (Washington, D.C.: Association of Research Libraries). For an explanation of the ranking algorithm, see URL: *http://www.lib.virginia.edu/socsci/arl/test-arl/arlindex.html*

spectus as a measurement of collections has declined during the past few years, perhaps implicitly reflecting growing skepticism that collection size or degree of comprehensiveness are, in themselves, adequate measures either of the collection's quality or of its benefit to the university community.

In addition to the ARL measures, "utility" measures of library collections are increasingly used as a basis for evaluation. The types of measurements that can generally gathered from automated circulation systems can document intensity or frequency of use, queuing for access to materials, academic discipline of users of various parts of the collection, or numbers and types of interlibrary borrowing requests. The results of these measurements can then be employed to determine or modify collection budgets among various academic departments, to select materials for remote rather than on-campus storage, and to make decisions about areas in which access agreements might substitute for ownership. A recent study by Bruce Kingma[3] provides methodology for determining when access rather than ownership of journals is more cost effective. But these measures of use and cost do not actually measure quality. A difficulty with most utility measures is that they neglect, or cannot measure, the qualitative effects of on-site browsability in large research library collections; nor can they assess intangible factors associated with the quality of scholarship or scholarly productivity. Is there a qualitative difference between a collection developed just in case it might be needed by a scholar and the availability of rapid access to items that a scholar decides are needed. How might that difference be measured?

Studies of information-seeking behavior[4] describe a recursive process of discovery in which scholars initiate research through a process of skimming and scanning sources of information, discussing the question with colleagues, and browsing in the library. The initial inquiry process leads to the development and classification of more highly structured questions, and these questions then result in a more formal process of research in-

---

[3] Bruce R. Kingma, "The Economics of Access versus Ownership: The Costs and Benefits of Access to Scholarly Articles via Interlibrary Loan and Journal Subscriptions." URL: *http://www-clr.stanford.edu/clr/econ/kingma.html* (January 27, 1997).

[4] See, for example, David Ellis, "A Behavioural Approach to Information Retrieval System Design," *Journal of Documentation* 45:3(September 1989):171–212; also Ellis, David, Deborah Cox, and Katherine Hall, "A Comparison of the Information Seeking Patterns of Researchers in the Physical and Social Sciences," *Journal of Documentation* 49:4 (December 1993): 356–369.

cluding reading, taking detailed notes on facts and ideas, outlining, following through on links among various sources, and additional skimming and scanning of information resources. During both the initial and intermediate stages of research, the scholar proceeds from source to source, chaining bits of information, following up on ideas and threads of previous research, and verifying information previously found. As the research process proceeds, information is ever more systematically extracted, synthesized, and questioned. In short, the scholar works from source to source, not in linear sequence, but in an every-widening ring of reference, citations, and discoveries; the research library has traditionally provided the environment in which much of this discovery process can take place.

Anecdotal evidence from individual scholars corroborates the research evidence. Rolland Stevens[5] describes the scholar's work thus:

> The library use of the social scientist and humanist is seldom restricted to the request of material by author and title. When he leaves the well-beaten paths of literature searching and explores byways in the hope of finding further information which may solve his problem or attempts to read widely for general background, he makes demands on the library . . . If this kind of library use is necessary to research, then it is essential that the social scientist or humanist have ready access to all the literature that is of potential use to him . . . Any . . . library policy which threatens to separate the scholar from his books ought to be re-examined in the light of his need of immediate access to research resources.

David Paisey[6] describes the process similarly:

> The precise mechanics of the process of humanities research in libraries are little understood and studied by planners, a fundamental gap in their equipment. This can lead to inadequate library structures based on interlending strategies in which scholars are seen as requiring single books, or single items of information, rather than related (often remotely related) groups of texts whose composition and configuration cannot be foreseen, with the back-up of limitless secondary materials, current and non-current, any or all of which may be cross-disciplinary.

Although research into information-seeking behavior and reports from scholars themselves both describe the importance of ready availability of a large corpus material to research, most items in research library collections are very little used, and a significant portion of the collections are

---

[5] Rolland Stevens, "The Study of the Research Use of Libraries," *Library Quarterly* 26:(1) (January 1956):41–51.

[6] David Paisey, "Review of *Buch, Bibliothek and geisteswissenschaftliche Forschung* by Bernhard Fabian," *The Library*, Sixth Series 6:3 (September 1984):299.

SUSAN ROSENBLATT

never used, bringing into question the actual value and cost-effectiveness of research library collections that aim at comprehensiveness rather than utility.

Skepticism about size of libraries as a measure of quality is not new. John Henry Newman, who characterized the library as the "embalming of dead genius"[7] also recognized the limitations of that concept, remarking on ". . . the mere multiplication and dissemination of volumes . . . as this most preposterous and pernicious of delusions."[8] More than one hundred years later, Daniel Gore, in his introduction to *Farewell to Alexandria*[9] states: "This collection of essays opens a new era for libraries, taking the first departure in 2,300 years from the durable model conceived by the librarians of Alexandria and endlessly replicated by every succeeding generation of librarians, right down to the present day. The Alexandrian model persists through the unexamined faith that to be good a library *must* be vast and always growing." In that same volume, Ellsworth Mason[10] questions prevalent assumptions about the relationship of size of collections and utility of libraries by summarizing six points derived from statistical data gathered at several libraries. He notes that scholars in many disciplines can successfully conduct research with little use of the library, that science and technology collections are much more heavily used than humanities or social science collections, that recent publications do not account for the overwhelming use of books, that materials that librarians and scholars consider important may be little used, and that improved bibliographic access to information about materials held elsewhere does not greatly increase the volume of interlibrary loans. If twenty years ago, prior to the hyperinflation of the 1980s and 1990s that significantly reduced acquisitions in all of the nation's research libraries and before digital information became widely availabile, collection size was questioned as a measure of quality, how much more complex might be the discussion today?

In contrast, evidence of a relationship between library size and aca-

---

[7] John Henry Newman, "Rise and Progress of Universities," in *Essays and Sketches* (New York: Longmans, Green, 1948),328

[8] John Henry Newman, *The Idea of a University Defined and Illustrated* (Oxford: Clarendon, 1976), I.vi.8

[9] Daniel Gore, *Farewell to Alexandria: Solutions to Space, Growth, and Performance Problems of Libraries.* (Westport, Conn., Greenwood Press, 1976), 3

[10] Ellsworth Mason, "Balbus; or the Future of Library Buildings," in *Farewell to Alexandria: Solutions to Space, Growth, and Performance Problems of Libraries* (Westport, Conn., Greenwood Press, 1976), 22–33.

demic quality was identified in *Assessment of Research-Doctorate Programs in the United States* (Washington, D.C.: National Academy Press, 1982). But the possible causality of the relationship is not tested; it could perhaps rather be associated simply with the resource base of the institutions being studied.

Additional measures of library quality are considered by accreditation bodies, including regional, disciplinary, and professional associations. Although assessment of the library is a key part of the institutional accreditation process, typically the library assessment is not integral to that of the university as a whole; therefore the quantitative and qualitative factors considered during the accreditation process may not adequately measure the contributions that the library makes to the academic programs of the university.[11]

Edward D. Garten provides a good summary of the current standards promulgated by regional commissions as well as disciplinary and professional associations for libraries, information technologies, and academic computing.[12] Garten's summary of the factors considered by the six regional commissions includes the following twelve categories of standards and expectations:

> Access to resources
> Adequacy and appropriateness of staff
> Audiovisual media
> Computing
> Evaluation and outcomes assessment
> Facilities
> Formal agreements with external libraries
> Information literacy and bibliographic instruction
> Linkages across support units
> Off-campus library services
> Resource selection/collection management
> Sufficiency of resources for curricular support

While these expectations extend beyond the collection size and expenditure emphasis of the ARL statistics, at least one half of them pertain

---

[11] See, for example, Ralph A Wolff, "Rethinking Library Self-Studies and Accreditation visits," in Edward D Garten, *The Challenge and Practice of Academic Accreditation; A Sourcebook for Library Administrators* (Westport, Conn.: Greenwood Press, 1994), 125–138.

[12] Edward D. Garten, ibid. See especially Part IV, 139–240.

largely either to resource sufficiency and availability or to adequacy of staff. Moreover, the accreditation bodies require no common methodology for measuring the performance of libraries in these areas.

Another approach to performance measurement is provided by Van House et al.[13] The authors of this handbook describe methodologies to gather quantitative data about various kinds of library performance, including the following:

1. *General User Satisfaction*
2. *Materials Availability and Use*
   a. Circulation
   b. In-library materials use
   c. Total materials use
   d. Materials availability
   e. Requested materials delay
3. *Facilities and Library Use*
   a. User visits
   b. Remote uses
   c. Total uses
   d. Facilities use rates
   e. Service point use
   f. Building use
4. *Information Services*
   a. Reference transactions
   b. Reference satisfaction
   c. On-line search evaluation

A chief benefit of this publication is that it provides easy methodologies for measurement of the factors listed, and can be replicated in order to provide a perspective about library performance over time. A shortcoming is that the work predates widespread introduction of digital library resources and the World Wide Web; thus there are no measures for ascertaining library performance in areas supported by new technologies.

Other efforts to develop performance measures pertain to operational efficiency, particularly in technical services. These measures include such factors as timeliness, accuracy, and cost per unit of work performed.

---

[13] Nancy A. VanHouse, Beth T. Weil, and Charles R. McClure, *Measuring Academic Library Performance: A Practical Approach* (Chicago: American Library Association, 1990).

Generally used to reengineer "back-room" operations to reduce expense, these measures of internal efficiency may be useful in assessing the relative cost-effectiveness of outsourcing such operations rather than performing them in-house. Lacking are commonly agreed upon units of work in the public service operations of libraries: selection, reference, and bibliographic instruction. Thus it has not been easy to compare costs and performance among libraries; nor has it been easy for any individual library to analyze the costs and benefits of alternative models for providing direct services to users.

Clearly, size of collections features prominently in traditional concepts of library quality, although measurements of efficiency and service quality are gaining in importance. Anecdotal evidence from individual scholars cites size and scope of particular collections as major factors contributing to the quality of their research. Yet, statistical evidence in many libraries indicates that only a small proportion of most research collections is actually used. The fundamental question is, What constitutes excellence in library collections and services? The practical question then follows: What quantitative and qualitative evidence can be gathered to measure the quality of the research library—how do we know how well it is performing?

THE SHIFT TO PERFORMANCE MEASURES OF LIBRARY QUALITY

While the information and publication explosion continues unabated, libraries' collection budgets fail to keep pace with inflation in the cost of library materials. Each library's collection represents a declining proportion of the world's output of scholarly information, so all libraries must depend to some extent on access to materials held elsewhere, rendering effectiveness of access an important performance measure complementing collection size. The proliferation of digital resources available over the Internet complicates further the development of performance measures for libraries. Some authors even question the need for a library as mediator or facilitator for digital information, suggesting that search engines, or the information providers individually might replace the functions of the library. If there is a role for the research library in selecting, organizing, providing access to, navigating, or helping faculty and students to use digital information, what might that role be? In other words, how can a research library add value to digital information, and how can the value be measured? How might the eventual availability of significant bodies of scholarly information available on line change the character of the library and its services? What is the relationship of the collections and services comprising the digital library to those of the traditional library? There is too much information for any single library to acquire, and the added burden of reliance on access to other collections and digital information simply adds to the complexity of the system and to the information overload experienced by both students and scholars. If technology raises questions about the library as *place*, and cost and quantity of information render its traditional collecting goals impossible to attain, then what is the role of the library in the university, and how can its effectiveness be judged?

The question for libraries is not dissimilar from the legitimation challenges to higher education at large. These challenges stem from rapidly rising costs and public perceptions that rising costs of higher education[14] are not justified in terms of the quality of education provided to their students. The technology revolution and the information explosion raise important questions not only for the library but also for the processes of teaching and learning. Just as there is too much information for any single library to acquire, or to provide access to; no individual can keep up with the output of information relevant to his or her course of study or research. In an era in which the rate of growth of information increases faster than humans or their institutions can apprehend it and in which technology changes the methods of delivery of that information, traditional assumptions about the mission and roles for both libraries and universities are open to question. If the quality of the library cannot be deduced from the size of its collections, numbers of circulation transactions, or seats available for study, by what measures will we know that it is meeting the needs of students and scholars?

Ralph W. Wolff[15] suggests that the technology revolution and knowledge explosion require that the mission of The Library be revised and

---

[14] "The New U: A Tough Market Is Reshaping Colleges" *Business Week* (December 22, 1997): 96–97, describes the fiscal challenges to higher education thus: "Over the past two decades . . . higher education has failed spectacularly to live within its means. From 1980 to 1994, the most recent year for which Education Dept. Data are available, instructional costs per full-time student at private universities increased 48% in real terms; public universities upped research expenses by 35%. In the same time, though, states reduced real, per student funding to public universities by 22% . . . That has produced an explosion in charges as institutions have sought to close the funding gap."

[15] Ralph A Wolff, "Using the Accreditation Process to Transform the Mission of the Library," *New Directions for Higher Education* 90 (Summer 1995):77–91.

brought into closer relationship to the mission of the university, particularly its teaching mission. For example, what is the role of the library in curriculum development, or in improving student learning? How can the library develop measurements of its effectiveness in teaching, learning, and research? How can the library help students gain "information literacy?" How can it develop "a culture of evidence" in which qualitative and quantitative evidence is gathered and used to evaluate library programs and overall quality? Wolff's work suggests that as the library becomes an integral part of the teaching mission and as digital information challenges its traditional role as primarily a repository of collections, measures of quality, such as collection size, or measures of activity, such as circulation, interlibrary loan, or reference transactions, become increasingly less relevant.

If the Library's role, as integral to research and teaching, defines the library of the future, then it must be evaluated primarily on its direct and indirect contributions to the larger mission of the university. The extent to which the size and nature of the collection contributes to this larger mission needs to be defined differently and measures developed to assess its success.

In his commentary on Newman's *Idea of the University*, Jaroslav Pelikan, echoing Wolff, writes that "the dynamic interrelation of research with teaching, and of both with the acquisition, preservation, and circulation of documents and artifacts applies . . . to libraries. In the future of the university and of the university library, moreover, the network of university and library can only become more intertwined."[16] He emphasizes the role of the library in teaching:

"The nature of the collegiality between library and faculty in undergraduate teaching calls for serious attention . . . even the undergraduate librarian at a university must be something of a research librarian, for it is the librarian's responsibility to build and maintain collections through which each successive generation will be inducted into the process."[17]

Pelikan also describes the role of the library in graduate education and research:

"Professional guidance can come only from subject bibliographers who are sensitive and thoroughly trained and whom research scholars recognize as their peers and colleagues in the raising up of future scholars. Graduate students . . .

---

[16] Jaroslav Pelikan, *The Idea of A University: A Reexamination* (New Haven, Conn.: Yale University Press, 1992), 113.
[17] Ibid., 114–115.

are also more likely, in their work as teachers of undergraduates, to recognize their colleagues in the library as genuine peers."[18]

If the quality of libraries is to be judged on their contributions to teaching, graduate education, and research, how can their performance be measured? The kinds of input and workload data currently collected by libraries do not measure contributions to teaching and learning; neither do measures of user satisfaction. What are the questions that libraries need to be asking about their performance, what data need to be collected; how can they be analyzed, and how can they be used to improve performance? The idea that library quality cannot be separated from the quality of teaching and research implies a fundamentally different role for the library: a more active role.

A more interactive role for the library within the university creates new expectations for the librarian. If librarians were formerly judged on the comprehensiveness of collections built and on the quality of reference services, now the librarian must be judged on the quality of his or her contributions to student learning, to research productivity by scholars, or to graduate education. These expectations constitute a qualitatively different role, one that traditional library education does not prepare librarians to perform.

This change in the mission of the library: from a collection, with services; to a set of programs, drawing on information resources, presents tremendous challenges during a long transition period in which print will be the dominant format for scholarly information. Not only must the idea of "collection" be redefined: what constitutes an adequate collection? What are the relationships among print collections, resources available through resource sharing agreements, and digital information? But now the definition of library is much more than collection, and cannot be separated from the contributions of its staff. The changing definition of the library thus requires that role of the librarian in support of the academic mission also be redefined. What is it that librarians do? How do librarians contribute to the undergraduate learning experience? How do they help the research process? How do they foster information literacy and lifelong learning? How can their contributions be measured?

If the collection no longer defines the library, some may infer a decline of the library's importance within the university. To maintain a signifi-

---

[17] Ibid., 115.

cant role, its relationship to the mission of the university must be more clearly articulated and strengthened and its contributions measured and assessed. The changing relationship between collections and information implies the need for librarians to develop fundamentally new roles within the academy—more active, more integrated, and more accountable.

A shift in perceived role for the library creates dual challenges for the library administrator. There are internal management questions: how to manage the changing library and assist librarians in developing new conceptualizations of their own roles; how to foster new competencies in staff. The second challenge is how to develop a productive dialogue about the library on the campus. To articulate a changing vision for the library and for the librarian is also to raise conflicts about values: about the nature and pace of the university library's response to technological change; about the university's role in scholarly communication, and about the effect of changes in the world at large on the academic community. Perhaps ultimately, creating a climate that fosters constructive dialogue about choices rather than iconoclastic debates is the greatest challenge of all for the library director. For it is only from the building of consensus about the role of the library that performance measures can be developed.

19

WHAT'S AHEAD?

The discontinuity of the future for higher education is the pervasive theme of this book. Digital technology has penetrated higher education, bringing transforming change to learning, instruction, research, management, and governance. Initially, the primary impact appeared to be confined to those units responsible for providing scholarly information resources—but as the various contributors to this volume demonstrate, both the enhancing and the debilitating effects of digital technology are now widespread throughout the enterprise. The single most important message underlying the series of essays, from the wide range of individual perspectives, is a shared conviction that, to flourish in the 21st century, the higher education community must accept the challenge of a fundamental restructuring. Because of the capacity of digital technology to eliminate barriers to information access and global communication, it is no longer possible to confine changes to individual units, institutions, or commercial organizations. New, pervasive interrelationships among all those who use digital technology present unprecedented financial and managerial challenges, as we seek to reinterpret social values and institutional missions in a reconfigured world.

Although tradition *per se* is rapidly becoming a millstone, academic institutions created *de nova* are not the solution. As the essays in the second section illustrate, a major challenge is the blending of new digital strengths with past and present values and assets in support of our concept of liberal education. The essayists raise valuable questions about the nature and future of scholarly communication in a digital university. Opinions vary as to whether the great print research collections—assembled as the repositories of human knowledge and maintained at great financial cost—will have a continuing role, or whether they will become burdensome white elephants, unused museums of the book.

Several essays point out the unhappy truth that while the continuing maintenance of traditional libraries is too costly to support, an equally large investment in research, training, and the conversion of materials will be required to provide electronic resources of similar value for the advancement of knowledge. The marketplace for scholarly information has changed radically with the advent of commercial publishing monopolies, the particular capacities of electronic publishing, and the unpredictable nature of the commercial value of scholarly disciplines as technology expands the frontiers of knowledge. Despite our enthusiasm for the *potential* of technology to eliminate the burdens of business as usual, it is also clear that there are serious obstacles, at least in the short run, to a smooth and affordable transition.

Perhaps the most serious limitation of all is one that faces society at large, and that is the acute shortage of talented and expert individuals to lead the revolution, to manage the transitional process, and to provide the continuing labor force necessary to sustain a digital society. The primary business of academic institutions is education, and we must now educate ourselves in an unprecedented manner in order to provide the creativity, the boldness, and the vision for a transformed society. The first step is a recognition that this is so. We hope that the essays in this volume will focus our collective mind on the crucial issues before us.

Brian Hawkins   *Patricia Battin*
Providence, RI   Washington, DC
May 1998

Index

Page numbers in *italics* denote figures or tables.